Endorsements and Reviews

Dr. Ian Hall has written an extremely valuable book on revivals and spiritual awakenings. Beginning with biblical narratives in the Old Testament and New Testament and continuing through the centuries to the present day, he highlights the primary revivals and spiritual awakenings throughout history. This comprehensive work reflects a lifetime of research.

In addition to all of the important and well-documented historical references, Dr. Hall also shares his personal experiences with revivals and spiritual awakenings, along with a sound biblical and practical theology, giving the reader ample material for spiritual inspiration and personal renewal. You will find here an abundant resource for the college or university classroom, the pulpit of a local church, or for any earnest follower of Jesus searching for a closer walk with God.

I thoroughly enjoyed the book; I learned much by reading it and my own heart was inspired to keep on praying, "Lord, do it again! Lord do it again!"

Dr. Donald G. Meyer
Retired President, University of Valley Forge

Reading *Times of Renewal* convinces one that Dr. Ian Hall has spent most of his life studying and teaching about revivals. The book is packed with helpful information regarding renewals throughout the ages, spanning biblical revivals in the Old and New Testaments and then up through the years to the present day. Ending with a theological perspective, *Times of Renewal* will provide a useful tool for anyone interested in God's work throughout history. As a professor teaching on revivals myself, I am more than happy to endorse this book and am particularly pleased that Dr. Hall has made this valuable resource available.

Carolyn Tennant, Ph.D.
Visiting Professor of Spiritual Formation
Assemblies of God Theological Seminary of Evangel University, Springfield, MO

The title of this book aptly describes its contents. This volume contains a lot of history. The book covers great moves of God in the Old Testament, the New Testament, and in subsequent church history, right down to the present time, the 21st century. The author includes dates, places, and the names of key individuals who were used by God during these times of spiritual stirring. The book contains accounts from around the world, it is global in scope. I dare say that no matter how well versed you are in the history of revival you will likely learn some new things by reading this book.

In the text Dr. Hall also interacts with the history he records. He addresses understandings of the word "revival" and identifies the key biblical elements of revival. He writes about what precedes it and what it accomplishes. In doing these things he presents a theology of revival. Those who read this book will learn much and find much to challenge and encourage them toward personal spiritual renewal.

John Lathrop, Author
M.A., Urban Ministry, Gordon-Conwell's Center for Urban Ministerial Education
Minister, International Fellowship of Christian Assemblies
Contributing editor, Pneuma Review

Dr. Ian Hall has filled a big gap by his book about revivals. He not only describes how God has given special refreshing times in distinct phases of history in various countries and areas of the world—he offers theological analyses for such visitations of God. Those special periods of God's move have been called renewal, awakening, or refreshing. Dr. Hall explains the terminology and puts it into the connections of the historical events. He explores the theological roots of revivals in the Old and New Testament. The reader is led through historical revival times, and also offers perspectives to more rarely visited phases like the role of the Nestorian missionaries among the Mongol and Turkic tribes in Central Asia in the 11th century.

The book is inspiring and widens the perspective of God's work in different periods of history. Dr. Hall offers a solid tool for the assessment of spiritual movements. It surely creates hunger for God's fresh visitation in our countries and churches.

Dr. Arto Hämäläinen

Chair of the Pentecostal Commission on Religious Liberty (PCRL)
Chair of the Africa Pentecostal Mission (APM)
Founding chair of the World Missions Commission of the Pentecostal World Fellowship (WMC/PWF)
Honorary member of the Mission Commission of the World Assemblies of God Fellowship (WAGF)
Adjunct Faculty Member of the Global University (GU)

A meticulous researcher, fine observer, and methodical writer, Dr. Ian Hall is a Pentecostal theologian who has personally undergone the journey of spiritual awakening, transitioning from atheist to Christian minister to theology professor to globe-trotting missionary.

As the book's subtitle implies, the author not only delves into the historical context of spiritual awakenings but also uses it to propose a concise yet seminal, Trinitarian-rooted, pneumatically-focused theology of revival. Arguing that the ultimate purpose of revival is to guide us back to Pentecost, the final section of the book is of particular value as it addresses critical aspects including the purpose of revival, its catalysts, occurrences, prerequisites, and the pivotal role played by the Holy Spirit.

Displaying a unique combination of historical accuracy, theological comprehensiveness, and pneumatological fervor, this book promises to ensure and enliven its readers to both the possibility and the imminence of Pentecost(al) revival.

Rev. Dr. Ciprian Gheorghe-Luca
Romanian Pentecostal pastor and public theologian

Times of Renewal is a fascinating journey through the history and theology of spiritual revival. The author delves deeply into topics such as biblical revival in the Old and New Testament, historical revival in the early Church, through medieval, Renaissance, and Reformation periods. Across captivating chapters, the book explores various spiritual awakenings, from the Great Reformers to those of the 20th century. With a comprehensive approach, this book not only informs but also inspires a deeper understanding of the significance of spiritual renewal. A must-read for those passionate about history and spiritual theology.

Rev. Nelu Filip
President, Pentecostal Union in Romania

Times of Renewal: A History and Theology of Revival and Spiritual Awakenings is an exceptional exploration of the profound and transformative moments of spiritual revitalization that took place throughout Christian history. Authored by Dr. Ian Hall, this captivating book is more than a mere recounting of events, for it also offers insightful examinations of factors that have ignited and sustained revivalist movements across cultures and epochs.

Undertaking meticulous research and offering a pertinent analysis, Dr. Ian Hall skillfully navigates through the annals of time, uncovering the patterns, catalysts, and enduring legacies of spiritual renewal. Starting with the biblical records and moving through the centuries up until modern-day revival movements, the tale told by the author paints a vivid portrait of the fervent devotion, community impact, and divine interventions that have been characteristic of this history.

Finally, the book is to be appreciated for the nuanced presentation of the theological underpinnings and implications of revivalism. Whether you are a scholar interested in researching revival movements, or just a curious reader intrigued by how God's Spirit moves "mysteriously" through human history, this book is a treasure trove that ought to be explored. It will undoubtedly enlarge your understanding of revivals and spiritual renewal patterns evident throughout history.

Dr. Marcel Valentin Macelaru Ph.D. Theology
Professor of Theology, Aurel Viacu University, Arad, Romania

TIMES
OF
RENEWAL

TIMES

OF

RENEWAL

A History and Theology of Revival

and Spiritual Awakenings

SECOND EDITION

IAN R. HALL

ENCOURAGE
PUBLISHING
NEW ALBANY, INDIANA

Printed in the United States of America

For worldwide distribution outside of Romania.

Library of Congress Control Number 2024935789

Cataloguing data:
Hall, Ian R.
Times of Renewal: A History and Theology of Revival and Spiritual Awakenings
1. Christian Church / History 2. Christian Education / Adult 3. Christian Ministry / Pastoral Resources 4. Christian Living / Spiritual Growth 5. Christian Theology / Pneumatology 6/ Christianity / Pentecostal & Charismatic

Dewey decimal classification: 248.25: Renewal and Growing in Faith; 269: Revivals; 220.95: Bible History

BISAC Codes: RELIGION/Christian Theology/Pneumatology
RELIGION/Christian Church/History

Cover and interior design by Jonathan Lewis
Edited by Dr. Donald G. Meyer
Editing team:
Lisa Grimenstein
Charlotte McNamee
Leslie Turner

Interior and cover design: Jonathan Lewis

ISBN 978-1-960166-21-0 (paperback and eBook)
ISBN 978-1-960166-22-7 (hardcover)

Published by:
Encourage Publishing, New Albany, Indiana
www.encouragepublishing.com

DEDICATION

This book is dedicated to Rev. Thomas Lars Johnson, Senior Pastor of New River Assembly of God, Red Wing, Minnesota, without whose constant encouragement this book would not have been completed.

Also, Rev. Laurentiu Pascuti, Oradea, Romania, who not only constantly encouraged me to complete the manuscript, but also was instrumental in the publishing of the first edition of this book in Romania.

I am indebted to these two dear pastor friends and to G. Paul Hendrickson of Massachusetts, who is responsible for the publishing of this updated edition in the United States.

Table of Contents

Dedication   xi

A True Story: From Atheist to Revivalist   1

Part I: The Foundation of Revival
1. The Dynamics of Revival   13
2. Understanding Revival   19
3. Old Testament Revival   27
4. New Testament Revival   43

Part II: Historical Revivals
5. Early Church (100–300 AD)   57
6. Imperial Church (300–600 AD)   67
7. Late Imperial Church (600–950 AD)   79
8. Early Medieval Period (950–1250 AD)   93
9. Medieval Period (1250–1350 AD)   107
10. Renaissance Period (1350–1525 AD)   119

Part III: Early Evangelical Awakenings
11. Reformation Period (1525–1575) 133
12. Puritan Awakenings (1575–1715) 151
13. The Great Awakening (1715–1770) 171
14. The Second Great Awakening (1770–1835) 195

Part IV: Late Evangelical Awakenings
15. Adventist Awakenings (1835–1845) 221
16. Mid-19th Century Awakening (1845–1870) 245
17. The Gospel Mission Awakening (1870–1900) 261
18. Early 20th Century Awakenings (1900–1940) 275
19. Post World War II Awakenings (1940–1960) 287
20. Charismatic Renewal (1960–1975) 299
21. Recent Stirrings (1975–Present) 311

Part V: The Theology of Revival
22. A Practical Theology of Revival 327
23. The Application of Revival Theology 343
Conclusion: Prospects of Revival 361

About Ian R. Hall 363

The Ministry of Ian and Sheila Hall 367

Bibliography 371

A True Story:
From Atheist to Revivalist

[YOU HOLD IN YOUR HANDS a work forty years in the making, coaxed into print in Romania by sheer determination and persistence, then republished in the United States, with only a few updates. For all of its setbacks, this edition seems to be releasing in perfect step with recent times of renewal experienced throughout the United States and other countries, and so we see God's timing in it.

However, the seed for this book, for all the study, experiences, and examination that went into it, was planted almost seven decades ago. To understand the depth and passion behind *TIMES OF RENEWAL*, let us begin with a brief but jaw-dropping story about the series of events that led Dr. Ian Hall to his first encounter of what many would refer to as a spiritual revival.]

Young Ian grew up in the small fishing village of Flamborough, in York-shire, England. His young mother struggled during her pregnancy and recovery, and, later in life, Ian was told that his father was serving in the military (during the height of Great Britain's involvement in World War II), when he went missing, as did thousands of others, never to return. Ian was cared for by an aunt until, at ten months, he was reluctantly given up to a foster family found through the now-famous Barnardo's children's foster care organization. Henry and Kharmion Cowton lovingly raised Ian and he saw his mother frequently while in their care. Ian was extremely bright and had a photographic memory, which he used to teach himself to read before his third birthday. Months before, as he began to talk, his foster parents noticed that Ian had a pronounced stutter, which they certainly hoped he would "grow out of" eventually. His foster family surrounded him with love and could easily recognize his brilliance; however, from the first day of school, Ian experienced immediate isolation, bullying, and abusive treatment in school.

As a young child, Ian also favored his left hand, which many considered a bad omen. In many parts of the world, being left-handed was thought to be sinister, a sign of evil and depravity. Every day when Ian arrived at school, his teacher would place a dog collar around his neck and chain his left hand behind his back, keeping it there until the end of the school day so that he would learn to write with his right hand. This treatment was both physically and emotionally tortuous and significantly worsened his speech impediment. Apart from a small number of girls, other children would not play with or talk to him, and he was the subject of constant ridicule. In this small village school, Ian would have the same teacher the following year, and so his painful and misguided treatment continued into his second grade—and his speech impediment worsened.

In October 1947, Ian's mother married Frank Hall, who worked as a lorry (truck) driver. The couple soon began a family and Ian was returned home to live with his mother, step-father, and eventually three brothers and a sister, starting fresh in a new school as well. While his dog-collar torture was over, his stutter had become completely debilitating, and for the rest of his public school education, he would suffer through endless taunts, total rejection, and isolation.

Ian's experience in a church setting was no different. Ian's foster family only attended church on holidays, and the Halls rarely attended church at all. When the family moved to Middlesbrough, Ian decided to visit the local St. George's Anglican Church, however, he was immediately escorted out and told not to return until he could speak and dress properly for church. He vowed never to return. The family later moved to Kingston upon Hull and Ian decided to attend the local Methodist church, where, once again, he was humiliated because of his speech impediment. By age thirteen he had renounced Christianity and called himself an atheist. "If God is real, how could he allow this to happen to me?" he wondered. Ian Hall wanted nothing to do with a God that would be so cruel. A high school teacher who was a Communist introduced him to the teachings of Marx, Lenin, and Stalin, and, for a time, he considered joining the Communist Party, but he was too young. "Even the Communists didn't want me," he would later quip.

By age fifteen, Ian had given up on completing his education. Though he was one of only four students qualified to go on to a prestigious high school, his family could not afford to send him there on a lorry driver's salary. He dropped out of school to join the British Royal Air Force with the intention of becoming an aircraft apprentice working on armaments—a job that required little communication. At this time, the deadly 1957 Asian influenza pandemic swept the country, and six months into his training, Ian fell severely ill. While he survived, he was left with epilepsy. Unable to serve, Ian was sent home to wait for his discharge papers.

This turn of events would be providential for the young man who had already faced so much adversity. Ian soon learned that, without a high school diploma, he could not earn enough to support himself. He started evening classes twice a week back at his old high school to complete his education, where he met David King, a young man also taking classes. After class, they would keep each other company on their walk home. David was full of fervor for God, and spoke constantly to Ian about becoming a Christian as they walked. Ian, unable to fully respond, could only listen and do his best to argue his atheistic point of view. From there, Ian picks up his story:

"I became a Christian believer through a life-transforming spiritual encounter with God in the city of Kingston upon Hull in England on Wednesday, November 27, 1957. A young man, David King, had been witnessing to me, a young atheist, about his Christian faith. In an attempt to demonstrate the falsity of his belief in the existence of God, I agreed to pray a simple prayer: 'God, be merciful to me a sinner.'

Although at first nothing happened, which is precisely what I expected, on the third time of repeating that prayer, I suddenly became conscious of an unseen presence whose overwhelming holiness exposed the sinfulness of my heart. The intensity of that experience humbled me in repentance and awakened me to the reality of God.

Ironically, that same day, I had received a letter from the British Royal Air Force containing my complete medical discharge papers.

The next time I saw David, he asked me, 'Did you pray?'

'Yes——I—did,' I slowly managed to reply.

'What happened?'

'I don't know——I feel strange inside——like——indigestion.'

'That's not indigestion, that's salvation!' David excitedly gave me specific instructions on what I was to do next. I must start going to church every Sunday and during the week, and read the Bible every morning and every night. 'And you need to hand out tracts,' he added. He said to start my Bible reading with 1 Thessalonians, then keep reading, and so I did.

As evening school entered Christmas break, I began attending the City Temple, an Elim Pentecostal church, with David. By the end of December, I had reached 2 Timothy 4. I read:

> '*I charge thee therefore before God, and the Lord Jesus Christ, who shall judge the quick and the dead at his appearing and his kingdom;*
>
> *Preach the word; be instant in season, out of season; reprove, rebuke, exhort with all long suffering and doctrine...endure afflictions, do the work of an evangelist, make full proof of thy ministry.*'

In that moment, God distinctly called me. I heard, 'I want you to be a preacher.'

I never returned to school that January, but instead got a job at a store stocking shelves. At the first opportunity, I told the church pastor that God had called me to be a preacher.

'That will never happen' was his immediate reply. He mocked the idea, coldly reminding me, 'You can never preach because you cannot speak! You have no high school diploma! And you're from a poor family—you could never afford to go to college.'

[Ian was a teenager. You can imagine that Ian had been "reminded" repeatedly all of his life of all the things he could never do, but this inexcusable

response must have been a deep sting for a brand-new Christian filled with hope for the first time.]

The pastor went on to say, 'Even if you did find a college to accept you, you would never find anybody to listen to you. I am going to write to (here he named some colleges) and tell them that if you ever apply, not to accept you because of your speech impediment and lack of a high school diploma.' Stunned, I walked away. He later told me he did write to two colleges. I left that church six months later. This was the same church Sheila Tinker attended."

Sheila and Ian would begin spending time together. Sheila's recollections demonstrate the lifetime of difficulties Ian had faced, obstacles that followed him into his young adult years.

"When I first met Ian and took him home to meet my mother, a widow, she asked me to not bring him home anymore because she could not bear to listen to his stutter and stammer. I remember he was asked to give his testimony during a Youth Sunday Special, and his stutter was so bad that the pastor asked him to sit down."

Sheila did as her mother asked. It would be three years before Ian would return to visit her home. Ian continues:

"Shortly afterwards, David recommended to me a book by a Scots revivalist, Duncan Campbell (1898–1972), which gave me a clearer perspective of my own experience, and also aroused in me a lifelong interest in revival. For the next year or so I continued to read the Bible and learned as much as I could about my new faith as the seeds of my own calling began to germinate. In the summer of 1959, I read in a Christian paper an advertisement for a preaching convention in the nearby city of Sheffield, the city where I was born, at which the main speaker would be the same Duncan Campbell. Although the convention was only a week away, I resolved to go and the pastor of the host church offered to accommodate me in his home. To my delight, I discovered that Campbell was also staying in the same home. To sit across the kitchen table from this venerable man of God after church each night until the early hours of the morning and to hear him describe the revivals in the Hebrides Islands in 1949 and 1957 was like heaven to me. I was hungry to learn more."

While Ian's desire to learn grew deep within, it was hard for anyone to imagine a path forward in ministry for this young, impoverished high school dropout with a stutter so pronounced that he could barely complete a sentence, much less witness to someone or deliver a sermon. Still, the call would not let him go. Undeterred, Ian thought, "If I can never speak, maybe God will use me if I can play piano." *He discovered years before that he did not stutter when he sang. He had watched Billy Graham and thought he could be an evangelist like Cliff Barrows, part of a musical team. He started going to a nearby Nazarene church where his piano teacher, Mrs. Hamilton, also attended. She quipped,* "I can tell you're a Christian because of the way you play—you never let your right hand know what your left hand is doing!"

Still, God had not called Ian to a music ministry; he had been called to preach.

In the same summer of 1959, about a year after Ian began attending the Nazarene church, Dr. Hugh Rae, the president of the British Isles Nazarene College, came as a guest speaker. As was the custom, at the end, the guest speaker would stand at the back and greet people as they filed out. Ian stood in line, and as he approached Dr. Rae, Ian recalls the dramatic, life-changing words he spoke:

"Dr. Rae pointed his finger at me and said, 'Young man, God has called you into the ministry, why are you not in college preparing for that ministry?'"

Ian was stunned. How did this stranger know he had been called? He proceeded to answer the question, listing the three crushing reasons the Elim Pentecostal minister had given, obstacles that he had allowed to become excuses. Ian continues:

"Dr. Rae admonished me, saying, 'Don't let that deter you.' He pulled an admissions application from his breast pocket and handed it to me. 'Fill out this application form and we will accept you on academic probation.' I was astonished. I did fill it out immediately and was accepted to start that October 1959, but my mother learned she was going to have another baby. She asked me to stay home to help her and care for the baby, and I agreed."

Despite this final setback, Ian persisted. Never before had he received such affirmation, nor had anyone once held him accountable and expressed their high expectations from him. On the recommendation of the college president, Dr. Hugh Rae, the British Isles Nazarene College agreed to admit Ian Hall, a high school dropout, under academic probation. On October 8, 1960, Ian left to begin the first leg of his academic journey, traveling with Tony Greenwood, a second-year student from Kingston upon Hull who had met Ian at church. Sheila retells the story:

"As the two were going into the front door of the college, Dr. Rae's wife mistook Ian in the half-light and said, 'Mr. Quick what are you doing here? Your classes do not begin until next Monday.' (Melvin Quick was a professor at the school.)

Ian responded, 'My name is not Quick; my name is Ian Hall and I am a new student.'

Tony Greenwood stared at him. 'Ian, you can speak!'

The President's wife questioned, 'Why wouldn't he be able to speak?'

Tony then explained: 'All of his life Ian has never been able to speak! He's had this terrible stutter and stammer!'

Mrs. Rae replied, 'Well, he speaks clearly enough now!'

God had instantaneously healed Ian."

Imagine what Ian must have been feeling after he had been healed from his speech impediment, the source of a lifetime of pain, loneliness and sorrow! As he was settling into his room later that day, the president came by.

"Ian?"

Ian turned to see Dr. Rae standing in the doorway. "Yes? Hello!"

Dr. Rae took in the scene. "You don't have a problem speaking now!" Dr. Rae's wife had told him about her encounter with Ian, and about his instant healing.

Dr. Rae smiled. "I'd like you to share your story in chapel tomorrow morning." Ian continues:

"In chapel the next day I gave my testimony, and I was soon invited to different churches to share the same testimony. At first, I went with older students who were there to preach, but later, I would give the sermon also. Usually, the church we were visiting would give me a gift, and that helped me pay for college, as well as a scholarship I received and money I had saved from my job.

My first semester, I got D's. All my life I had relied on my photographic memory to get me through school; I never had to study to do well. But in college a photographic memory doesn't help you think, reason, and understand. The president said, 'You're on academic probation; if you don't pull your grades up we'll have to dismiss you.'

I prayed, 'God, You're the one who got me into this! You'll have to teach me how to study.' I worked hard that next semester, teaching myself how to study. By the end of my second semester, I was getting A's and B's and was asked to teach other incoming freshmen how to study. By my third year, I taught classes on my method, which I called 'Hall's Efficient Learning Process (HELP).'"

Through this process, Ian also learned that he had a gift for teaching and for developing curriculum. He authored courses on homiletics and preparing to preach that later became textbooks. Every hardship so far in his life had only served to prepare him for his calling and Dr. Rae continued to challenge and push him forward. Now, there was only the matter of this young lady back home. Toward the end of his first year in college, Tony Greenwood went to work helping the two reconnect. He told Sheila that Ian would like for her to write to him and did the same to Ian. Soon the two began writing, and after that school year ended, Ian arranged to see her in person. He had never mentioned to her in his letters about his miraculous healing; until that moment, and until he saw her and spoke, Sheila had no idea his speech impediment was gone.

With fresh encouragement, Ian soon proved himself, and over his years at the college earned several academic awards on his way to earning his certificate and license to serve as a minister. October 3, 1964, Ian and Sheila were wed.

Years later Sheila asked Dr. Rae, "Why did you take a chance on Ian?"

He responded, "Because years ago somebody took a chance on me."

Now the stage has been set for the experience that would determine the trajectory of Ian's lifelong passion for revival, a date that was still long into the future. Ian describes his long journey toward his own first revival experience:

"Although I entered Christian education and ministry in 1960 with the full expectation that God would surely send another revival, it was not until August 4, 1974, almost fifteen years later, that expectation was realized in my own personal experience.

Since 1969 my wife and I had been pastoring a struggling Elim Pentecostal church in Ryde, Isle of Wight, with modest success. Unexpectedly, in the morning service that August Sunday in 1974, a very refined older lady in the congregation spontaneously began to sing in the Spirit. Quickly, the singing spread until the whole congregation had joined in this 'song without words.' That marked the beginning of a remarkable thirteen months of spiritual awakening, which, by the time it ended, had transformed virtually every congregation on the island, resulting in, among others, the proliferating of interdenominational prayer groups in every parish on the island and the doubling of church attendance."

For the young pastor, this time of refreshing was the launch point from where he soon began to further his studies, ultimately earning his Ph.D. in Theology. While an Associate Professor at North Central Bible College (NCU), Ian stepped out into mission work which placed him in Romania for over thirty years, far away from the comfort and security of home. His service, together with his wife, Sheila, is summarized at the end of this book and is a testament to the work God can accomplish through us, despite our weaknesses, when we answer his call. From that moment, over fifty years ago as of this writing, sprung the work found in your hands now, and so much more—a lifetime of service, challenge, and growth, marked by miracles and wonders—and a deep personal understanding of the power, the purpose, and the source of revival. Dr. Hall recounts simply these early wonders:

"God healed me completely from my epileptic seizures one month after I prayed that prayer, 'God be merciful to me, a sinner.' The day I first entered college to begin my pastoral studies, October 8, 1960, my speech impediment was completely healed."

It would seem God was, indeed, merciful to him.

[Now that you have a deeper understanding of Dr. Hall's passion for the subject of revival, ask God to show you the threads of revival in your own life as you follow the path laid out in this book, from the beginning of history until today.]

Part I

The Foundation
of Revival

Chapter 1

The Dynamics
of Revival

Revival is a major topic of interest in the Christian world today. Newspaper and magazine articles, both religious and secular, sporadically feature reports from every inhabited continent bringing news of a revitalization of the spiritual life of the church. For some three years in the mid-nineties, an obscure Toronto charismatic church became the surprising venue for hundreds of thousands of visitors from virtually every country around the world, because revival, or at least "a refreshing" was reported to be occurring there. As interest waned, a northwest Florida Pentecostal church claimed the spotlight for some two years. Then, in 2008, a central Florida church briefly seized the Christian world's attention. Most recently, in February 2023, there has been the news of a fresh awakening at several Christian colleges and universities in the US and in other countries. In 1996 the American Assemblies of God renamed its "Signs and Wonders" Conference in Springfield, Missouri, "Revival Now." What does it all mean?

The Significance of Revival. For some, revival is an arcane topic of interest only to religious zealots longing for the good old days of the nineteenth century. When our world is about to self-destruct in sociological and economic chaos, the study of revival seems as helpful as meditating during an earthquake would be. Nevertheless, from very different theological perspectives William G. McLoughlin (1922–1992) and Timothy L. Smith (1924–1997) rooted historical revitalizations of society in religious revivals.[1]

Even some evangelical Christians see the interest in revival as a pious distraction from the individual believer's responsibility to fulfill the Great Commission.[2] Ignoring the millions rushing to a lost eternity past his window, the revival student sits, morbidly examining himself in his spiritual mirror, alternatively lamenting and exulting in what he sees. In reality, far from the pursuit of revival distracting Christians from world evangelization, every major forward movement of Christianity throughout its two millennia of history was a bursting forth of new life from a revived church.[3] As we shall see, revival is essential to the growth and well-being of both church and society. It determines the barometric pressure governing the spiritual weather of our world.

The Definition of Revival. In North America in particular, revival is used in two different ways. Webster's Dictionary defines **revival** as "an awakening, in a church or community, of interest in and care for matters relating to personal religion; (and) a service or a series of services for the purpose of effecting a religious awakening."[4] We may therefore speak of a **revival** in the older and more widely used sense of a spiritual awakening affecting a whole community. We may also speak of a revival in the peculiarly American sense of a type of evangelistic crusade that is intended hopefully to revitalize the believers and to awaken the surrounding community.

This American usage of revival is usually traced back to the teaching of Charles G. Finney (1792–1875), the renowned nineteenth-century revivalist. He asserted that:

A revival is the result of the right use of the appropriate means. The means which God has enjoined for the production of a revival, doubtless have a natural tendency to produce a revival. . . . A revival is as naturally a result of the appropriate means as a crop is of the use of its appropriate means.[5]

By linking revival to "the right use of the appropriate means," Finney taught that revival is the result of something that we do. He did, however, acknowledge that of themselves "means will not produce a revival, we all know, without the blessing of God."[6] Nevertheless, among his followers, revival came to be used for the means themselves, not solely for the intended result of those means.

If these variant usages are not clearly distinguished, we may encounter such confusing comments as: "We had a revival, but nobody was revived," or, "We had a revival in our church, and, in the middle of it, God sent us a revival." If our terms are not clear, our language confuses rather than communicates our meaning. Dr. J. Edwin Orr (1912–1987), the renowned revival scholar, told of passing a church in Southern California that advertised: "Revival – every night except Monday." At the same time a neighboring church was advertising: "Revival – every night except Friday." Orr wondered why one could not have revival on a Monday and the other could not have revival on a Friday. Could the Lord be too busy to be present every night? Or, were the believers too busy with other things to be revived every night?

Although the term **"revival"** may suggest a scheduled revival crusade to the American mind, our use is in the sense of a quickening or renewing by the Holy Spirit of the spiritual life of the believers, individually and as the body of Christ in a given community, which prompts a return to New Testament Christianity. Thus, Orr defined an **evangelical awakening**, his preferred term for an authentic revival, as:

> An Evangelical Awakening is a movement of the Holy Spirit bringing about a revival of New Testament Christianity in the Church of Christ and its related community. Such an awakening may change in a significant way an individual only; or it may affect a larger group of believers; or it may move a congregation, or the churches of a city or a district, or the whole body of believers throughout a country or a continent; or indeed the larger body of believers throughout the world.[7]

Orr's definition most precisely describes what has happened in the historical revivals of Christianity, and corresponds with my personal experience of the work of God.

A Personal Journey in Revival. As recounted in the opening story of this book, "From Atheist to Revivalist," I became a Christian believer through a life-transforming spiritual encounter with God in 1957. For all of my expectation, it would be another seventeen years before I would experience, and witness, revival within my own life, in our church, and well beyond those walls, throughout every congregation of every denomination on the Isle of Wight.[8]

News of what had occurred on the Isle of Wight began to spread and as a result Edwin Orr invited me to teach in the "Oxford Reading and Research Conference on Revival" at Regent's Park College, Oxford in July 1977, so beginning an association that lasted until Orr's death almost ten years later. Orr's encouragement prompted me to turn my interest in revival into an intense study and careful analysis of the whole subject, resulting in a series of lectures delivered each year at North Central Bible College (now North Central University) in Minneapolis, Minnesota, throughout the 1980s, and in many churches, conferences, seminars, and other Bible colleges in the US and Europe. This present volume, *Times of Renewal: The History and Theology of Revival and Spiritual Awakenings*, is based upon those lectures, augmented by additional research and further experiences of revival, which occurred during my pastoral ministry in the London borough of Ilford, and in my ministry as a missionary-evangelist in Germany and Romania.

Although I have tried to be as accurate and comprehensive as possible, so much new material has recently been brought to my attention by the many friends who have provided encouragement and advice that I am increasingly aware that "the half has not been told." My appreciation for all who have contributed news and views on this topic cannot be adequately expressed, especially to my wife, Sheila, and to our son, Jonathan. All errors and omissions are solely my own.

As the church enters its third millennium, there is apparent not only an increasing sense of apprehension and anticipation, but also a great hunger for personal and corporate revival in the body of Christ worldwide. I pray that this volume in some small way will help inspire faith and expectancy for a fresh outpouring of the Holy Spirit in our day.

Endnotes

1 W. G. McLoughlin, *Revivals, Awakenings, and Reform: An Essay on Religion and Social Change in America*, 1607–1977 (Chicago, IL: University of Chicago, 1978); T. L. Smith: *Revivalism and Social Reform in Mid-Nineteenth-Century America* (New York, NY: Harper, 1957).

2 Matthew 28:19–20; Mark 16:15.

3 K. S. Latourette, *A History of the Expansion of Christianity* (Exeter, UK.: Paternoster, 1971 edn.), 7 volumes.

4 *New Webster's Dictionary of the English Language* (New York, NY: Delair Publishing, 1981), 822.

5 C. G. Finney, *Revivals of Religion* (London, UK: Morgan and Scott, 1913, second edition), 5 (emphasis original).

6 Finney, *Revivals of Religion*.

7 J. E. Orr, *The Eager Feet: Evangelical Awakenings*, 1790–1830 (Chicago, IL: Moody, 1975), vii.

8 Minutes of the Ryde Ministerial Fraternal, July 17, 1975.

Chapter 2

Understanding Revival

In some circles, the term **revival** is distasteful, conjuring up images of the excesses associated, often unjustly, with the "Frontier Revivals" of nineteenth century America or of the "hot-gospel" tent meetings stereotyped in Sinclair Lewis's *Elmer Gantry*. Many prefer synonyms such as **renewal**, **awakening**, or **refreshing**. Since the topic is so much in the news and in the hearts of people today, it is necessary to be clear about the meaning of the terms that are used, and about the marks of an authentic revival.

A Distinction of Terms. To understand revival, it is important to distinguish between the various terms used. Historically, at different times, different expressions have been popular, according to the aspect of the experience that was most prominent. Although in popular speech some terms tend to be used synonymously, each has a specific meaning.

Revival is the most commonly used term, yet it properly applies only to the believer, not to the unbeliever. It is impossible to restore life, consciousness, vigor, or health to that which has never been alive. Only that which has been alive can truly be revived.

The terms **evangelical awakening** or **spiritual awakening** are often used interchangeably with **revival**. These describe the rousing of a sleeping nominal church or a careless community to the power of the gospel (evangel) message and to spiritual realities. Some, like Orr, prefer to use **awakening** as the general term while restricting **revival** to its stricter application to the believers.[1] In an earlier work, however, Orr acknowledged that:

> The logic of words suggests "revival" for the revitalizing of a body of Christian believers, and an "awakening" for the stirring of interest in the Christian faith in the related community of nominal Christians or unbelievers.[2]

In the Bible the apostle Peter used the phrase **times of refreshing**[3] which is a good description of what happens in a revival. God refreshes the church and restores it to a condition of newness. In some Christian circles, particularly in relation to the more recent movement emanating from Toronto, Canada, a **time of refreshing** is considered as distinct from a revival and to be the preparation for a coming revival. Although the term **time of visitation**, particularly in the Old Testament, usually referred to a period of judgment, it could also be used for an occasion of blessing.[4] It came to be used throughout church history for any time when God drew near to his people.

Among early Protestants, particularly the Puritans of colonial America, such periods were variously called a **stirring**, a **harvest time**, or a **quickening**, descriptive of the particular aspect of the awakening most apparent to the participants. More recently, the term **renewal** has been in vogue. Christian literature since the sixties has been full of different types of **renewal** such as charismatic renewal, evangelical renewal, spiritual renewal, and personal renewal. While not synonymous, such terms suggest a revitalizing of church structures and of individual faith.

Noteworthy in world missions studies is the "**Folk Movement**" or "**Mass Movement**" phenomenon, which describes a spiritual awakening in a non-Christian ethnic community resulting in a general move toward Christianity, sometimes paralleling, and at others resulting from a revival within the church. Despite the obvious deficiencies of large-scale group conversions, Latourette observed that the growth of Christianity in Asia,

Africa, and Latin America, in the last two centuries especially, has been largely the result of such **mass movements.**[5]

A personal favorite is the phrase **outpouring of God's Spirit** because of its focus on the source. Revival is the direct result of an **outpouring of God's Spirit** on individuals and on the community at large. Orr described the Spirit of God as "the Divine Dynamic causing all such Awakenings."[6] The history of revivals and spiritual awakenings is the history of the Holy Spirit's activity in the church and in the world.

The Pattern of Revival. From the revivals and spiritual awakenings of history it is possible to discern a pattern of events taking place. This revival pattern emerges directly from the account of the first recorded revival in the Old Testament, that under Moses at Mount Sinai.

The revival pattern begins with **a period of declension** in which there was gross sin among the ungodly and a measure of apathy among the religious. This declension is one of the tragic hallmarks of modern society, especially in the West. In some areas there are clear signs of an approaching revival, but much of the United States of America, and North America generally, is somewhere between declension and contrition.

There has not yet appeared **the heart-felt contrition or repentance**, so typical of true revival, coming fully into focus. There has been no general repentance, although there are some individuals who are adopting a truly penitent attitude toward sin. They are becoming deeply aware of sin, and walking sensitively with the Lord because they wish to be right with him in their relationships and in their attitudes.

Following repentance comes **intercession**, not just repenting of personal sins and getting right with God but also interceding for the community, for the need of the hour, getting under the burden for prayer. Periodically there have been concerts of prayer held in many parts of the US and other countries. Although recently, unlike in past generations, they have not sparked a revival, the frequency of these concerts of prayer undoubtedly is moving nations in the direction of revival.

Those whom God has convicted and brought into a place of intercession may be called into **a prophetic ministry**, which is the fourth phase in the revival pattern. A prophetic ministry will do two things: it will challenge the current attitudes of both the ungodly and the religious, and it will encourage the convicted to heartfelt repentance while there is still opportunity. Some set themselves up as prophets and adopt the old Puritan "jeremiad" style of preaching, in which the author laments over the shortcomings of the church in general, adopts a critical tone in relation to the spiritual life of professing Christians, highlighting from Scripture perceived failures, and calling those convinced to repentance. The ministry of Jeremiah, from whom the term "jeremiad" comes, did not precipitate revival; instead it heralded judgment upon the community, because the community did not repent. This warning of coming judgment is an important aspect of prophetic ministry. Jonah's prophesying was primarily a warning: "Forty days from now Nineveh will be destroyed,"[7] and it did result in a widespread repentance. The prophetic ministry challenges the current attitudes by pinpointing the sin, awakening people to the consequences of those sins, warning of the judgment to come, and encouraging people to adopt a repentant attitude.

What produces repentance? Conviction of sin. Who convicts of sin? The Holy Spirit.[8] Our telling everybody what is wrong with them will not inevitably prompt any change. Even if we know what is wrong with us, we may not feel it deeply enough to do anything about it. We may resolve that we will be different, but we seldom **are** different until the Holy Spirit makes us uncomfortable with our present condition. Then we will do something about it. The Holy Spirit may inspire a "jeremiad," or that may just be our way of bolstering our own ego by putting everybody else down. What is wrong with the church? The church does not pray enough, fast enough, live up to its responsibilities before God, depend upon the power of the Holy Spirit, and so on. The one who so perceptively describes the failures of others may feel very self-satisfied because he is not responsible for the current state of affairs. In reality, his self-righteousness and critical spirit may prove a hindrance to revival and a stumbling-block to others.

The prayers of the Old Testament are striking in the way the intercessors identified themselves with the needs of those for whom they were praying. Nehemiah, for example, prayed the following (emphasis mine):

22

I confess the sins **we** Israelites, including **myself** and my father's house, have committed against you. **We** have acted very wickedly toward you. **We** have not obeyed. –Nehemiah 1:6–7

The intercessor identified himself with the needs of the people. Judgment had come. This was not the time to point the finger of accusation, but to seek the Lord in repentance for restoration.

The role of the prophet then was not to attribute blame, but to identify the attitudes and actions that had brought that judgment. Only the prophet, who recognizes as Isaiah did, "I am a man of unclean lips, and I live among a people of unclean lips,"[9] can rightly minister the Word of the Lord. Out of his own heartfelt conviction Isaiah was revived and preached a reviving message to the community. The person who has never been broken over his own sin can never speak to the hearts of those broken by sin. A true revival comes when there is an awakening of the believers. A prophetic ministry brings people to that place of awakening.

There are two distinct aspects to the awakening: there is **the renewing of the spiritual life**, and there also is **a recovery of spiritual truth**. Truths already present in the Word of God but that have been neglected, ignored, or overlooked are brought back into bold relief. Every evangelical awakening from the Reformation onward has focused upon one or another particular truth. The Reformation itself focused on the truth of personal justification by faith. The Puritan awakening saw the church as a separated body of believers. The Wesleyan or Great Awakening highlighted the need for a personal sanctifying relationship with God. The revival at the beginning of the nineteenth century focused on the missionary vision of the church and thrust forth missionaries to the farthest parts of the earth. Twenty-five years later the revival stressed the second coming of Christ. In the mid-century awakening, the emphasis was on Christian holiness, which prepared the way for the concept of the baptism in the Holy Spirit, the focus of the decade of revival with which the twentieth century opened. In the years following World War II, the promotion of healing evangelism was succeeded by a general emphasis on the restoration of the charismata to the church. Such an obvious pattern in the evangelical awakenings of history suggests that each revival has had its own particular focus of truth. The result was often a preparation of the church for future trials, both by a separation from the world and by a fortification against the Enemy.

Endnotes

1 Orr, *The Eager Feet*, vii.
2 J. E. Orr, *The Flaming Tongue: The Impact of 20th Century Revivals.* (Chicago, IL: Moody, 1973), ix.
3 Acts 3:19–20.
4 Isaiah 10:3; Hosea 9:7; cf. Job 10:12; Luke 19:44.
5 Latourette, *History of the Expansion*, 5:104ff, 492ff; 6:89ff; 7:292ff.
6 Orr, *The Eager Feet*, vii.
7 Jonah 3:4.
8 John 16:8.
9 Isaiah 6:5.

Chapter 3

Old Testament

In this chapter we begin an examination of biblical revivals, focusing especially on the revivals described in the Old Testament. From what we have already noted relating to spiritual awakenings and revival periods, we see that much current revival teaching stems from the Old Testament experience. The Old Testament exemplifies the kind of community comparable to much of the Christianized world, especially from the medieval period onward. The Old Testament revivals therefore model procedures and patterns that provide insights for our experience today.

In the next chapter we shall look at the New Testament where we encounter a different kind of situation. Christianity was making its way in an essentially hostile and predominantly pagan environment. Christians were the embattled minority in a world of competing religions and yet still the Spirit of God was poured out, renewing the church and sweeping great multitudes of pagans into the kingdom of God, which has also happened in some of the modern awakenings in the non-Christianized or post-Christian world.

Old Testament Revivals. In our examination of Old Testament revivals we will, first of all, make a survey of the many instances of revival recorded in the Old Testament to ascertain the characteristics exhibited, and then choose a particular model revival to analyze in relation to the revival cycle identified in Chapter Two. In the Psalms the sons of Korah prayed a heart-rending, heart-felt prayer for revival:

Restore us again, O God our Savior, and put away your displeasure toward us. Will you be angry with us forever? Will you prolong your anger through all generations? Will you not revive us again, that your people may rejoice in you? –Psalms 85:4-6

Terminology. The most common word used is one that is used here for revive, the Hebrew word *chayah*, which speaks of renewing that which has become old and worn out, of restoring to usefulness. The prayer is on a corporate level. The experience may also take place on an individual level, as in the prophecy of Isaiah:

For this is what the high and lofty One says—he who lives forever, whose name is holy: "I live in a high and holy place, but also with the one who is contrite and lowly in spirit, to revive the spirit of the lowly and to revive the heart of the contrite." –Isaiah 57:15

Again that same word is used indicating a quickening and renewing, of restoring to a place of usefulness and favor. God is calling his people not just to a corporate renewal but to an individual renewal. Another significant term is used in the prayer of Ezra:

But now, for a brief moment, the LORD our God has been gracious in leaving us a remnant and giving us a firm place in his sanctuary, so our God gives light for our eyes and little relief in our bondage. Though we are slaves, our God has not forsaken us in our bondage. He has shown us kindness in the sight of the kings of Persia: He has granted us new life to rebuild the house of our God and repair its ruins, and he has given us a wall of protection in Judah and Jerusalem. –Ezra 9:8, 9

The phrase "*He has granted us new life*" is the other Hebrew word *michyah*. It does not carry the connotation of restoring that which was old and decrepit so much as moving on into a new experience. Throughout the Old Testament the particular emphasis of revival is that revival is intended both to restore and to advance the work of God in the life of the community and in the lives of the individuals.

History. Dr. Ron Davies appropriately noted: "There is considerable disagreement among writers concerning which Old Testament events may be described as revivals."[1] Although Jonathan Edwards attributed Genesis 4:26b—*"At that time men began to call on the name of the LORD"*—to "a remarkable pouring out of the Spirit of God,"[2] there is no clear evidence to support the latter. Throughout human history there have been notable instances of personal encounters with God that have transformed individual lives and even affected whole communities, but without more information it is difficult to identify such as revivals and spiritual awakenings.

Baker identified the report of the encounter with God by Moses and Aaron at the mountain of God prior to the exodus as resulting in revival among the captive Israelites.[3] How extensive was the move of God's Spirit at the time of the exodus? The prophet Amos compared the activity of God in relation to Israel with his activity in other nations:

> "'Are not you Israelites the same to me as the Cushites?' declares the LORD. 'Did I not bring Israel up from Egypt, the Philistines from Caphtor and the Arameans from Kir?'"(Amos 9:7)

This may indicate the possibility of a more general movement of God's Spirit at this time.

History records a major people movement after the middle of the second millennium before Christ, in which the Philistines left their ancient Minoan kingdom centered upon Crete, abandoning inexplicably and almost intact their ancient capital of Knossos, and set out for Palestine. There these "Sea Peoples" were repulsed by the Egyptian forces of Pharaoh Rameses II, but nevertheless arrived in Palestine about the same time as the Israelites did.

Other "Sea Peoples" had also settled in the northwest. Centuries later, Hiram king of Tyre, a close friend of King David of Israel, and his fellow Phoenicians, as those northwestern settlers became known, show evidence of having some knowledge of and respect for the God of Israel.[4] Such faith as they had, was later greatly overlaid with superstition and resulted in ultimately the judgment of God falling upon Tyre and Sidon, their principal cities, and their destruction. A similar fate befell their principal city in the West, Carthage in North Africa. The historical evidence suggests that initially they may have had some faith in the true God and been conscious of his presence.

History also records a major people movement from the northeast, involving the Arameans, the people who were to inhabit and settle to the northeast of Palestine. The relationship between Israel and the Arameans/Syrians was not always enmity. There were times when much of Syria came under the suzerainty of the Israelite kings, especially after King David married Maacah, the daughter of Talmai, king of Geshur, a major Aramean city.[5] Damascus was always a home for many Jews, and at times was allied with Israel and at other times was not.

It took almost a millennium before the decline in godliness there had reached such a level and paganism had become so prevalent that those cities too were destroyed. But even in the days of Elisha, Naaman, a Syrian leader, came to the prophet of God seeking cleansing from his leprosy.[6] This showed some measure of confidence in the God of Israel, a remnant of an ancient faith that was long in decline among that group.

Although there is little evidence available of a move of God among the people known as Cushites (Nubia or Ethiopia), Scripture described Moses' wife as a Cushite,[7] and if she was the same person as Zipporah, the daughter of Jethro, the Midianite priest,[8] this would indicate a similar faith in God to that of Israel. Archeological explorations in Africa do indicate a southward people movement that populated much of central and southern Africa. Were they a people led on by the Lord, as were the Israelites coming out of Egyptian bondage? The move of God that ultimately brought Israel out of captivity may well have been part of a much more general stirring that was affecting many different communities.

More extensive details are available in Scripture regarding the divine encounter under Moses at Mount Sinai at the time of the giving of the law.[9] This serves as a model of Old Testament revivals, because not only are there many details recorded, but also the sequence of events is typical of many Old Testament revivals. Davies, however, doubted that this was a true revival in the classic sense, noting:

> The conduct of Israel in the wilderness, as well as the explicit statement in Deut. 29:4, would seem to indicate that there was no genuine spiritual work taking place in the hearts of the adult generation who left Egypt.[10]

However, it should be noted that in any historical revival, not all who are affected will respond positively, and some who do so initially may subsequently backslide. Possibly the renewing of the covenant, to which Davies referred, indicated a spiritual awakening among the younger generation that would enter the promised land, as Edwards believed.[11]

A generation later at Shechem in Canaan was another revival under Joshua in which the people with one accord committed themselves to serving God:[12]

> "Now then," said Joshua, "throw away the foreign gods that are among you and yield your hearts to the Lord, the God of Israel." And the people said to Joshua, "We will serve the Lord our God and obey him."
> On that day Joshua made a covenant for the people, and there at Shechem he reaffirmed for them decrees and laws. And Joshua recorded these things in the Book of the Law of God. Then he took a large stone and set it up there under the oak near the holy place of the Lord.–Joshua 24:23-26

Under Samuel there was a further revival, about 1075 BC, when Samuel summoned those people back to faith in God. The ark of the covenant had been returned from its Philistine bondage and the people of God turned, with one accord, albeit briefly, to seek the Lord.[13]

> Then all the people of Israel turned back to the Lord. So Samuel said to all the Israelites, 'If you are returning to the Lord with all your hearts, then rid yourselves of the foreign gods and the Ashtoreths and commit yourselves to the Lord and serve him only, and he

will deliver you out of the hand of the Philistines.' So the Israelites put away their Baals and Ashtoreths, and served the Lord only.
–1 Samuel 7:2b-4

Despite the greatness of men like King Saul and David, there is no indication of any revival taking place during their reigns. However, at the building of the temple in Solomon's day about 960 BC, the Shekinah glory of God came down in such intensity that even the priests in the temple were not able to stand to minister, such was the immediacy of God's presence in their midst.[14]

> When Solomon finished praying, fire came down from heaven and consumed the burnt offering and the sacrifices, and the glory of the Lord filled the temple. The priests could not enter the temple of the Lord because the glory of the Lord filled it. When all the Israelites saw the fire coming down and the glory of the Lord above the temple, they knelt on the pavement with their faces to the ground, and they worshiped and gave thanks to the Lord, saying, "He is good; his love endures forever."–2 Chronicles 7:1-3

More than a generation passed before there was a further outpouring of God's Spirit in the divided kingdom of Judah in the days of Asa.[15] A generation later in the time of Jehoshaphat in Judah and Elijah in northern Israel, there was a fresh awakening of God's people, first in the south, and then at the time of the climactic events on Mount Carmel when the idolatrous northern kingdom briefly returned to the ancient faith.[16]

The lengthy ministry of Elisha, the great successor of Elijah, had a significant impact on both the northern Israelites and beyond into Aram (Syria).[17] Toward the end of Elisha's life came another awakening in the south, in the days of King Joash, when once again there was a returning to God, and a restoring of the temple worship in Jerusalem.[18] A generation later as the Northern Kingdom of Israel was teetering toward its ultimate collapse, there was a further move of God's Spirit, not in Israel but in its eventual conqueror, Assyria, when Jonah went reluctantly to Nineveh and preached a message bringing repentance and spiritual awakening there.[19]

The Ninevites believed God. A fast was proclaimed, and all of them, from the greatest to the least, put on sackcloth.

When Jonah's warning reached the king of Nineveh, he rose from his throne, took off his royal robes, covered himself with sackcloth and sat down in the dust. This is the proclamation he issued in Nineveh: "By the decree of the king and his nobles:

Do not let people or animals, herds or flocks, taste anything; do not let them eat or drink. But let people and animals be covered with sackcloth. Let everyone call urgently on God. Let them give up their evil ways and their violence. Who knows? God may yet relent and with compassion turn from his fierce anger so that we will not perish."

When God saw what they did and how they turned from their evil ways, he relented and did not bring on them the destruction he had threatened. –Jonah 3:5-10

God does not restrict his activities to just one group of people, but often when God pours out his Spirit, he moves in many different communities.

The revival a generation later under King Hezekiah in Judah around 715 BC seems to have been largely confined to his kingdom,[20] whereas the next recorded revival under King Josiah penetrated into the remnant of northern Israel, now called Samaria, the bulk of the population having been carried away into Assyrian captivity in Hezekiah's day.[21] That did not stop the Spirit of God from including the remnant in his visitation of God's ancient people. Many from the remaining Israelite tribes came down to Jerusalem to worship and gather with the southern tribes, reuniting the remnant of the north with the south.

There was a further stirring of God's Spirit during the time of captivity in the days of Zerubbabel, when Zechariah and Haggai, the great prophets, proclaimed a restoration at least in part to the promised land.[22] The last major revival period in the Old Testament came some seventy-five years later under the leadership of Ezra the scribe, Nehemiah the governor, and Malachi the prophet. The last remnants of paganism were rooted out of

Israel and from this time onward the role of the teachers of the law became very influential.[23]

Although the accounts of historical events between the closing of the Old Testament in the days of Nehemiah and Ezra and the opening of the New Testament are limited, we do know that God had not stopped moving upon his people. In the post-biblical period about 200 BC God moved, bringing the people out of their oppression and compromising relationships with the Greeks into a more faithful service of him.

Early in the third century among the Jewish diaspora in Egypt the Hebrew/Aramaic Old Testament was translated into Koine Greek (the Septuagint), similar to the language of the New Testament, which was spoken by the majority of the population in northern Egypt, across North Africa and throughout much of the eastern Mediterranean. Such a major enterprise is unlikely to have been undertaken unless prompted by an increasing interest in the God of Israel.

Although the Maccabean revolt is usually described as a period of military conflict against the Seleucid successors to Alexander's Macedonian Empire, there apparently was a strong religious element, even a spiritual awakening, in the initial phases of the uprising,[24] especially from 166–164 BC, culminating in the desecrated Jerusalem Temple being restored, as commemorated in the Feast of Dedication. The anticipated golden age of Jewish independence quickly tarnished under the later Hasmonean rulers, leading to the probable withdrawal of the Essenes and other sectarians from normal Jewish life.[25]

The "Therapeutae," the healing monks of Egyptian Judaism, who flourished around Alexandria near Lake Mareotis in the years immediately before and after the beginning of the Christian era, have at times been associated with the Essenes. Some early Christian writers thought they may have been or become Judeo-Christian monks.[26] The stories of notable miracles of healing and restoration and prophesying attributed to them and their contemporaries certainly indicate a remarkable faith in and consciousness of God.[27] Throughout the old covenant period it seems that scarcely a generation goes by without there being a renewing and visitation by the Holy Spirit.

A Model Old Testament Revival. The revival that occurred with Moses at Sinai has served as a model, providing the various elements of the revival cycle: a period of decline was followed by an increasing sense of contrition, and the emergence of a prophetic ministry resulting in the awakening of believers, which in many instances served a preparation for future trials for the people of God.

The Bible records much detail relating to what happened at Sinai. God came down and communicated with his servant Moses. Tragically, while Moses was on the mountain with God, **decline** set in among the people. They made a golden calf; they wanted visible gods to go before them. Paganism had a great attraction for them after some four hundred years in Egypt. There were three clear aspects to the sin of the people as depicted in Exodus:[28] idolatry, immorality, and a corrupted priesthood. Even Aaron, the brother of Moses and the divinely chosen high priest, was corrupted by this gross sin.

> Then the Lord said to Moses, "Go down, because your people, whom you brought up out of Egypt, have become corrupt. They have been quick to turn away from what I commanded them and have made themselves an idol cast in the shape of a calf. They have bowed down to it and sacrificed to it and have said, 'These are your gods, Israel, who brought you up out of Egypt.'"–Exodus 32:7-8

As the prospect of divine judgment loomed over the people because of their stubborn sinfulness, Moses engaged in intercessory prayer for them. **Intercession** involves identification, not criticism and condemnation. Instead of standing before God on behalf of the needy, some want to judge the guilty and condemn them to their well-deserved fate. Nehemiah recorded a model intercessory prayer (emphasis mine):

> Lord, the God of heaven, the great and awesome God, who keeps his covenant of love with those who love him and keep his commandments, let your ear be attentive and your eyes open to hear the prayer your servant is praying before you day and night for your servants, the people of Israel. **I** confess the sins **we** Israelites,

including **myself** and **my father's family**, have committed against you. **We** have acted very wickedly toward you. **We** have not obeyed the commands, decrees and laws you gave your servant Moses.
–Nehemiah 1:5-7

He took their guilt upon himself as he prayed on behalf of the people. True intercession involves **identification**.

Similarly, Daniel wrote (emphasis mine):

I prayed to the Lord my God and confessed:
"Lord, the great and awesome God, who keeps his covenant of love with those who love him and keep his commandments, **we** have sinned and done wrong. **We** have been wicked and have rebelled; **we** have turned away from your commands and laws. **We** have not listened to your servants the prophets, who spoke in your name to our kings, our princes and our ancestors, and to all the people of the land.
"Lord, you are righteous, but this day **we** are covered with shame— the people of Judah and the inhabitants of Jerusalem and all Israel, both near and far, in all the countries where you have scattered us because of our unfaithfulness to you. **We** and our kings, our princes and our ancestors are covered with shame, Lord, because **we** have sinned against you. The Lord our God is merciful and forgiving, even though **we** have rebelled against him; **we** have not obeyed the Lord our God or kept the laws he gave us through his servants the prophets. All Israel has transgressed your law and turned away, refusing to obey you.
Therefore the curses and sworn judgments written in the Law of Moses, the servant of God, have been poured out on us, because **we** have sinned against you. –Daniel 9:4-11

Throughout these prayers it is not *they*; it is *we*. The intercessor identified himself with the people. That is real intercession—to identify with and pray through on behalf of those who need the Lord.

Moses then moved into **a prophetic ministry**. Returning from his divine encounter with the inscribed tablets of the testimony, Moses approached the camp and saw the calf and the dancing. Incensed, he threw the tablets to the ground, shattering them. Taking the calf they had made, he burned it in the fire, ground it to powder, scattered it on the water and made the Israelites drink it. He challenged the mood of the age, taking a strong and clear stand against the festivity, the merrymaking, the compromising, the sinning, and the immorality. He also called his brother Aaron to account for his lack of faithful leadership.[29]

He then called the people to a fresh commitment to God:

"He stood at the entrance to the camp and said, 'Whoever is for the LORD, come to me.' And all the Levites rallied to him."–Exodus 32:26

God always calls us to commitment. It is may be difficult to step out from the crowd and be different, but the prophetic ministry challenges us to the kind of commitment that requires us to separate ourselves and to be what God wants us to be.

As Moses returned to his intercession on behalf of the rebellious and unheeding people, he learned of the inevitability of divine judgment.

The LORD replied to Moses, "Whoever has sinned against me I will blot out of my book. Now go, lead the people to the place I spoke of, and my angel will go before you. However, when the time comes for me to punish, I will punish them for their sin."

And the LORD struck the people with a plague because of what they did with the calf Aaron had made. –Exodus 32:33-35

Sin brings its consequences. The prophet's role is to warn the people of those coming consequences, so that those who will listen may repent, return to God, and be prepared for the revival that is also coming.

The revival itself was marked initially by widespread **repentance**.[30] Conviction of sin is one of the Holy Spirit's primary activities in dealing with mankind,[31] which produces repentance on the part of those awakened to their relationship to God. Prior to Mount Sinai, whenever anyone desired an encounter with the Lord, they had to go to the tent of meeting outside the camp,[32] but now the tent of meeting was to be incorporated in the tabernacle, which was to be built according to the Lord's instructions and to be located symbolically in the midst of the Israelite camp.[33] Although there was not the physical separation henceforth as in the earlier day, there was a real separation from the world around on the part of the revived. Too often today there is no clear line of demarcation between the church and the world. Not geographically but certainly spiritually the church must be separated from the attitudes and impact of the world.

The location of the tent of meeting indicated **a sensible presence of God**.[34] Sometimes in periods of revival the presence of God is so real that it seems as though if a person opened his eyes during prayer he would actually see God standing there. In 1974 at the Tuesday evening prayer meeting following the outpouring of God's Spirit on the church in Ryde, Isle of Wight, there came such an intense sense of the presence of God that the whole congregation stood in worship for more than an hour, unconscious of the passing of time. God himself was right there.

Similarly in the BFP Church in Gaildorf, Bavaria, on February 5, 1995, as the Sunday morning service was concluding, there came such a sense of God's presence that the musicians leading worship stopped in the middle of a song and the searchlight of the Holy Spirit moved from person to person until everyone present had had a personal and transforming encounter with God, culminating in a spontaneous outburst of worship as the sense of sin and separation from God was gone. Perhaps Isaiah's experience in the temple, when he saw the Lord high and lifted up,[35] was of the same order.

This was followed at Mount Sinai by **a fresh revelation of God's glory**. As Moses stood there in the cleft in the rock, God proclaimed his glorious name and character to his friend, and restored the broken tablets.[36] Even Moses' face was radiant from his transforming encounter with the Lord.[37]

The effects of a revival then can be summarized as: first, **a greater sensibility to the presence of God**.[38] We do not just sing, "In Him we live and move and have our being," but that is our experience—a personal awareness of the presence of God.

Secondly, **an awareness of who He is:**

The Lord, the Lord, the compassionate and gracious God, slow to anger, abounding in love and faithfulness, maintaining love to thousands, forgiving wickedness, rebellion and sin.[39] –Exodus 34:6-7a

Such a consciousness of what God is really like transforms our character, conduct, and society.

Thirdly, **a reestablished covenant:**

Then the Lord said: "I am making a covenant with you. Before all your people I will do wonders never before done in any nation in all the world. The people you live among will see how awesome is the work that I, the Lord, will do for you. Obey what I command you today. I will drive out before you the Amorites, Canaanites, Hittites, Perizzites, Hivites and Jebusites."–Exodus 34:10-11

If the world is to see the awesome work of God in the church, we must return to implicit obedience to his commands.

Fourthly, **an anointed leadership.** When Moses came down from Mount Sinai with the two tablets of the testimony in his hands he was not aware that his face was radiant because he had spoken with the Lord. People were afraid to come near him because his face glowed with the presence of God. Such an anointing may not be externally visible, but in 2 Corinthians we are reminded our very lives are to reflect his glory.

And we all, who with unveiled faces contemplate the Lord's glory, are being transformed into his image with ever-increasing glory, which comes from the Lord, who is the Spirit. –2 Corinthians 3:18

Finally, **a revitalized worship.** Moses assembled the whole community together and detailed the building of the tabernacle where God would meet with them, where the sacrifices of praise and adoration and for the atonement of sin would be offered, where there would be cleansings, and where there would be sensible demonstrations of the divine presence and confirmations of the covenant that God had made with them.[40] This revitalized worship makes a powerful impact upon the community that is touched by the revival fire.

Endnotes

1   R. E. Davies: *I Will Pour Out My Spirit* (Tunbridge Wells, UK: Monarch, 1992), 43

2   J. Edwards: *The Works of Jonathan Edwards: Volume 9 – A History of Redemption.* (New Haven, CT: Yale, 1989), 142

3   Exodus 4:29-31; E. Baker: *The Revivals of the Bible* (London: Kingsgate Press, 1906), 9–17

4   2 Chronicles 2:11–14

5   2 Samuel 3:3

6   2 Kings 5:1ff.

7   Numbers 12:1

8   Exodus 2:16ff.

9   Exodus 32–34

10 Davies, op. cit., 45

11 Edwards, op. cit., 189–192

12 Joshua 24:1–27

13 1 Samuel 7:2ff.

14 1 Kings 8:1 ff; 2 Chronicles 5–7

15 1 Kings 15:9 ff; 2 Chronicles 14–16

16 1 Kings 18-22; 2 Chronicles 17–20

17 2 Kings 2–9

18 2 Chronicles 24

19 Jonah 1:1ff.

20 2 Chronicles 29:3ff.

21 2 Chronicles 34:1ff.

22 Ezra 1–6; Haggai; Zechariah

23 Ezra 7–10; Nehemiah; Malachi

24 1 Maccabees 2:15-27 (NRSVCE)

25 G. W. Buchanan: art. "Essenes" in G. W. Bromiley (ed.): *The International Standard Bible Encyclopedia* (Grand Rapids, MI: Eerdmans, 1982), 2.147–155

26 Eusebius: *Ecclesiastical History*, II.17

27 References in I. R. Hall: *Charismatic Phenomena in the Ante-Nicene Church* (Leeds, UK: MPhil Dissertation, 1984 available on line), 25ff

28 Exodus 32:1–6

29 Exodus 32:19–24

30 Exodus 33:4–6

31 John 16:8

32 Exodus 33:7–11

33 D. W. Gooding: art. "Tabernacle" in I. H. Marshall et.al. (eds.): *New Bible Dictionary* (Downers Grove, IL: InterVarsity, 1996), 1145

34 Exodus 33:14; 40:34ff

35 Isaiah 6:1ff

36 Exodus 33:18ff

37 Exodus 34:29–35

38 Exodus 33:14

39 Exodus 34:5ff

40 Exodus 35:1ff

Chapter 4

New Testament

New Testament revivals are probably the most frequently reproduced in Christian history. Orr observed: "The major marks of an Evangelical Awakening are always some repetition of the phenomena of the Acts of the Apostles."[1] The role of the Spirit of God in revivals would naturally lead us to expect such a reproduction of the phenomena associated with his recorded activity in Acts. Furthermore, since Scripture provides a model for faith, doctrine, and life for succeeding generations, we would expect to be able to evaluate and validate subsequent revival phenomena from the biblical record.

The Revival in the Gospels. The revivals of the New Testament are not limited to those recorded in the Acts of the Apostles. The New Testament begins with an account of a transitional revival period as described in the Gospels, associated with the ministry of John the Baptist and the early ministry of the Lord Jesus. Although it occurred in the New Testament, it actually marks the last of the Old Testament revivals. The Lord Jesus described the ministry of John as marking the transition between the testaments: *"The Law and the Prophets were proclaimed until John. Since that time, the good news of the kingdom of God is being preached..."* —Luke 16:16

The events recorded in the Gospels carry all the marks of a typical Old Testament revival. John's prophetic ministry challenged current attitudes regarding sin and morality. Matthew recorded his stinging rebuke of the religious leaders,[2] to which Luke added John's equally challenging words to the tax collectors, the soldiers, the common people in general, summoning them to repentance.[3]

> John said to the crowds coming out to be baptized by him, "You brood of vipers! Who warned you to flee from the coming wrath? Produce fruit in keeping with repentance. And do not begin to say to yourselves, 'We have Abraham as our father.' For I tell you that out of these stones God can raise up children for Abraham. The ax is already at the root of the trees, and every tree that does not produce good fruit will be cut down and thrown into the fire." –Luke 3:7-9

Even the ruler, Herod the tetrarch, was subjected to the prophetic denunciation of John.[4] The Lord Jesus himself described the ministry of John as among the greatest of the prophets.[5] It precipitated a great repenting and turning to God among the multitudes drawn to his preaching *"from Jerusalem and all Judea and the whole region of the Jordan."* –Matthew 3:5

The early ministry of the Lord Jesus extended the revival into the northern region of Galilee, preaching substantially the same message of repentance,[6] attested by baptism in water.[7] Apart from the additional theme of summoning the hearers to faith in himself, the major difference between the ministry of the Lord Jesus and that of John was that the older revivalist's work was not marked by the miraculous signs accompanying that of the Lord Jesus.[8] After the death of John the Baptist the revival apparently continued for a short time under the ministry of the Lord Jesus and his apostles until the miraculous feeding of the five thousand, when, following the bread of life discourse, there was a substantial diminishing of followers, as the Gospel of John recorded: *"From this time many of his disciples turned back and no longer followed him."* –John 6:66 Although great crowds continued to be attracted by his ministry on specific occasions,[9] there was an apparent polarizing in the community and even a resistance to his ministry on occasions.[10] The revival was obviously waning, even though many of those touched by the revival would remain loyal to him and ultimately they would comprise the core of the church that would continue his ministry.[11]

Approximately the first year and a half to two years of the Lord Jesus' ministry may be placed during this great revival period, in which the whole nation was being shaken. To see the ministry of the Lord Jesus from this perspective gives a fresh insight into the significance of the flow of events recorded in the Gospels. Davies also noted that: "the ministries of the Twelve and the Seventy were accompanied by revival phenomena,"[12] which would be expected from their occurrence during this same period.

The Revivals in Acts. The Resurrection of the Lord Jesus, for all its importance for Christian theology and in restoring the confidence of the disciples, did not itself apparently precipitate a general spiritual awakening, but rather prepared the leaders for that which was to come.

A. The Day of Pentecost. The next revival was the result of the outpouring of the Holy Spirit on the day of Pentecost.[13] This particular revival provides an excellent model as the Scriptures recorded in detail its causes, its effects, and its results. Primarily concentrated around the city of Jerusalem, the revival may have been carried further afield by those present from other parts of the Roman Empire and beyond its boundaries.[14] Scripture is silent on that point. It came in two waves, described in Acts 2 and in Acts 4–6. Some scholars separate the two and talk about two different revivals. In my opinion there was but a brief pause in the flow of the revival of Acts 2 before, regaining its momentum in Acts 4, it moved forward in even greater power, sweeping the church to a position of considerable influence in the Jewish community.[15]

B. The Samaritan Awakening. The next revival, described in Acts 8, was in Samaria. In the persecution following the death of Stephen, the disciples had been scattered abroad.[16] Some even traveled as far as Phoenicia, Cyprus, and Antioch.[17] One of the elders of the church appointed in Acts 6 had gone to Samaria, probably to the city of Shechem, or Gitta,[18] and there had begun an effective preaching ministry, proclaiming that Jesus is the Christ, accompanied by significant miracles of healing. The impact on the city was enormous: crowds thronged Philip, large numbers were converted, and *"there was great joy in the city."*[19]

> Philip went down to a city in Samaria and proclaimed the Messiah there. When the crowds heard Philip and saw the signs he performed, they all paid close attention to what he said. For with shrieks, impure spirits came out of many, and many who were paralyzed or lame were healed. So there was great joy in that city. –Acts 8:5-8

Not only did the Samaritans accept Jesus as the Messiah, but also as a consequence of Peter and John's visit, there was an outpouring of the Holy Spirit and an extension of the revival into many Samaritan villages.[20] Truly a substantial move of God had taken place among a people who were despised by the Jews but now were the recipients of an outpouring of God's Spirit comparable to that on the day of Pentecost.

Nor were the Samaritans the only people affected by this revival. As the wording of Acts 9 indicates, the conversion of Saul of Tarsus was part of that same movement of God. *"Meanwhile, Saul was still breathing out murderous threats against the Lord's disciples."*–Acts 9:1 At the same time as the awakening was transforming Samaria, Saul was pursuing the church beyond the borders of Palestine to Damascus.[21] Whether the Christian church had been established in Damascus as a result of the initial outpouring on the day of Pentecost, or as a result of the scattering of the Christians following the death of Stephen, is unclear in Scripture; however, it is obvious that some Jewish Christians had fled from Jerusalem to Damascus, since Ananias had heard of Saul's assault on the church.[22] Certainly the number of disciples in Damascus was substantial enough to warrant a special commission being given to Saul to go there and to bring back any Jewish Christians, who may have fled there and were engaged in propagating the Way, the early term for the Christian faith. Thank God for those revival converts: they would make a major impact in years to come.

The revival that took place, however, had largely come to an end by the time Saul, later known as Paul, returned to Judea.[23] Approximately three years had elapsed since his conversion and, at the time of his return to

Jerusalem, there does not seem to have been a noticeable revival occurring in Judea. What we do know is that Paul engaged in debate and discussion with the Hellenistic Jews.[24] To save him from an assassination plot, he was then sent back to his homeland of Tarsus in Asia Minor and the church enjoyed a time of peace and consolidation.[25] The major part of the church at this time was to be found in Judea, Samaria, Galilee, and Syria. Palestine generally had been powerfully affected by the revivals.

C. The North-West Judean Revival. This marked a new phase in revival development. The goal of revival became not just the conversion of individuals and the renewing of the existing church, but also the establishing of the church among hitherto unreached groups. The church was already present in this area; as Peter traveled about the countryside, he went to visit the saints in Lydda[26] where there already was an established church. Nevertheless, a new revival was about to come.

This new revival in northwestern Judea was prompted by the healing of a bedridden paralytic, Aeneas.

> There he found a man named Aeneas, who was paralyzed and had been bedridden for eight years. "Aeneas," Peter said to him, "Jesus Christ heals you. Get up and roll up your mat." Immediately Aeneas got up. All those who lived in Lydda and Sharon saw him and turned to the Lord. –Acts 9:33-35

The great turning to God that started in these twin cities moved up the coast to Joppa where, through the raising of the disciple Dorcas, many more people believed in the Lord.[27] From there it spilled over into Caesarea to the home of an influential Gentile named Cornelius. That there was an outpouring of God's Spirit upon Gentiles in this revival was astonishing to the hitherto exclusively Jewish Church.[28] Furthermore, this substantial movement of God's Spirit both prepared for an exponential growth of the church and was ultimately to change the texture of Christianity for all time.

D. The North Syrian Revival. The next revival in Acts 11 was briefly mentioned, almost in passing:

Now those who had been scattered by the persecution that broke out when Stephen was killed traveled as far as Phoenicia, Cyprus and Antioch, spreading the word only among Jews. Some of them, however, men from Cyprus and Cyrene, went to Antioch and began to speak to Greeks also, telling them the good news about the Lord Jesus. The Lord's hand was with them, and a great number of people believed and turned to the Lord.

News of this reached the church in Jerusalem, and they sent Barnabas to Antioch. When he arrived and saw what the grace of God had done, he was glad and encouraged them all to remain true to the Lord with all their hearts. He was a good man, full of the Holy Spirit and faith, and a great number of people were brought to the Lord.

Then Barnabas went to Tarsus to look for Saul, and when he found him, he brought him to Antioch. So for a whole year Barnabas and Saul met with the church and taught great numbers of people. The disciples were called Christians first at Antioch. –Acts 11:19-25

Barnabas himself, described in this passage as *"a man full of the Holy Spirit,"* had a prophetic ministry, and scripture tells us *"a great number of people were brought to the Lord through his ministry."* Paul joined him in this revival and the revival continued at a great pace; large numbers of people were brought into the church and discipled through the prophetic ministry manifested there in Antioch.

Despite the paucity of details regarding the Antiochian revival, from the information included by Luke it is apparent that Antioch in Syria experienced a special outpouring of God's Spirit, with a great sense of conviction, many conversions, and outstanding miracles. Although we do not know how far that revival spread, we do know that it made a substantial impact beyond the city of Antioch and the northern Palestine region of Syria, so much so that the outreach to the Gentiles largely resulted from this revival.

In many revivals God raises up a missionary force to send the gospel out to the uttermost parts of the earth. Each one of the revivals noted resulted in the sounding forth of the gospel to unevangelized communities. It began with the building up of the church, with the bringing of the church back into a right relationship with God, and with the stirring, quickening, and inspiring of believers with the prospects of what God was going to do.

E. The Ephesian Revival. This is the last major revival recorded in the New Testament.[29] The preparatory ministry was that of the great preacher from Alexandria, Apollos, who had been brought to Christ through those affected by the revival in the days of John the Baptist.[30] He apparently knew nothing about the earlier outpourings of God's Spirit recorded in Acts. His line came through Alexandria. Upon Paul's return to Ephesus, he encountered twelve men, converted through Apollos's ministry. There followed an outpouring of God's Spirit upon the small group that proved to be the key that opened up, not just Ephesus itself, but also the whole of the province of Asia, to a spiritual awakening that continued for two years and ultimately touched every person in the province.[31]

Throughout that time period there were extraordinary miracles through Paul's ministry. Handkerchiefs and aprons that had touched him were taken to the sick; their illnesses were cured; evil spirits left them; the name of Jesus was held in high honor; people were seized with fear; believers came and surrendered their magic scrolls to be burned; and there was a clear separation between the church and the world. Truly this was a great move of God, which Luke summarized: *"In this way the word of the Lord spread widely and grew in power."*–Acts 19:20 What began with an outpouring of God's Spirit, spilled over into miracles, conviction, separation, holiness, increasing and abounding godliness and the Word of God spreading until the whole of that region was encompassed within the framework of that spiritual awakening.

It came to an end in a riot. Wherever Paul went, his ministry seemingly was accompanied by revival and riot. At times revivals produce a reaction on the part of the unconverted multitudes. They may have been affected by the revival, but revival can have a polarizing effect. Not everybody is converted. Some, when they hear the gospel and experience the outpouring of God's Spirit upon the community, fall under conviction and rather than submit to the conviction and repent of their sins, take a strong stand against it. They may repudiate that conviction, refuse to repent, and even react violently against the convicting power of the Holy Spirit. Every revival in history has been marked by this. While the revival is spreading rapidly and public opinion is favorable, the opposition may remain quiescent, but at the first opportunity there may come an uprising of antipathy toward the revival and those affected by it.

The Model Revival. The revival on the day of Pentecost serves as a significant model of a New Testament revival. In Baker's estimation, "the revival at Jerusalem on the day of Pentecost was the greatest of all time."[32] Luke's account certainly provides a canonical basis for evaluating all subsequent outpourings of the Holy Spirit as was the practice in the early church.[33]

First, **the preconditions**. What did the disciples do that prepared the way for the revival? The community at large had rejected the Messiah. The vast majority of the Jews were not aware of the resurrection appearances of Jesus. Those resurrection appearances had now ended, and Jesus had ascended to glory.

From the outset, Acts 1:12–14 tells us they engaged in consistent, corporate prayer:

> Then the apostles returned to Jerusalem from the hill called the Mount of Olives, a Sabbath day's walk from the city. When they arrived, they went upstairs to the room where they were staying. Those present were Peter, John, James and Andrew; Philip and Thomas, Bartholomew and Matthew; James son of Alphaeus and Simon the Zealot, and Judas son of James. They all joined together constantly in prayer, along with the women and Mary the mother of Jesus, and with his brothers.–Acts 1:12-14

Prayer is always basic to revivals. Matthew Henry (1662–1714), the renowned Puritan Bible commentator, is reputed to have declared: "When God intends great mercy for His people, the first thing He does is set them a-praying." By turning their hearts toward prayer, they engaged in the right action and in the right place. In Acts 1:4 the Lord Jesus said *Do not leave*

Jerusalem," and in Jerusalem they stayed. In obedience they did what Jesus told them to do in the right place.

Acts 1:12-14 also shows us they had the right attitude—one of substantial unity. The Greek adverb *homothumadon* indicates a singleness of mind and purpose. Those who would see revival must learn to flow in the direction that God determines. Too often in church prayer meetings one wants to pray about one thing and another about something else. Each has his own direction and although the participants may be physically in one place, they are not united in purpose and mind as the disciples were united in purpose and mind.

Secondly, **the pattern of the revival.** Not only was the Holy Spirit poured out upon the gathered disciples on the day of Pentecost, but also there was a recurrence of prophetic ministry. The Greek verb *apophthengomai* was generally used for an inspired utterance and was applied by Luke both to the initial speaking in tongues (*glossolalia*) and to Peter's address to the wondering crowd.[34] Furthermore, Peter explained the earlier tongues-speaking as the fulfillment of the prophet Joel's promise of a recurrence of prophesying as a result of the outpouring of the Spirit.[35] The use of this term for Peter's address indicated it was not a homiletically prepared sermon as we would understand it today, but a divinely inspired utterance or prophecy.

The effect of this upon his hearers was dramatic as implied by the use of the Greek verb *katanussomai*,[36] for an overwhelming sense of conviction. In his letter to the Romans, Paul used the related noun to express the prophet Isaiah's reference to *"a deep sleep."*[37] Perhaps this experience corresponds to the more recent revival phenomenon of "being slain in the Spirit." Certainly the hearers' question "Brothers, what shall we do?" was more than a mild curiosity. It was a cry from the heart because of an overwhelming sense of conviction by the Holy Spirit.

Thirdly, **the results of the revival**. The results may be summarized as: the daily growth of the church by the addition of those who were being saved; the renewal of the church as the newly converted devoted themselves to the apostles' teaching, fellowship, worship, and prayer; and the recurrence of miraculous manifestations:

They devoted themselves to the apostles' teaching and to fellowship, to the breaking of bread and to prayer. Everyone was filled with awe at the many wonders and signs performed by the apostles. All the believers were together and had everything in common. They sold property and possessions to give to anyone who had need. Every day they continued to meet together in the temple courts. They broke bread in their homes and ate together with glad and sincere hearts, praising God and enjoying the favor of all the people. And the Lord added to their number daily those who were being saved. –Acts 2:42-47

Despite the inspiration of the resurrection of the Lord Jesus and the dramatic challenge of the commission to take the gospel to the whole world, with the promise of miraculous signs in confirmation of the message proclaimed,[38] there was no recurrence of miraculous manifestations until the Holy Spirit was poured out. Then the miraculous was restored to the church, and continued for a considerable time afterward. As Orr appropriately noted there has been a repetition of many of the phenomena of the Acts of the Apostles in subsequent evangelical awakenings.[39]

Endnotes

1   Orr, *The Fervent Prayer*, vii
2   Matthew 3:7–10
3   Luke 3:7–19
4   Matthew 14:3, 4; Mark 6:17–19
5   Matthew 11:7–15; Luke 7:24–28
6   Matthew 4:12, 17; Mark 1:14, 15
7   John 3:22; 4:1, 2
8   John 10:41
9   Matthew 15:30, 31; 19:2; 20:29; Luke 19:37
10 John 7:1ff; Matthew 16:21; Luke 9:51–56
11 Acts 1:1ff
12 Davies, op. cit., 49, 50
13 Acts 2:1ff
14 Acts 2:9, 10
15 Acts 5:13, 14; 6:7
16 Acts 8:1–4
17 Acts 11:19
18 R. N. Longenecker: "The Acts of the Apostles" in F. E. Gaebelein (ed.): *The Expositor's Bible Commentary* (Grand Rapids, MI: Regency, 1981), 9.356
19 Acts 8:5–8
20 Acts 8:14–17, 25
21 Acts 26:9–12
22 Acts 9:13, 14
23 Galatians 1:17, 18
24 Acts 9:28, 29
25 Acts 9:31
26 Acts 9:32
27 Acts 9:42
28 Acts 10; 11:1–18
29 Acts 19:1ff
30 Acts 18:24ff
31 Acts 19:10

32 Baker, op. cit.,136

33 Acts 10:47; 11:15–17; 15:8, 9

34 Acts 2:4, 14

35 Acts 2:16ff cf. Joel 2:28, 29

36 Acts 2:37

37 Romans 11:8 cf. Isaiah 29:10

38 Mark 16:15–18

39 Orr, op. cit., vii

Part II

Historical Revivals

Chapter 5

Early Church

100–300 AD

By the end of the first century, there were churches in a large part of the Mediterranean area, not only in Rome, Greece, Crete, throughout Asia Minor and the eastern Mediterranean, along its southern coast from Egypt to Libya, but also beyond the Roman Empire in Mesopotamia, Media, and Parthia. With the extensive penetration of the church into the eastern Mediterranean and Middle East came great potential for future spiritual awakenings. Certainly, according to the writings of the last surviving apostle, there was a great need for a spiritual awakening among the seven churches of Asia Minor mentioned in his *Apocalypse.*[1]

Although, due to "the fragmentary nature of the evidence for what happened,"[2] there are no specific accounts of spiritual awakenings between the end of Paul's life and the middle of the second century, there are indications that such probably occurred—for example, Pliny the Younger wrote to the Emperor Trajan in about AD 112 regarding the growth of Christianity and demise of paganism in Bithynia in the recent past:

The contagion of this superstition has spread not only in the cities, but in the rural districts as well; …the temples…have been almost

57

deserted, …the sacred rites…have been long neglected…and (for) sacrificial victims…[until] recently, a buyer was rarely to be found.[3]

Such hints suggest that much more had happened than we can now trace, for example, the rise of the Jewish-Christian prophet Elkesai (c. 100) and the movement centered upon his ministry in northern Mesopotamia that subsequently overflowed from Mesopotamia to Antioch in Syria, across southern Asia Minor, down into Egypt, and ultimately to Rome. Eusebius also noted that through the ministry of Quadratus (c. 120), bishop of Athens in succession to the martyred Publius, "the faith of the people [was] revived by his exertions."[4] Quadratus was also "said to have been distinguished for his prophetical gifts" and, together with others:

performed the office of evangelists to those who had not yet heard the faith. . . . The holy Spirit also, wrought many wonders as yet through them, so that as soon as the gospel was heard, men voluntarily in crowds, and eagerly, embraced the true faith with their whole minds.[5]

Church historians usually account for the growth of the church in the post-apostolic period in terms of the unifying language and culture, the relative ease of travel in the *pax Romana* (Roman peace), the Jewish Diaspora, the growth of the mystery religions replacing the old paganism, the admirable ethics, and the communal evangelism of the early Christian church.[6] The role of the supernatural, so obvious in the apostolic church,[7] should not simply be attributed to legend, but recognized as a recurrent factor emerging from successive outpourings of the Spirit.

The Second-Century Awakenings. The first clear indicators of another revival period do not come until the middle of the second century. A spiritual awakening began about AD 150 in the area around Phrygia in **Asia Minor**. It later spilled over into the Phrygian missionary area of Lyons (Lugdunum) in Gaul, where Irenaeus (c. 115–202) exercised a powerful ministry; to Carthage, where Tertullian (c. 160–215) later also had a notable ministry; and to Alexandria, where Origen (c. 185–254) was one of the great teachers, and from where missionary activity reached down into Ethiopia, along the Persian Gulf, and out to what are now the Gulf States but then were nomadic Arabian tribes. This awakening even affected Rome itself.

By the end of the second century, more than half of the Mediterranean basin had been Christianized. Most of Palestine had been well and thoroughly evangelized. In northern Egypt, the Libyan area from Carthage westward to modern Mauritania, southern France, the area around Rome and throughout southern Italy, Greece, especially down the east coast, in the Peloponnesus, and along the west coast of Macedonia to Illyricum, and outside of the Roman Empire in the Mesopotamian valley, there were indications of a powerful Christian presence. The penetration of Christianity in those areas is indicative of the impact made.

The Third-Century Awakenings. Further in the third century there was another outbreak of revival. Once again in the west, in Rome under Novatian (c. 200–258) and his counterpart Novatus (c. 240) in Carthage and also in Rome, both cities were strongly affected. Among those affected by this awakening the puritanical Donatist movement arose almost a century later. Also, at this time in Pontus, Asia Minor, the famous revivalist, Gregory Thaumaturgus (c. 213–270), exercised a powerful ministry attested by many miraculous healings, from which he received his name "wonder-worker." When Gregory became bishop of Pontus, it is reported, "he found only seventeen Christians in his see and at his death (thirty years later) only seventeen remained pagan."[8]

Also, in the Mesopotamian area among the followers of the Jewish-Christian prophet Elkesai, came a fresh move of God's Spirit. Mani (216–277), from whom the later Manichean movement was named, was raised in Seleucia-Ctesiphon, a chief city of Mesopotamia, among Jewish Christians where there was a genuine move of the Holy Spirit. Mani himself had a succession of visions of the Lord, the first of which when he was twelve years of age resulted in an apparently life-changing experience of repentance and conversion to Christ. As a result of the second vision about the age of fifteen, he was baptized in the Holy Spirit and from his third vision at about the age of twenty-two he began his powerful prophetic ministry that initially had a considerable impact.

When persecution came from the predominant Zoroastrianism, however, Mani did not head westward into the area of orthodox Christianity, but he fled eastward and in his travels into northern India he came into contact with Hinduism and Buddhism, from which he acquired some new ideas and teachings, which by his return he had welded together into a hodgepodge system that was no longer truly Christian. Tragically, what could have been a great revival movement on the borders of the Roman Empire ended up being perverted into a non-Christian movement. For several centuries thereafter Christianity found itself battling against the Manichean movement.

By the end of the third century, the expansion of Christianity was quite phenomenal. Much of western Asia, especially Asia Minor and Palestine, southern Europe and northern Africa were thoroughly Christianized. The leaders of the Roman Empire realized that the temples of the old gods were forsaken and Christianity was now the dominant faith of the empire. Tertullian had boasted, almost a century earlier, "All we have left you is the temples!"[9] If that was true in North Africa at the beginning of the third century, it was certainly true throughout the empire by its end. It has been conservatively estimated that at least 10 percent of the population professed to be Christian by this time.[10]

The great Diocletian persecution at the beginning of the fourth century, the last persecution the church endured, was prompted by the pagan priestly cult that felt that if Christianity were not eliminated then they would be wiped out. It was a struggle to the death because of the effective penetration that Christianity had made at that point in time into pagan society, which was being revolutionized by Christianity even where it did not want to be. It could not avoid the influence of Christian teaching. It was not surprising that Constantine (c. 274–337) recognized the way things were going and declared for Christianity. By so doing he allied himself with the single most powerful force in the empire of that day, Christianity.

At the close of the third century, history records the remarkable folk movement outside the Roman Empire in the kingdom of Armenia under

Gregory the Illuminator (c.240–332), the Apostle of Armenia, who, after an extensive imprisonment of some twelve years in a pit near Artashat for attempting to evangelize, not only successfully prayed for the restoration of the sanity of King Tiridates III, his persecutor, but led the whole royal court, the nobility, and ultimately, at least nominally, the whole nation to faith in Christ.[11]

The Model Revival. The second-century revival has been called "A Second Century Pentecost."[12] The epicenter of the awakening apparently was Phrygia in Asia Minor, which is not surprising because Asia Minor had some of the oldest Christian communities outside of Palestine, which, south of Syria, had been devastated by the second Jewish war about AD 130. Although Montanus's name and reputation in later centuries came to dominate the awakening, the movement preceded and extended beyond his influence.

The revival itself apparently began about AD 150. By the end of the century, this outpouring of God's Spirit, or the New Prophecy movement, as its proponents apparently called it,[13] had impacted a substantial part of the Roman Empire, from its beginning in western Asia, extending into North Africa, from Alexandria to Carthage, and northward into France among the Gauls of Lyons. Some even saw signs of it in Vienna, although the evidence from Vienna is rather limited. In Rome, also, there seems to have been a major move of God's Spirit.

Although the conversion of Justin Martyr (c. 100–165) probably preceded the awakening, from the dating of his writings, *First Apology* (c. 152), *Second Apology* (c. 153), and *Dialogue with Trypho* (c. 160), his prominence as an apologist coincided with this time. He saw confirmation of Jesus' messiahship in the contemporary and continuing presence of God's Spirit in the church.[14]

Some of Montanus's early followers claimed to have entered into their experience through the earlier prophet, Quadratus of Athens (c. 80–138) or through his female contemporary, Ammia of Philadelphia (c. 100–150).[15] Probably about AD 156[16] Montanus, of Ardabau in Mysia, was soundly converted to Christ, experienced a powerful baptism with the Holy Spirit and subsequently began to prophesy. Although later writers, following the lead of Didymus the Blind[17] (c. 309–398), described him as a priest of Cybele[18] or Magna Mater,[19] contemporary evidence does not support this. Nevertheless, his obvious leadership abilities enabled him to attract a considerable following, although he himself was an immature new convert.[20] Age and prior leadership does not guarantee Christian maturity. Paul warned about the practice of putting a novice in a position of leadership.[21] It can be destructive to him and to the church that he leads. When leaders in the non-Christian world come into the church, sometimes they are thrust into positions of leadership that their spiritual maturity does not warrant. Inflated with pride, they can easily go astray. Montanus is a classic example; because of his background he quickly came into a position of leadership and when his practices and his teachings were challenged, he refused to submit his ministry and his life to the judgment of his peers.

Despite several attempts by the institutional church bishops of the area to dissuade Montanus and his fellow leaders, the prophetesses Maximilla and Priscilla, they apparently repudiated the bishops' authority, believing that the Montanists alone represented the genuine revival and outpouring of God's Spirit. They apparently refused to allow their prophecies or practices to be judged in accordance with Scripture. By thus moving away from biblical accountability, they placed themselves and their followers in danger. Even when initially there may be no evidence of doctrinal heresy, when leaders think that they alone are able to hear the voice of God and correctly interpret his will, they are moving in the wrong direction.

Montanus and the other leaders of the New Prophecy movement apparently preached a strong Bible message, calling for a return to the basic standards of primitive Christianity, which is what appealed to Montanism's most prominent convert, Tertullian of Carthage (c. 160–220). Montanus's message also included a strong emphasis on the soon coming of Christ, which was to be a major feature of many of the pre-Reformation revivals.

Although the movement still stressed Christian teachings, it began steadily moving away from basic biblical truths. By the end of the second century, the major part of the revival movement in the East had severed its connections with orthodox Christianity and formed a separate group. The strand of the revival associated with Montanus came to be viewed as error, not because of theological or doctrinal heresy,[22] but because the way in which prophesying was performed.

The revival in the West maintained its strong connection with the institutional church because not only was Lyons a metropolitan center but also Irenaeus, who was so prominent in the awakening, was the second missionary bishop of the expanding work begun by Pothinus (c. 87–177) among the Gauls in Southern France. As a bishop of the church, he could ensure that the revival kept true to orthodox Christianity and free from the problems that had emerged at the eastern edge of the movement in Asia Minor. Irenaeus was a disciple of Polycarp of Smyrna (c. 70–155), who in turn was a disciple of the last of the original Twelve, John the Evangelist (d. 98?). He was renowned as a very godly man, with a strong reputation for opposing heresies. In his most famous book *Against Heresies* (c. 180), he spoke clearly about the current outpouring of God's Spirit and the miracles that he knew were being manifested.[23] His other extant book *Demonstration of the Apostolic Preaching* (c. 178) also bears the hallmarks of a revival publication providing instruction for recent Christian converts.

Although little is known about the ministry of Pantaenus (d. 190) in Alexandria, Eusebius reported that:

> …[Pantaenus] displayed such ardor, and so zealous a disposition, respecting the divine word, that he was constituted a herald of the gospel of Christ to the nations of the east, and advanced even as far as India. There were even there yet many evangelists of the word, who were ardently striving to employ their inspired zeal after the apostolic example, to increase and build up the divine word.[24]

The growth of the work in Egypt was such as to warrant the establishing of a catechetical school with both an evangelistic and training purpose, which on his return from his missionary travels, Pantaenus headed until his death in AD 190. His illustrious successors, Clement of Alexandria (c. 155–220) and Origen (c. 185–254), both former students of the school, continued in the same spirit. The latter in his rebuttal of the pagan philosopher, Celsus, appealed to the continuation of miraculous manifestations as evidence of divine anointing.[25] On being exiled from Alexandria, Origen established a similar school in Caesarea in Palestine, from where a former student, Gregory Thaumaturgus, became bishop of Neo-Caesarea in Pontus and was extensively involved in the next major spiritual awakening.

Further to the west in North Africa the awakening continued to bear fruit in the city of Carthage, where Tertullian, a doctor of law and a brilliant mind, was converted. At first a strong champion of orthodoxy, he later became disillusioned over the rejection of the New Prophecy revival movement by the institutional church. Ultimately, within the church in North Africa a new movement, called Tertullianism emerged, seeking to retain the best of the revival emphases matched with orthodox teaching. Eventually this too separated and was not to reunite with the main body of the church in North Africa for some two centuries until the time of Augustine.

In Rome the awakening initially was welcomed. As a result of the intervention of the Asian bishops, however, the movement came to be rejected, or at least, viewed with great suspicion except for that in Gaul, where Irenaeus maintained beneficent oversight.

This revival then had a mixed influence upon the church. On the one hand, the Eastern Orthodox Christians tended to be very skeptical about future revival movements, having seen the mainly negative impact that had been made on the most Christianized part of the empire, Asia Minor, by the New Prophecy movement. On the other hand, along the southern shore of the Mediterranean there was some ambivalence toward such movements in the future because of the mixed results there. In the West, however, there was a greater openness toward subsequent revival movements because of the benevolent impact made. Not surprisingly then, the whole missionary advance of the church among the tribes of western Europe came about as a result of successive waves of revival.

Endnotes

1 Revelation ch. 2–3.

2 R. E. Davies, op. cit., 55.

3 Pliny: "Epistle to Trajan" in H. Bettenson, (ed.): *Documents of the Christian Church* (London: Oxford U., 1963 edn.), 4.

4 Eusebius, op. cit., IV.23.

5 Ibid. III.37.

6 W. W. Gasque: "The Church Expands: Jerusalem to Rome" in T. Dowley (ed.): *Eerdmans' Handbook to the History of Christianity* (Grand Rapids, MI: Eerdmans, 1977), 68ff.

7 Mark 16:20; Acts 8:4–8; 10:32ff; 14:3ff, 27; 15:3, 4, 12; Romans 15:8, 9; 1 Cor. 4:20; 1 Thess. 1:5.

8 K. S. Latourette: *A History of Christianity* (New York, NY: Harper & Row, 1975 edn. Revised), I.76.

9 Tertullian: *Apology*, xxxvii.5.

10 J. H. Kane: *A Concise History of the Christian World Mission* (Grand Rapids, MI: Baker, 1982), 17.

11 Latourette: *History of the Expansion of Christianity* (Exeter, UK: Paternoster, 1971), I.105–106; Davies, op. cit., 57.

12 D. Allen: *A Second Century Pentecost in Redemption Tidings*, 12. January, 1978, 3.

13 D. E. Aune: *Prophecy in Early Christianity* (Grand Rapids, MI: Eerdmans, 1983), 313.

14 Justin: *Dialogue with Trypho*, 88.

15 Eusebius, op. cit., V.17.

16 Epiphanius: *Panarion*, 48.1 contra Eusebius, op. cit., V.16.

17 Didymus: *On the Trinity*, III.41.

18 Latourette: *History of the Expansion*, op. cit., I.346; S. M. Burgess: art. "Holy Spirit, Doctrine of: The Ancient Fathers" in *The New Dictionary of Pentecostal and Charismatic Movements*, 732.

19 G. H. Williams & E. Waldvogel: art. "A History of Speaking in Tongues and Related Gifts" in M. P. Hamilton (ed.), *The Charismatic Movement* (Grand Rapids, MI: Eerdmans, 1975), 65.

20 Eusebius, ibid., V.16.

21 1 Timothy 3:6.
22 Davies, op. cit., 57.
23 Irenaeus: *Against Heresies*, II.xxxii.4–5.
24 Eusebius, op. cit., V.10.
25 Origen: *Against Celsus*, I.6, and III.24.

Chapter 6

Imperial Church

300-600 AD

From the beginning of the fourth century, as Christianity moved into the Imperial Church period, there was a succession of powerful moves of God. The fourth century itself was marked by some remarkable events. A category of preachers came up in the years following the accession of Constantine in AD 306 that was to have a most powerful effect on the future of the church. Some of the names of these preachers will not be as familiar as others. At the same time as Ulfilas (310–388), the apostle to the Goths, was impacting the barbarian Germanic tribes' people across the Danube frontier of the Roman Empire, Gregory Nazianzus (330–389) was exercising a powerful charismatic ministry in Asia Minor, and the renowned and eloquent Ambrose of Milan (339–397) had a similar ministry in northern Italy. These remarkable contemporaries were followed by the equally influential patriarch of Constantinople, John Chrysostom (c. 350–407), "the golden mouthed" orator of the early church, who drew great crowds to hear God's Word; the disciple of Ambrose, Augustine (354–430), bishop of Hippo, North Africa, whose theological writings were to influence many generations within the Roman and Protestant Churches; the learned Jerome (c. 345–419), translator of the Latin Vulgate Bible; and the controversial yet brilliant Theodore of Mopsuestia (c. 350–428).

It is by no means coincidental that such people arose to prominence at approximately the same time. The church had entered into a new era of opportunity, which these men recognized.

Because it became fashionable for pagans to worship in the Christian churches, many joined without a real conversion experience. Many clergy, without realizing the effect their actions would have, opened the churches and welcomed them in. Influential figures in the Imperial Court could hardly be denied the right to speak and even to vote on church affairs, when Constantine himself, while still unbaptized, had presided over the Council of Nicaea (325). His officials, therefore, could expect to be accorded the same privileges and be given similar seats of honor and prestige.

The Fourth-Century Awakenings. The Monastic Movement. While the major part of the institutional church was embroiled in theological controversy, God chose to pour his Spirit on specific individuals who made a significant impact on people groups, often outside the Roman Empire proper. Antony of Egypt (c. 251–356), the father of anchoritic monasticism, after a life-transforming encounter with God at the age of twenty, retreated from contemporary society to seek the Lord. Within a short time, according to his younger contemporary and biographer, Athanasius (c. 296–373), he became "responsible for a strong spiritual movement as large numbers followed him in taking up the monastic life and as he performed many miracles, healings, (and) exorcisms."[1] Inspired by the example of Antony and other anchorites, Pachomius (c. 287–346) pioneered cenobitic monasticism, establishing his first of eleven centers in Tabennisi on the Nile (c. 320) as a self-supporting training center for both personal devotion and service for the Lord. From these centers thousands of cenobites ranged out into the surrounding communities spreading the gospel and inspiring multitudes to turn to the Lord.[2] Also inspired by Antony and his biographer, Athanasius, Martin of Tours (c. 335–400) founded a monastic community in Liguge in Gaul, later moved to Marmoutier. From his bishopric in Tours, like the majority of the Gallic bishops, he and his monks proceeded to evangelize the surrounding pagan population accompanied by miraculous signs and exorcisms.[3] Subsequently, other anchorites, like Simeon the Stylite (c. 390–459), made their home on the top of pillars, from which vantage point they preached to the thousands attracted to their ministries.[4]

The Gothic Awakening. Outside the Roman Empire, Ulfilas, the great missionary evangelist to the Goths, had a powerful impact on the barbarian tribespeople. Variously described as being descended from Gothic or Cappadocian Christian captives,[5] much of Ulfila's life is shrouded in history and legend, other than the fact that at about the age of thirty he was consecrated as bishop of the Gothic Christians by the Arian, Eusebius of Nicomedia (d. 341), who was briefly bishop of Constantinople during the reign of Emperor Constantius II (reigned 337–361). During his evangelistic ministry, not only was he credited with devising a Gothic alphabet so that he could translate the Bible into the language of those among whom he was ministering, but also, he reportedly chopped down a sacred tree with impunity and built a church with its wood. From that center his ministry, often attested by miracles of healing and deliverance, apparently had a major impact over the whole Gothic nation, resulting in their espousal of the Christian faith, albeit of an Arian theology.

The Late Fourth Century. Toward the end of the fourth century came a further move of God's Spirit, which effected a remarkable transformation within the Christian church. Among the renowned Cappadocian Fathers, the outstanding preaching ministry of Gregory Nazianzus was noted for the miracles, which were reported to have accompanied it, particularly visual and auditory manifestations, and miracles of healing, and deliverance, resulting in outstanding numbers of converts. At this time emerged the powerful ministry of Ambrose in Milan. To encourage congregational participation as in the pre-imperial church, Ambrose developed a more extensive liturgy, modeled on the Old Testament psalmody. Many coming into the institutional church were unfamiliar with the participatory and charismatic worship derived from the Jewish synagogue,[6] but were accustomed to a temple style of worship, in which the attendees simply observed the professionals offering worship on their behalf. Ambrose's desire undoubtedly was to involve the worshippers directly in appropriate worship.

Some prominent converts were gained, such as the renowned Latin church father, Augustine. Converted partly through the ministry of Ambrose of Milan, and partly through reading the story of Antony's conversion,[7] he became one of the most influential people from the Imperial Church period. Whatever influence his earlier Manichaeism may have had on his Christian theology, his remarkable conversion experience undoubtedly helped form it. In the late summer of AD 386, while in the garden of a house in Milan, he heard a child's voice say: "Tole Lege" (Take and read). His eyes lighted on an open Bible and taking it up he read:

Let us behave decently, as in the daytime, not in orgies and drunkenness, not in sexual immorality and debauchery, not in dissension and jealousy. Rather, clothe yourselves with the Lord Jesus Christ, and do not think about how to gratify the desires of the sinful nature."[8]

As is often the case in revivals, his conversion included a direct auditory or visual phenomenon. Many are deeply challenged through the straightforward preaching of the Word. Others are brought face-to-face with a truth that they have been unwilling to respond to, by visions or by auditory phenomena, as God, in a salutary fashion, breaks into their world. Augustine had known for some time that he ought to break with his immoral lifestyle; nevertheless it took that transforming encounter to finally persuade him. Despite his outstanding conversion experience, throughout his subsequent lengthy bishopric in Hippo, near Carthage in North Africa, there is no evidence of any revival or spiritual awakening under his ministry. Conversely, he vigorously opposed the Donatists, and Pelagians, and sought to embrace the last remnants of the Tertullian revival movement within the ambit of the institutional church.

Equally renowned as a preacher and church leader was John Chrysostom, bishop of Constantinople, whose phenomenal ministry attracted great crowds and was attested to by miraculous signs, indicative of a divine anointing.

The Fifth-Century Awakenings. As the new century dawned the Roman Empire was reeling under the barbarian invasion; Rome itself was sacked by Alaric and his Visigoths in AD 410; the Arian Vandals, together with the pagan Alans and Suevi, swept through Gaul to occupy Spain and much of north Africa; and the Franks and Burgundians occupied the now devastated Gaul. The church in the west was embroiled in the controversy over the British theologian Pelagius (c. 350–425), the nemesis of Augustine; and the church in the east faced its own controversies over Nestorianism and Eutychianism. A time less conducive to spiritual awakening could hardly be imagined.

Nevertheless, an awakening was to come in a limited but historically significant area. Off the west coast of the mainland of Britain lies the island now called **Ireland**. Ireland's barbarian tribes were ruled over by five kings with one a high king, who had kept the land virtually inviolate from any real Christian penetration, despite several attempts from the South. As Roman authority in the west disintegrated, especially after the withdrawal of the legions (398–402) from Britain, the Irish began raiding the west coast for slaves.

One such slave, taken in one of the Irish high king Niall's raids around AD 405[9] was a young man with the Celtic name of Succat, better known by his Latin name, Patricius or Patrick (c.390–461). Taken from his comfortable Christian home on his family estate, Bannavem Taburniae, near Old Kilpatrick, Dumbarton,[10] he became the slave of Miliucc, a landowner of Slemish, near Ballymena, County Antrim, Northern Ireland.[11] During his six years of captivity he experienced a personal encounter with God:

And there the Lord opened my mind to an awareness of my unbelief, in order that, even so late, I might remember my transgressions and turn with all my heart to the Lord my God.[12]

While caring for the flocks and herds of his captor, Patrick devoted himself to prayer and fasting, "because the Spirit was burning in (him) at that time."[13] During one such period, he heard a voice commending his devotion and promising his soon return home.[14] After a remarkable sea journey to the west coast of Gaul, now devastated by the Vandals and their allies, several notable experiences of divine provision and deliverance, and a brief stay in the monastery on St. Honorat, one of the two Lerins Islands, Patrick finally returned home to his kinsfolk, where:

in a vision of the night, I saw a man whose name was Victoricus coming as if from Ireland with innumerable letters, and he gave me one of them, and I read the beginning of the letter: The Voice of the Irish; and . . . I seemed to hear the voice of those who were beside the forest of Focluth which is near the western sea, . . . crying as if with one voice: We beg you, holy youth, that you shall come and shall walk again among us.[15]

Finally, about 432, following a period of theological study under Germanus of Auxerre (c.378–448), a now middle-aged Patrick returned to Ireland as the recognized bishop.[16] He landed in the region of Tara as the pagan Druid priests were holding their Spring festival. Traditionally all fires would be extinguished the day before the celebratory festival, when they would lighten the darkness by rekindling the fires. Realizing what was about to happen, Patrick hurried to the nearest hill, built a gigantic bonfire, which he set ablaze, causing a furor. The king of Tara, who was also high king of Ireland, Laoghaire, son of Niall, (reigned 428–464) and soldiers came, ready to execute him for contravening their religious observances. However, through a series of miracles, God intervened, changing the king's heart. Many of the king's followers became ardent Christians and in the ensuing awakening, most of the king's family was soundly converted. His son, Fedilmid, donated his estate at Trim on the Boyne to establish a permanent center from which the evangelization of Ireland could proceed.

For the next thirty years his ministry among the Irish continued with phenomenal results, including many miracles. While some of the stories told about him were clearly legendary, there must have been some basis in reality for them to gain credence, especially those recounted during his lifetime and that of his contemporaries. It is estimated that during those years he established 365 churches and gained some 120,000 converts.[17] From the impact Patrick's ministry made, the large numbers converted to the Christian faith, and the churches he established, a remarkable move of God undoubtedly occurred, which inspired a new generation not only to evangelize the barbarian conquerors of the British mainland, but extend their efforts throughout post-Roman Europe.

Even there, change was underway. Clovis, king of the Franks (reigned 481–511), influenced by his catholic Christian wife, Clothilda, a Burgundian princess, decided to become a Christian and, together with three thousand of his followers, was baptized on Christmas Day, 496, at Reims, opening the door for the reevangelization of Europe.

The Sixth-Century Awakenings. In the east, despite the pressure on the Byzantine Empire from the barbarian invasions and the internal conflicts in the church, the apostolic missionary impulse was not absent, especially in the wake of spiritual awakenings, resulting in the evangelization of Nubia (c. 545), and the spread of the Jacobite and Nestorian churches throughout the Persian Empire, India, central Asia, and China.

The Jacobite Churches were named after Jacob Baradaeus, bishop of Edessa (d. 578), who was converted during the awakening around 540 and began almost four decades of itinerant ministry from the Nile to the Euphrates, preaching, establishing churches and monasteries, and ordaining a hundred thousand clergy, eighty-nine bishops, and two patriarchs.[18] Despite the losses from Imperial persecution as Monophysites and from the Muslim conquests in the succeeding centuries, the Jacobite churches continue to exist. "Of all the branches of Christianity east of the Euphrates, the Nestorians were the most numerous. Into the Nestorian fellowship went the descendants of most of the early Christian communities of the region."[19] Periodic stirrings through awakenings ensured a steady stream of monastic candidates to take up the missionary challenge and maintain the existence of such churches despite a succession of barbarian and Muslim conquests.

With the decline of the western Roman Empire, the newly established monasteries became the principal centers both for preserving the records of the faith and for extending that faith to new generations. Although later monasticism may have developed in a somewhat different direction, initially it served as a vehicle for gathering together the revived and their converts into communities for prayer, for study, and for copying the Scriptures, and from which they could go forth on evangelistic missions into the surrounding community. Until recent times, this continued as the primary method of missionary advance within the Roman Catholic communion. The church would send in a small group of monks as missionary evangelists who would establish a center, gather converts, train them in those centers, and then send them forth as preachers and evangelists back into their villages.

Wales. Despite the legendary efforts of Arthur of Camelot, regarding whom little of historical certainty is known, the brief respite resulting from the British victory in the Battle of Mons Badonicus (c. 500), and the limited assistance from Armorica (Brittany), the remnants of Roman British society retreated to the Welsh hills. Among the warriors from Armorica was Illtud (c. 500), a great-nephew of Germanus, who following a life-transforming experience, had a significant ministry in ensuring the continuation and growth of the church in Wales. From his monastic school in Llantwit Fawr, Glamorgan, his students proceeded to become leaders in the resurgence of Christianity in the western part of Britain and beyond; David (500–589), later to become the patron saint of Wales; Gildas the Wise (c. 500–570), the monk and historian; Paul Aurelian (c.435–575) and Samson of Dol (485–565), who reevangelized a newly fallen Brittany and its neighbors.

Ireland. Meanwhile in Ireland itself a fresh revival movement broke out about 540 associated with Finnian of Clonard (470–549). On one occasion, it is said, as he was preaching, a rainbow suddenly appeared as a confirmation of his message on a bright, clear day with not a cloud in the sky and no sign of rain, nor had there been rain for some time. In his center in Clonard, Finnian devoted himself to preparing "the Twelve Apostles of Ireland" to complete the evangelistic work of his mentor, Patrick. The move of the Holy Spirit through his ministry became so extensive that at one point some three thousand students were under instruction at Clonard.[20] Among those students of Finnian was the renowned missionary evangelist, Columba (521–597), the great-great grandson of Patrick's captor, King Niall. Although named as one of the Apostles of Ireland, Columba's renown came from his ministry across the sea in Scotland.

Scotland. Christianity among the southern Picts of Scotland had preceded Patrick, who in his *Letter to Coroticus* referred to them as "apostate Picts."[21] Whether Ninian (d. 432?), the apostle to the southern Picts, was responsible for their initial evangelization or their reevangelization is uncertain. Ninian reportedly was a Briton, who had studied in Rome, and met Martin of Tours, in honor of whose *Candida Casa* monastery in Marmoutier, he named his foundation in Galloway—Whithorn, from where an extensive evangelism of southern Scotland was undertaken with many reported miracles. Among those trained there was Finnian of Moville (495–589), who on his return to his native Ulster, established a further training center for the evangelization of the northwest of Ireland. Among his treasures was a copy of Jerome's Vulgate Latin Bible.

In about 560 Columba, who may have earlier been a student at Moville, while visiting Finnian, was caught surreptitiously copying part of the Latin Bible. His refusal to surrender it to Finnian caused the matter to be referred to the high king Diarmaid for his verdict. As the ruling favored Finnian, Columba's supporters responded with a pitched battle at Culdreimhne, north of Sligo (561), resulting in some three thousand deaths. Columba was held responsible and exiled to Scotland, promising not to return until he had won to Christ as many as had lost their lives in the conflict.[22]

With twelve companions he departed for Scotland's west coast, eventually landing on a small island, Iona, where in 563 he established a center for evangelizing the remaining pagan Picts. Two years later, accompanied by Cainnech (517–600) and Comgall (517–601), Columba visited the Pictish high King Brude in Inverness, as a result of which the door was opened for evangelizing the whole of his realm. In the awakening that followed, Columba "turned that nation to faith in Christ by word and by example."[23]

Further south, Kentigern, or Mungo (c. 518–603) as he is sometimes called, especially among the Scots, in 543 began a decade-long, highly effective evangelistic outreach on the Clyde among the southern and western Scots until a rising anti-Christian reaction in Strathclyde under King Morken (d. 572) compelled him to flee south to work with David in Wales, where he established a monastic training center in Llanelwy. On the Christian king, Rhydderch Hael's accession to the throne of Strathclyde in 572, he appealed to the aging Kentigern to return and restore the Christian faith throughout his realm. For the next thirty years from his new center on the Clyde, which he called *Clas-gu* (dear family), whence the modern name *Glasgow*, missionary activity radiated from Galloway in the south to Aberdeen in the north and out to the Orkney Islands. The city motto "Let Glasgow flourish by the preaching of His Word and the praising of His name" reflects the continuing impact of Kentigern's ministry.

The Model Awakening. Among the renowned Celtic "peregrini," i.e., Irish monks who traveled incessantly evangelizing post-Roman Europe, was Columbanus (543–615), who had been part of the monastic community of Bangor in Ulster, established by Columba's companion Comgall in 558. After some twenty years in Bangor, in 589, Columbanus felt constrained, together with twelve fellow evangelists, to travel to Brittany in France, where they were eagerly welcomed by Gontram (d. 592), King of Burgundy, thus opening the way for extensive travels throughout the Merovingian domains of southern France and beyond, evangelizing, preaching the most earnest Christian life and endeavoring to bring the hearers to a firm commitment to Christ.

In the foothills of the Vosges mountains at Annegray he found an abandoned Roman fortress where he established a center to which those, who wished to seek God, could come and be spiritually awakened. It became such an attraction that the next year (590) King Gontram granted him an old Gallo-Roman castle some eight miles away at Luxeuil, for a further monastic community. In Fontaines, he proceeded to establish yet another community. From these centers a substantial amount of the evangelizing of the south and western France was to take place.

His ministry and the awakening continued into the next century, focusing on summoning people to a life of holiness before God. After Gontram's death the crown passed to his nephew Childebert II and then to his sons Theodebert II and Theodorus (Thierry II). As they were minors, their grandmother, Brunhilda, became their guardian and took great exception to the strong preaching of Columbanus, insisting that he be expelled from the realm. Finally, in 611, he was escorted by armed guards to Nantes, Brittany, to be shipped back to Ireland. Taken out to the ship in a small boat, he waited while they loaded the cargo onto the ship. The seamen boarded and the ship sailed, oblivious to the fact that Columbanus was still in the small boat. A strong wind came and blew his little boat back to the shore, by which time the royal escort had returned home reporting that the evangelist had been successfully banished from the domain.

Resuming his evangelistic pilgrimage across the continent, Columbanus crossed France to southern Germany, Austria, Switzerland, preaching wherever the opportunity afforded. His remarkable ministry and the churches resulting from his travels, testify to the effect that this one missionary had and to the spiritual awakening that accompanied his ministry. He stands out as a great model of the early Christian missionary who saw everything as part of the plan and purpose of God for his life and ministry.

Several, who had been associated with him in his monasteries also followed a similar pattern for ministry. Valeri (Walric) of Leuconay (d. 622), the gardener at Luxeuil, responded to the call to northwestern Gaul and there won many pagans to faith in Christ. Eustace (560–629), who succeeded Columbanus as abbot at Luxeuil, successfully evangelized the invading tribes who came into that area. Eligius (588–660), together with his associate Dado, followed the North Sea coast evangelizing the Flemings, Frisians, and Suevi. Another companion of Columbanus, Gall (550–640) had a powerful ministry alongside of that of his mentor throughout much of the area, evangelized much of Switzerland especially around the Lake of Zurich, commemorated by the city of St. Gallen which has a long history of Christian work.

At the time of his death Columbanus was planning a further outreach to the Wens, a Slavic tribes' people, who had populated much of the area of Hungary and western Yugoslavia. To bolster support for his outreach he traveled down into northern Italy, to raise support and to recruit others to join in with him, in the process establishing the notable monastery at Bobbio in 614, on land given by the recently converted King Agilulf (d. 616). The next year he died before his plans for evangelizing the pagan Slavs could be realized.

His ministry and the accompanying awakening effectively bridge the gap between the sixth century and the seventh century and set the scene for the even stronger forward movement of missionary activity among the unevangelized tribes of Europe that was to come.

Endnotes

1 R. E. Davies, op. cit., 58.
2 D. F . Wright: art. "Pachomius" in NIDCC, 741.
3 Latourette, *History of the Expansion*, I.201.
4 P. Toon: art. "Simeon the Stylite" in NIDCC, 905.
5 Latourette, op. cit., I.213.
6 1 Corinthians 14:26.
7 Augustine: *Confessions*, viii.12.
8 Romans 13:13–14 NIV1984.
9 P. Salway: *Roman Britain* (Oxford, UK: Oxford U.P., 1981), 463.
10 Patrick: *The Confession of St. Patrick*, 1.
11 F. F. Bruce: *The Spreading Flame* (Exeter, UK: Paternoster, 1958), 373.
12 Patrick, op. cit., 2.
13 Ibid., 16.
14 Ibid., 17.
15 Ibid., 23.
16 Bruce, op. cit., 374.
17 M. Taylor: *Exploring Evangelism* (Kansas, MO: Beacon Hill, 1964), 95.
18 Ibid., 265.
19 Ibid., 267.
20 W. H. Gratton-Flood: art. "The Twelve Apostles of Erin" in *Catholic Encyclopedia* (New York, NY: Robert Appleton, 1913) (quoted in Wikipedia art. "Columba," 7/15/2011).
21 Quoted in J. H. Todd: *St. Patrick, Apostle of Ireland* (Dublin: Hodges & Smith, 1864), 384.
22 Bruce, op. cit., 387.
23 Bede: *Ecclesiastical History of the English Nation*, III.4.

Chapter 7

The Late Imperial Church

600–950 AD

In this chapter, the focus is on the historical revivals in the late Imperial period. A common impression is that after the close of the Roman Empire in the West, there was real no forward move within Christianity until people like Dominic Guzman (1170–1221) and Francis of Assisi (1182–1226) appeared on the scene. Some classical works of church history trace the progress of Christianity in individual countries, especially in western Europe, but give no correlation between developments in different countries, nor is the background of those events fully explored. Investigation into the background, into the events taking place based on the testimony of contemporary witnesses, leads to the conclusion that God continued pouring out his Spirit throughout the Dark Ages and the whole of Christian history.

Out of the revivals of the fourth and fifth centuries came a great missionary movement leading to some of the most exciting developments in Christianity in the following centuries. Because of the rapid changes taking place in western Europe in the late Imperial period it seemed that no sooner was an area evangelized and the pagan tribes converted to Christianity than new barbarian tribes would invade and the Christians, reluctant to take up arms against their fellow man, were driven out. A fresh outreach had to be made into the now pagan area in order to reevangelize and restore the Christian faith there. As God continued to pour out his Spirit, and to revive his people, they reached out in evangelism to touch the lives of these new settlers. The losses that the church experienced in the west through barbarian invasions in the sixth and seventh centuries were more than offset by the considerable conversion rate that followed. In the east however, the story was different, especially in the oldest Christian lands of western Asia and North Africa where the new syncretistic religion of Islam largely replaced the older Christian faith.

The Rise of Islam. From the Arabian Peninsula, the new religion of Islam swept north, east, and west, taking advantage of local discontent and ethnic conflicts, sweeping away the older kingdoms, devastating the Byzantine Empire, destroying the Sassanid Persian Empire, like an uncontainable flood. Within a century of the death of Mohammed (c. 570–632) the Muslim Empire stretched from the Atlantic Ocean, across North Africa, the Middle East, central Asia, to China, and from the Silk Road south to the Nilotic Kingdoms. Although the success of Islam, especially in the formerly Christian lands, has been attributed directly to the failure of Christian orthodoxy, "the causes were in part political, in part quasi-national."[1] Furthermore, much of the eastern and African Christian world would be deemed heretical by the orthodox and catholic church. Harried and oppressed by the Byzantine government, many welcomed the respite that the Muslim overlords would bring. The Roman provinces of North Africa, for example, had been occupied by predominantly Arian tribes, the Vandals and their Visigoth allies, whose faith had some similarities to Islam. The Byzantine reconquest of North Africa in 533, rather than bringing peace, heralded repeated upsurges of African claims to independence against imperial and papal assertions of authority.[2] That, combined with the declining economic situation due to the frequent droughts, made the region an easy target for the Muslim invasion, which was also welcomed by many of the Moorish and Berber tribes' people as a relief from the Roman and Byzantine oppressors.

Exhausted from its long struggle with the Sassanid Persian Empire and the Slavic Avar kingdom of central Europe, and its attempts to reestablish imperial rule in Italy in the face of the Lombard threat, and in North Africa over the Vandals, the Byzantine Empire was in no condition to resist the rising tide of Islam. The church in the Empire also was facing its own internal conflicts, first the Monophysite/Monothelite controversy, settled by the Sixth Ecumenical Council, Constantinople III (680–681), the impact of the Paulician revival (c. 640 onwards), and then the Iconoclast Controversy (717–843). It is debatable whether the latter controversy arose as a reaction to the menace of Islam or from the primitivistic influence of the Paulicians. By the end of the seventh century the oldest Christian lands were firmly under the control of Islam.

From North Africa, the Muslim invaders crossed into Europe through the Iberian Peninsula (711–718), destroying the Christian Visigothic kingdom of Roderic (d. 712), and establishing the Umayyad Caliphate of Al-Andalus. The Christians of France and the surrounding nations in the face of such peril began to seek the Lord's protection and God responded by moving in power in their midst once more. The Muslim advance into France was stalled first at the Battle of Toulouse (721) by Duke Odo of Aquitaine, and then ended by Charles Martel at the Battle of Tours (732). Although the reconquest of the Iberian Peninsula would not be completed until the fall of Granada in 1492, the Muslim threat had been contained and the revitalization of the Christian faith in western Europe resulted in the evangelization of the remaining pagan Germanic tribes, Scandinavia, and Greater Moravia.

The Seventh-Century Awakenings. Despite the losses to Islam, the church continued to grow both within the Byzantine Empire, among its neighbors, and in the West. Often the expansion of the church resulted from imperial or royal pressure in the form of treaties, or conquest; at other times from the monastic schools established by zealous missionary-monks, in the wake of the individual efforts of traveling merchants, pilgrims, or even captives, who readily shared their faith.[3]

Following the Council of Ephesus (431), the vibrant **Nestorian Christian Church** had separated from the Imperial Church and established its main center, first in Edessa, Persia, then in Nisibis and Seleucia-Ctesiphon on the Tigris River (from 489), and finally in Baghdad (from 775).

"Nestorians were active missionaries and founded communities in Arabia, India (Malabar Christians), and Turkestan."[4] Early in the seventh century God began stirring them yet again with a vision for the unreached lands of the East. *The Nestorian Monument of Hsianfu* (erected in 781) tells of the coming of Christianity to China. "In the year 635 one A-lo-pen had come from Ta-Ch'in (the Near East), bringing the Scriptures. . . . A-lo-pen was welcomed by the Emperor."[5] This Emperor, Taizong (reigned 626–649) ordered the Scriptures translated into Chinese for his examination and on his approving their message, commanded their propagation throughout his empire. His successor, Gaozong (d. 683) had Christian monastic training centers established in every district of the empire, however his successor, Empress Wu Hou (reigned 690–705) was an ardent Buddhist and initiated an anti-Christian reaction that brought the rapid growth of the faith to an end within China, but not in the neighboring countries.

In the middle of the seventh century came a significant awakening, affecting both east and west. When the Spirit of God was poured out upon the predominantly **Manichaean** village of Mananali in Mesopotamia, a man named Constantine came to a vital faith in Christ, was filled with the Holy Spirit, and sensed a divine call to a prophetic ministry. Taking the name of Sylvanus, one of Paul's companions,[6] he began a remarkable ministry about 657, characterized by a predominantly Pauline theology, because the only Scriptures available were the Gospels and the Epistles of Paul, hence the name given to his followers: Paulicians. After more than a quarter century of extremely fruitful ministry mainly in the Kibossa area of Armenia, resulting in some 30,000 people coming to faith in Christ, and more than a thousand churches established, he was martyred in 684. Upon his death his executioner Simeon came to faith in Christ and taking the name of Titus, became the leader of the Paulicians. The awakening continued until his own martyrdom in 690. The spread of the movement was not inhibited by the rising tide of Islam nor by sporadic Imperial opposition. The iconoclastic emperors, Leo III and his successor, Constantine V Copronymus (741–775), allowed it to flourish and the latter was rumored to be himself a Paulician.[7]

In the West, unlike the apostolic evangelization of the Roman Empire, the conversion of **the Germanic tribes** under the auspices of the Roman church usually followed the imperial model of Emperor Theodosius, who in 380 declared the Roman Empire Christian and enacted a series of laws proscribing pagan practices. The rulers and nobility of the Germanic tribes once converted would consequently impose their new faith on their subjects. This "top down" approach meant that effectively Christian and earlier pagan practices and beliefs coexisted among the subjects sometimes for centuries, for example, the conversion of Clovis I in 498 meant that the Franks were officially Christian, but the population did not abandon many of its pagan customs until the spiritual awakenings of the seventh century swept across the Frankish realm. When Amandus (c. 584–679) began his ministry among the Frisians of Flanders, he requested the Merovingian king Dagobert I (reigned 628–639) to make baptism compulsory, and he attempted to eliminate pagan traditions. The resulting tumult temporarily ended his work there.[8] Twenty years later, during the awakening he returned as the bishop of Maastricht (647), and his ministry then made a lasting impact.

Some of the most notable missionary activity from this time period was inspired by the example of earlier **missionary-monks** like Ninian and Martin of Tours, who effectively evangelized the unreached tribes that had lain beyond the reach of the church or had newly moved into the region. Once an area had been largely evangelized, such as in Ireland, individuals and groups traveled across the Irish Sea to their kinsfolk in Scotland, to the English mainland, and to the European continent, engaging in outright evangelism, and in establishing churches and monasteries for recruiting and training the next generation of missionaries.

Because in the monastic centers the focus was on prayer and fasting and preparation for ministry, periodic outpourings of the Spirit of God would thrust out the more zealous monks to evangelize the next unreached tribe. By the end of the seventh century in Ireland, as a result of the departure of so many of the more capable monks, some of the monasteries were largely stripped of occupants and began to fall into decay. When the barbarian Vikings from Scandinavia began their invasions across the North Sea there was little remaining to resist them. Much of Ireland, Scotland, and the north of England fell before them. As beneficial as the missionary movement was for the extension of the church, it was not always so for the ongoing life of the community and for the civilization left behind.

On **the British mainland**, the old Celtic church had fled westward, leaving almost all the country to the pagan Germanic invaders, the Angles, Saxons, and Jutes. Toward the end of the sixth century Pope Gregory I (the Great) (540–604), inspired by the sight of Anglian slaves, determined to see their countrymen brought into the Christian faith, committing the task to Augustine of Canterbury (d. 604) and a party of monks. In 597, Augustine and his companions eventually landed on the Isle of Thanet, near the coast of the Jute kingdom of Kent, where Ethelbert (c. 560–616) with his Christian Frankish bride, Bertha, reigned. Granting them the use of the ancient Romano-British Church of St. Martin in Canterbury, Ethelbert soon requested baptism as a Christian, following which some ten thousand of his subjects also were baptized.[9] That this was more than a formality is obvious from Pope Gregory's letter to Augustine in 601 "exhorting him not to be puffed up with pride that great miracles were taking place during the course of his missionary endeavors in Britain."[10] From the Jute kingdom in quick succession the East Saxons and East Anglians adopted the Christian faith, and bishoprics were established in London and Rochester. The passing of Augustine three years later and of King Ethelbert after another decade led to a pagan reaction under King Eadbald (reigned 616–640), with the East Saxons and East Anglians quickly following suit and expelling their bishops. With Eadbald's own conversion around 624, the Christian advance resumed.

Similarly, in Northumbria, Edwin (584–633), the pagan king, in 616 had banished his rivals, Oswald (d. 642) and his brothers, to the Gaelic kingdom of Dalriata, where through the influence of the Irish monks on Iona, they were converted and baptized. Through his marriage to Eadbald's daughter, Edwin was himself converted in 627, but his fellow Saxons were reluctant to adopt the Catholic faith of the southern kingdoms. On regaining the throne of Northumbria in 634, Oswald determined to bring his subjects into the Christian faith following the Irish rather than the Catholic pattern. Although the first bishop, Corman, sent from the monastery of Iona, returned there in frustration, his replacement Aidan (d. 651), accompanied by twelve monks, persisted, establishing a training center and bishopric on the island of Lindisfarne, close to the royal fortress of Bamburgh. In the awakening that followed Aidan, "the Apostle to the English" and his companions walked from village to village, preaching, healing the sick, and working miracles until the whole of Northumbria was evangelized.

Within twenty years of Aidan's death came a fresh wave of revival to Lindisfarne. Among the English students there were Cuthbert (634–687), known as "the Wonder-worker of Britain" from his miraculous ministry throughout Northumbria, and Wilfrid (634–709), who shortly thereafter received an empowering vision for evangelism. Leaving his charge in York, he traveled throughout England to the south, evangelized the last pagan stronghold of the Isle of Wight, continued into France in 677, and headed north to Frisia (Holland and Belgium), spreading the gospel with miraculous confirmation all the way. His powerful ministry prepared the way for Willibrord (658–739), the "Apostle to the Frisians" who had been his student in Ripon, Yorkshire.

In 659, Hilda (614–680), the great niece of King Edwin of Northumbria, and abbess of the convent of Hartlepool in County Durham, felt impressed by God to found a double monastery for both men and women at Streonaeshalch (modern Whitby) in Yorkshire. Within a short time, the spiritual awakening that had affected Lindisfarne spread to that area, not through the abbess or an influential leader but through an uneducated, illiterate cowherd named **Caedmon** (d. 680). As the monks were concluding a feast by singing Latin hymns to the harp, Caedmon, understanding neither Latin nor poetry, retreated to his cowshed to sleep. In his dream one approached him asking him to sing of "the beginning of created things." Inspired by the Spirit of God he composed a nine-line alliterative praise poem *Caedmon's Hymn*,[11] one of the earliest known examples of poetry in Old English or in any Germanic language.

The next day on recounting his dream and song to one of the monks, he was taken to see the abbess Hilda, who upon hearing the story and being satisfied as to its veracity, tested him to produce a further poem based upon a Scripture passage, which he did. As a result, Hilda ordered Caedmon be admitted to the monastery and taught biblical history, which, without understanding a word of the instruction in Latin, after a night of prayer and meditation, under the inspiration of the Holy Spirit, Caedmon would render into verse, singing in the English tongue of "the creation of the world and the early history of mankind; the journey of Israel from Egypt to the land of promise; the Incarnation and all the cardinal doctrines of the Christian faith; the terrors of judgment, the pains of hell, and the delight of heaven."[12] Not only is Caedmon renowned as "the father of English Sacred Song,"[13] but his poetry was the first known attempt to translate any portion of the Bible into the English language. As a result of hearing for the first time the Word of God in their own language, many responded by converting to the Christian faith. As Bede some sixty years later, commented: "By his verses the minds of many were often excited to despise the world, and to aspire to heaven."[14] Some subsequently entered the monastery for training as missionaries to the unreached parts of the European continent, which led to the recognition of Whitby as the main center from which the pagan Germanic people would be evangelized.

The Eighth-Century Awakenings. As the seventh century closed, yet another stirring came that prepared the way for a succession of revivals throughout the next century. In 690, **Willibrord** and eleven apostolic companions crossed the English Channel to Frankish Frisia (Holland and Belgium), where with the support of Pepin of Heristal (635–714), the Mayor of the Palace under the declining Merovingian monarchy, they proceeded to evangelize the pagan Frisians. Establishing his base in Utrecht (695) and a monastic training center in Echternach, Luxembourg, three years later, Willibrord's work prepared the way for a succession of awakenings which through his own forty-year-long ministry, and that of his companions, saw the Christian faith take hold not only of Frisia and Germany, but also of Scandinavia.

Boniface (680–755), born Winfrid, or Wynfryth in Crediton, Devon, and educated in the monastery school at Exeter, and later at Nursling, in the awakening around 716 followed a missionary call to work with

Willibrord in Frisia. Frustrated initially by the conflict between Charles Martel (686–741), ruler of the Franks and defeater of the Muslims, and the last pagan ruler of the northern Frisians, Radbod (d. 719), Winfrid returned briefly to Nursling. Finding the missionary call inescapable, he resumed his ministry, traveling throughout Thuringia and Bavaria, where the awakening resulted in thousands of Hessians being baptized.[15] His Latin-speaking companions gave him the name Boniface (the doer of good deeds), because of the proliferation of miracles in his ministry. Commissioned as bishop and later metropolitan over all Germany east of the Rhine, Boniface sought to bring all into the Christian faith.

His death came at the hands of pagan tribespeople who, following a great baptismal service near Dokkum, between Franeker and Groningen, raided his camp determined to wipe out the Christians. Although some wanted to defend themselves, Boniface insisted that they should lay down swords and not engage in warlike activity. The result was that all, including Boniface himself, were slaughtered and their possessions stolen. Among the booty were copies of the Scriptures, which the pagans concluded must be valuable and so they secreted them away until they could capture someone to reveal the valuable content of these books. Before long a man named Luke was captured, who read the books to his captors, which resulted in the conversion of many of the same raiders. Even out of seeming tragedy God brought a powerful confirmation of his Word and his call on the life of a remarkable revivalist and missionary.

The Ninth-Century Awakenings. The Holy Roman Empire. Much of western Europe by the ninth century had been brought into the Christian fold, yet the northern barbarians of Scandinavia and the Slavic people of central Europe were almost totally unreached. The revivals of the ninth century inspired a significant attempt to reach them with the gospel of Christ.

When Charlemagne (742–814) succeeded his father, Pepin the Short, as ruler of the Frankish kingdom in 771, he saw himself as a Christian ruler over a Christian kingdom. Following the Roman Imperial model, he forcibly converted the conquered people of Saxony (772–798), Lombardy (northern Italy) (774), the Spanish Marches (781–806), and Pannonia (796–803). As the ninth century dawned Charlemagne achieved his great ambition being crowned emperor of the renewed Holy Roman Empire that would last at least nominally for a millennium. Crowned on Christmas Day, 800, by Pope Leo III as the Holy Roman Emperor, he promoted the Carolingian Renaissance of the arts and theology, organized his realm into dioceses, modeled on the political divisions of the early Roman Empire, with lesser kings over the various subject peoples.

Among the new dioceses were those of Minden (780), Bremen (787) and Hamburg (804), with the responsibility of evangelizing the last unreached people in western Europe, the Vikings of Scandinavia. Charlemagne was not to live to see his vision fulfilled, but God would give that same vision in the awakening of 825 to young Frankish monks, named Ansgar (800–865). Although a century earlier Willibrord and his companions had attempted with limited success to reach the Norsemen with the gospel, it was the appointing of Ansgar as archbishop of Hamburg in 831 by Charlemagne's successor Emperor Louis I (the Pious) (778–840) that was to prove decisive. Even before his official recognition as "Apostle of the North," Ansgar's deep concern for the souls of the Vikings had sent him on several evangelistic forays into Scandinavia. From his new base in northern Germany he and his missionary team of monks were to regularly cross the Baltic, traveling as far as the Arctic Ocean and winning some thirty Viking kings to the Christian faith. Under the old Viking system as went the king, so went his subjects. If he was baptized, his subjects would follow. Although the evangelization of Scandinavia would not be completed for another century, Ansgar's missionary vision, born in revival and reinforced by subsequent stirrings in the Carolingian Empire, prepared the way for the conversion of the Vikings.

Central and Eastern Europe. As God was moving in the West, he also continued to stir hearts in central Europe and in the East. After a century of theological and political conflict the church in the East was ready for a forward movement leading to the evangelization of the Slavic people who occupied central Europe. The Avar Khaganate that covered most of the region, especially Pannonia, had battled repeatedly against both the Byzantine Empire in the Balkans and against the Frankish Empire in the West. Finally defeated by Charlemagne in 796 and 802–803 and forsaken by its Wendish allies (Western Slavs), the Avar rule collapsed in 804, opening the way for missionary outreach to the Slavic people.

Although the Emperor Heraclius (575–642) had sent Roman missionaries to evangelize the Serbian Slavs with some temporary success, two centuries later Emperor Basil I (reigned 867–886) compelled the defeated Serbian pirates to submit to baptism, prompting the Serbian king, Mutimir (c.850–891) to request missionaries from Constantinople, formally converting the Serbian people to the faith.[16] Similarly, the request of the Bulgarian ruler Boris I (reigned 852–889) for Christian baptism in 864, began the process of bringing his empire, which covered modern Bulgaria, Transylvania, and southeast Pannonia, into the Christian faith. As the southern Slavs were formally adopting Christianity, Rastislav, the prince of Moravia (reigned 846–869), having been converted while a hostage in the Frankish King Louis the German's court, sought to bring his whole realm into the Christian faith, by requesting teachers of Christianity, first and unsuccessfully from Rome (863), and then from Constantinople (864).

Chosen for the task were two brothers, Constantine (later known as Cyril) (826–869) and Methodius (815–885) from Thessalonica. Constantine had participated in earlier missions to the Abbasid Caliphate (859) and the Khazar Khaganate (860). Despite lack of success in these missions, the Byzantine emperor Michael III (reigned 842–867) and the Patriarch of Constantinople, Photius (810–893), Constantine's former university professor, committed the work to the two brothers, whose mother may have been part-Slav herself. The first task undertaken by Constantine was to develop an alphabet for the previously unwritten language so that the Scriptures and liturgy would be available in the language of the people. "This script, known as Glagolitic, was the forerunner of the form of writing now used in south-eastern Europe and Russia, which is called Cyrillic, after the younger brother."[17] Armed with the Word of God and empowered by the Holy Spirit, they began a work, which would not only bring the western Slavs into the faith, but also reinforce the conversion of their southern kinsfolk, and ultimately lead to the conversion of the eastern Slavs. The outstanding success of their mission brought them recognition by both Constantinople and Rome as "the Apostles to the Slavs," despite the subsequent loss of much of Greater Moravia to the invading Magyars.

Following the conversion of Tsar Boris, the evangelization of the Bulgarian Empire was accelerated by the arrival of the disciples of Methodius, under the leadership of Clement of Ohrid (840–916) and Naum of Preslav (830–918), who were expelled from Bohemia during the anti-Byzantine reaction in 885. In the awakening that accompanied their arrival, so many desired to prepare for ministry that Naum alone was responsible for educating some 3,500 students from 886–893. In the middle of the awakening (889), Tsar Boris resigned to devote himself to prayer and study at the monastery of St. Panteleimon, near Ohrid (modern Macedonia). Although his successor, Vladimir, spearheaded a short-lived pagan reaction, Boris returned from his monastic retirement to install his younger son, Simeon (reigned 893–927), who had himself been trained as a monk.

The Paulicians. The same awakening that so radically impacted Scandinavia and the central European Slavs also was to revitalize the Paulicians on the eastern edge of the Byzantine Empire. The growth of the Paulicians under the iconoclastic emperors had given way to periods of sporadic persecution, but it seemed as though they multiplied as fast as they were being killed, especially under the remarkable leadership of Sergius-Tychicus (801–835), spreading their message throughout Asia Minor. A wave of savage persecution under the Empress Theodora (842–857) in Armenia resulted in some one hundred thousand deaths, and eventually led to a war of extermination under Emperor Basil I (reigned 867–886).

This war was accompanied by a fresh wave of revival under the leadership of Carbeas (d. 863) and Chrysocheir (d. 873). The latter acquired his name, meaning "anointed hands," because of his reputed practice, following a battle, of venturing back onto the battlefield and laying hands upon the wounded, whether his own soldiers or the Imperial troops. Reputedly many were instantly and miraculously restored to perfect health. Often, however, the Imperial soldiers who were healed also converted to the Paulician cause, swelling their ranks. Basil, under the subterfuge of a peace conference, had Chrysocheir assassinated. The now leaderless Paulicians scattered, and their main center, Tephrike (modern Divrigi), in upper Mesopotamia, was destroyed.[18]

Although particularly in Western Europe the Dark Ages marked the end of the Imperial Church, which was developing into medieval Roman Catholicism, God continued moving powerfully through many individuals. In each awakening four convictions characterized the resultant movement: that the ministry of the Holy Spirit was continuing unchanged from apostolic days; that the true believers needed to separate themselves from worldliness and ungodly pursuits; that ministry was to be exercised by the whole body of Christ—laity and clergy alike; and finally, that the return of the Lord Jesus was imminent. As the first Christian millennium neared its close, a growing conviction inspired the monastic missionaries to attempt the evangelization of the world as the church's preparation for the millennial reign of Christ.

Endnotes

1 S. Neill: *A History of Christian Missions* (Harmondsworth, UK: Penguin, 1964), 64.

2 D. F. Wright: art. "Africa, North" in NIDCC, 16.

3 Latourette, *History of the Expansion*, II.15–17, 223–262, 271.

4 P. Toon: art. "Nestorianism; Nestorius" in NIDCC, 700.

5 Ibid., 278.

6 Acts 15:22 et.al.

7 P. D. Steeves: art. "The Paulicians and the Bogomils" in *Eerdmans' Handbook to the History of Christianity* (Grand Rapids, MI: Eerdmans, 1977), 246.

8 Latourette, *History of the Expansion*, II.80.

9 Neill, op. cit., 68.

10 R. M. Riss: *A Survey of 20th Century Revival Movements in North America* (Peabody, MA: Hendrickson, 1988), 8.

11 Bede, op. cit., IV, 24.

12 F. M. Stenton: *Anglo-Saxon England* (Oxford, UK: Oxford U.P., 1971, 3rd Edn.), 196.

13 Memorial to Caedmon, St. Mary's Churchyard, Whitby, Yorkshire, UK.

14 Bede, op. cit.

15 C. G. Thorne: art. "Boniface" in NIDCC, 142.

16 Latourette, *History of the Expansion*, II.240.

17 P. D. Steeves: art. "The Orthodox Church in Eastern Europe and Russia" in Eerdman's Handbook, op. cit., 310.

18 J. G. G. Norman: art. "Paulicians" in NIDCC, 755; Latourette, *History of the Expansion*, II.440ff.

Chapter 8

Early Medieval Period

950–1250 AD

This chapter focuses on the historical revivals in the early medieval period or the later Dark Ages. In the previous chapter we emphasized how revivals spread Christianity through the forward movements from the seventh century onward, bringing many of the Germanic and Slavic tribes into the faith. In the early medieval period, a succession of revival movements thrust missionaries to the northwest to continue the evangelization of Scandinavia, and to the northeast into Russia and beyond. Wherever Christianity spread, it was affected and at times amended by the fresh outpouring of God's Spirit, which was impelling the new missionary expansion.

With the decline of the Carolingian Empire in the latter half of the ninth century came a deterioration in the life of the church in general and of the former major driving force for renewal and missions, the monastic movement. Many monasteries had been raided, even destroyed by invading Vikings and Magyars, leaving the monks totally dependent on local rulers and an often-corrupt ecclesiastical system. In 909, Duke William I (the Pious) of Aquitaine (875–918) founded a small monastery at his former hunting lodge at Cluny to be directly responsible to the Pope and led by a reform-minded Benedictine monk Berno (d. 926). The vision of Berno and his successors led to a movement that reformed and revitalized not only the Western monastic movement, but ultimately the whole Western church through the reforming Cluniac popes, Leo IX (1002–1054) and Gregory VII (1023–1085).

The Tenth-Century Awakenings. Western Europe. As the Carolingian Empire declined, the Viking Norsemen took advantage of the power vacuum. Raids gave way to settlements throughout the British Isles and Continental Europe. Many of the Viking settlers intermarried with the local population and accepted the faith of the lands occupied, alongside their ancestral religions. The first Duke of Normandy, Rollo (c. 846–931), in 911, accepted Christian conversion as part of the treaty legitimatizing the Viking occupation of area, but pagan reaction followed, augmented by a fresh Viking invasion in 943.[1] A decade later, however, in the wake of the new awakening the Christian faith resumed its advance in the Viking settlements.

Otto (the Great) (912–973) succeeded his father, Henry (the Fowler) (876–936) as king of the Germans in 936 and sought to revive Charlemagne's vision of a Holy Roman Empire that would both unite the Christians of Continental Europe and protect them from the growing menace of the Magyar raiders from the East. After his decisive defeat of the invaders at the Lechfeld, near Augsburg in 955, he was able extend the German Christianization of the lands east of the Elbe River and south into Italy, culminating in his being crowned as Holy Roman Emperor by Pope John XII in 962.[2] Although his attempts to promote the Christian faith across the northern frontier of his German realm had had minimal success, his coronation as emperor coincided with a spiritual awakening that was rejuvenating much of Europe and would have major repercussions for Scandinavia.

Scandinavia. The earliest recorded missionary efforts in Scandinavia have been traced back to Willibrord, the apostle to the Frisians, whose efforts in the second decade of the eighth century (710–718) met with limited success. A century later the mission of Ansgar, the Apostle of the North, brought more success but the lasting breakthrough was not to come until the awakening in the last half of the tenth century, especially after the conversion (c. 960) of Harald Bluetooth Gormsson (c. 911–986), king of Denmark and overlord of Norway, as a result of a demonstration of miracles by a Frisian missionary bishop Poppo (d. 1016). Although before his conversion Harald had allowed missionary preaching from 935 and suffragan bishops were functioning by 948, the evangelization of Denmark accelerated after the king's formal conversion. "Poppo became famous as a missionary in Denmark and is said to have won 'many thousands' to the Christian faith."[3]

The evangelization of Norway, unsuccessfully attempted by local rulers such as Haakon the Good (reigned 934–961) and his successor, Harald Greyhide (reigned 961–976), proved more difficult. A royal prince, Olaf Tryggvason (c. 963–1000) was converted in 986, following an encounter with a Christian prophet during a raid on the Isles of Scilly. On ascending to the throne as King Olaf I in 995, he made the evangelization of his country and its dependencies of Iceland and Greenland a priority. Despite the brevity of his reign and the pagan reaction that followed during the rule of the Jarls of Lade, a further awakening in the next century was to see Christianity firmly established in much of Scandinavia.

Eastern Europe. At the same time as the Vikings were raiding and settling in western Europe, fellow Scandinavians, mainly from the Rusland area of Sweden, swept through the Slavic lands of eastern Europe, even plundering Constantinople (860). From their northern colony of Novgorod and their southern capital of Kiev, they came to dominate and give their name to the whole region of Russia. The patriarch, Photius, sought to follow up the success of Cyril and Methodius' mission to the Slavs with a mission to the Kievan Rus with some success, as a consequence of which Emperor Basil I sent the first missionary bishop. The interaction with the Byzantine Empire undoubtedly produced some Christian conversions, but it was not until the middle of the tenth century that a decisive breakthrough occurred.

Olga (890–969), the widow of King Igor (913–945), was converted the year of Igor's death and reigned as regent for their infant son, Svyatoslav (d. 972). The Christian community grew throughout her reign but Svyatoslav remained pagan. His son, Vladimir (956–1015), however, was converted and ardently promoted the evangelization of all Russians, making

Christianity the official faith. Although to describe what happened as "a folk movement" has been questioned, the stories of the mass baptisms of the populations of Kiev (c. 987) and Novgorod (c. 991) would support such a description.

In the first Bulgarian Empire, Tsar Simeon proved an even greater ruler than his father, Tsar Boris I, and by the end of his reign, the evangelization of the Bulgar people, who covered most of the upper Balkans, was completed. The same year (927) Dimitriy I, the chief bishop of the Bulgarian Church, who had been powerfully involved in the awakening, was recognized as a patriarch alongside the historic Patriarchates. As the strength of the Kievan Rus under Olga and Svyatoslav increased and the Bulgarian Empire weakened under the later tsars, Byzantine emperor John I Tzimiskes (925–976) launched a series of wars (970–971) that brought an end to an independent Bulgaria.

Seeking to pacify the Paulicians who were recovering from the earlier wars with the Byzantine Empire, John Tzimiskes offered them land in Philippopolis (modern Plovdiv), Thrace (modern Bulgaria) for settlements (970–973).[4] His intention was to use them as a buffer against the Kievan Rus and the rising menace of the Magyars, who eventually would establish themselves in Hungary. Some two hundred thousand Armenian Paulicians migrated to Bulgaria, where they were initially known as *Pavlikiani*, and later as *Bogomils* after their leader Theophilus (Bogomil in Bulgarian). Periods of spiritual awakening interspersed with persecution helped their faith spread throughout the Balkan region, posing a threat to the Orthodox Church in Bulgaria and the surrounding countries. Being now introduced into Europe, they would spread westward across the continent and feature in a succession of revival movements in the medieval period.

Outside the Byzantine Empire the Muslim advance through Central Asia had been stymied by the Nestorian Church of the East. Avid missionaries, the Nestorians had spread the Christian message throughout central Asia. Although the outreach in China had been frustrated at the end of the Tang Dynasty, their evangelistic outreach continued in other lands spurred on by periodic awakenings.

The Eleventh-Century Awakenings. Asia. At the dawn of the new millennium Christianity faced a new situation: the ancient Christian lands in the eastern Mediterranean were now dominated by the Muslim religion; the Muslim advance into Europe had been halted; the barbarian tribes who had replaced the Christianized Roman Empire in Europe, had themselves adopted the Christian faith and were attempting to unify the region as the Holy Roman Empire; millennialist movements inspired by the prospect of the imminent return of Christ, were impacting church life throughout Europe; the Norsemen of Scandinavia were in process of converting to the Christian faith, as were the Slavic tribes of Europe and northern Asia; and the Nestorian Church of the East, caught between an expanding Islam and a resurgent Buddhism, was ardently evangelizing throughout central and southern Asia. The passing of the old millennium was bringing the church a new day of opportunity.

The zealous Nestorian missionaries, undaunted by the Muslim threat ,set their sights on the Mongol and Turkic tribes of central Asia. According to the thirteenth-century Jacobite historian, Gregory Bar Hebraeus, early in the eleventh century (c. 1007) the ruler of the Kerait tribe apparently lost his way in a snowstorm while hunting in the mountains. Abandoning hope, he was preparing to die when a saint appeared in a vision, declaring: "If you will believe in Christ, I will lead you lest you perish." Returning home safely the king sought out Nestorian Christian merchants, who led him to faith in Christ. At their suggestion he requested Abdisho (reigned c. 987–1009), the Metropolitan of Merv (modern Mary, Turkmenistan), to send missionaries to baptize him and his tribe. The awakening that followed the arrival of a single priest and a deacon resulted in 200,000 converting to Christianity.[5] This was one of the few instances of a tribe converting from the Muslim to the Christian faith. The medieval story of Prester John, the enigmatic ruler of the east, who would come to the aid of the beleaguered Latin Kingdoms during the period of the Crusades, probably originated from this folk movement. The movement spread to embrace other Mongol tribes, such as the Naimans, the Merkit, the Ongud, and, to a lesser extent, the Kara Khitan, leading to a substantial and influential Christian presence throughout the Mongol domains.

Eastern Europe. Following the defeat of the Magyars by Emperor Otto I in 955, Bishop Pilgrim of Passau (d. 991) had sent missionaries into Hungary and even undertaken an evangelistic tour there himself. On his return about 973, "he reported to the Pope that 5,000 Magyars had been baptized."[6] That year as the awakening continued, Geisa (reigned 972–997), the prince of Hungary, married a Christian princess, Adelheid of Poland, and two years later was himself baptized together with his infant son, Stephen (975–1038). The number of Christians multiplied as Geisa sought to advance the faith. When Stephen came to the throne in 997 Hungary, was declared to be a Christian nation. The king had a reputation for preaching to his subjects and performing miracles of healing. Despite a brief pagan reaction under Ladislaus I (1045–1095) following Stephen's death, the forward movement of the Christian faith would not be halted.

Northern Europe. Throughout the British Isles the Celtic, Irish, and Anglo-Saxon communities had been plagued by the Norsemen for more than two centuries, but the spread of Christianity in Scandinavia gave the threat from the north a different complexion. When Canute (985–1035), the son of Sweyn Forkbeard, became king of England in 1016, he was already a convinced Christian determined to promote the cause of Christ. On his accession to the throne of Denmark (1018), Norway, and part of Sweden (1028), he vigorously sought to consolidate his rule through the conversion of his subjects. Sweden proved difficult, as earlier attempts by Ansgar (830), Unni of Hamburg (936), and King Olof Skotkonung (990–1020) had born little lasting fruit. Only the spiritual awakening accompanying the restoration to the Swedish throne of King Inge the Elder (d. 1105) in 1087 saw the Christian faith finally established there and the first tentative attempts to reach across the Baltic Sea to Finland.

Continental Europe. As the new millennium dawned the talented, educated, and deeply religious Otto III (reigned 983–1002) was Holy Roman Emperor and first installed his cousin Bruno as Pope Gregory V in 996, and following Gregory's death in 999, elevated his former tutor, Gerbert of Aurillac (940–1003), as Pope Sylvester II. Otto's desire for Christian renewal in the empire dominated the reign of his son and successor, Henry II (973–1024), who was viewed as "the model Christian ruler."[7] In his zealous promotion of reform within the Western church, Henry was able to call on the growing influence of the Cluniac movement, regarding which Clouse observed: "Growing out of the reform movement of the monastery at Cluny a great renewal came to eleventh-century Christianity."[8] Emperor Henry III (1017–1056), who "thought of himself as a *priest-king*,"[9] was an equally ardent promoter of the Cluniac renewal and in 1043 declared that he would forgive his personal enemies, renouncing all thought of vengeance, and encouraging all his nobles to do the same, thus precipitating further renewal throughout his realm.

The rising tide of Christian enthusiasm in the west toward the end of the century coincided with the growing power of the Seljuk Turks in the Middle East. The defeat of the Byzantine forces at the Battle of Manzikert (1071) leading to the loss of Asia Minor to the Turks, and the appeal of Emperor Alexius I Comnenus (reigned 1081–1118), for aid from the West, prompted Pope Urban II (reigned 1088–1099) at the Council of Clermont (1095) to proclaim the First Crusade to deliver the Holy Land from the Muslim occupiers.[10] For the next two centuries the crusades would direct the enthusiasm of much of the medieval church to the elusive objective of liberating the Middle East from Muslim control. For some, however, the new millennium turned their attention in a somewhat different direction.

The Twelfth-Century Awakenings. The twelfth century was marked by several significant movements, some arising from the awakenings of the preceding centuries, and others from the rising interest in the return of Christ observed as the new millennium approached. In Western Europe the Cluniac movement, which had made a notable impact for renewal and reformation for more than century, was beginning to lose its energy. Thorne commented: "Even though it grew weak because of its vastness, its mission was admirably accomplished. Cluny renewed the ideals of its predecessors as Citeaux was to do for Cluny."[11]

During the renewal in the reign of Emperor Henry III, a young nobleman, Robert (of Molesme) (c. 1027–1111), inspired to devote himself to prayer, entered the abbey of Moutier-la-Celle and quickly rose to become the prior. After several attempts at renewal there and in other monasteries, he agreed to join a group of zealous hermits to form the Abbey of Molesme, in the forest of Colan in 1075. As the awakening spread, more attempted to join them, some bringing different ideals, as a result of which Robert, Alberic (d. 1109), and Stephen Harding (d. 1134) departed to a desolate valley deep in the forest near Dijon, France, donated by Viscount Renaud of Beaune, where in 1098 they founded a new abbey, Citeaux, dedicated to the ideals of prayer and self-support. As the awakening continued Robert returned to Molesme in 1100 to continue his leadership there, and first Alberic and then Stephen succeeded him at Citeaux. Under Stephen's leadership the new Cistercian order spread to twelve houses and welcomed its most renowned participant, Bernard (of Clairvaux) (1090–1153).

Bernard of Clairvaux. Within four years of entering the order, Bernard was asked to establish a new monastery in a former hideout for robbers known as "the Valley of Wormwood," which he renamed Clairvaux (1115), "the Valley of Light," and which was to become the center of the order and the renewal movement associated with it.[12] Renowned for his eloquence in preaching, enthusiasm in evangelism, devotion to Christ, and ministry of healing, Pierard described him as "the dominant figure in twelfth-century Latin Christendom."[13] As controversial as he was principled, Bernard condemned Cluny for its failings, also the rising scholastic movement in theology and the growing millennialist movements.

Millennialist Movements. The new millennium brought a flurry of itinerant preachers, prophets, and pseudo-christs, who gathered followers from among the poor and dispossessed, threatening the stability of medieval society, especially when so many of the nobles and their armies were absent participating in the Crusades. While some were undoubtedly heretical, like Eon (Eudo de Stella) (d. 1148), others began within the church, became critical of its corruption, and either moved outside or sought to reform the church from within, like Tanchelm of Antwerp (d. 1115), Robert of Arbrissel (c. 1045–1116), Peter de Bruys (d. 1131), Henry of Lausanne (d. 1148), Norbert of Xanten (1080–1134), and Arnold of Brescia (c. 1090–1155).

Tanchelm of Antwerp was a powerful proponent of the awakening in the second decade of the twelfth century, attracting huge crowds and enjoying the favor of Count Robert II of Flanders (d. 1111). Following his patron's death, Tanchelm and his associates began attacking the corruption in the Roman Catholic Church, teaching that sacraments administered by unworthy clerics were invalid. This fed into the current social unrest in the Low Countries, threatening the stability of church and state. To counter Tanchelm's influence, a younger renowned revival preacher, Norbert of Xanten, founder of the community at Premontre (1120) and "famed as a worker of miracles, a healer of the sick and insane,"[14] was summoned to Antwerp to win Tanchelm's followers back to the Roman Catholic faith. His success, his friendship with Bernard of Clairvaux, and the approval of his *Premonstratensian* order of regular clerics by Pope Honorius II (d.1130) in 1126 gave his order phenomenal growth so that by the end of the century it included more than six hundred communities.

Robert of Arbrissel, founder of the monastery of La Roe (1096) and then of Fontevrault (1099), exercised a similar ministry to that of Norbert in western France but his impact upon the prostitutes of the area was such that Abbot Geoffrey of Vendome and Bishop Marbodius of Rennes suspected him and his followers of sexual indiscretions. Peter de Bruys, from orthodox beginnings as the priest of an Alpine village church, ultimately rejected the established church and its doctrines, teaching that "infant baptism was not valid, as only personal faith could bring salvation."[15] He also rejected the use of crucifixes, the new Roman Catholic doctrine of transubstantiation, and even the erection of buildings as churches, since the true church is spiritual, not physical. His followers, by the time of his death reputedly numbering several hundred thousand, were known as *Petrobrussians* and later as *Henricians,* from Peter's successor Henry of Lausanne, a former Benedictine monk of Cluny, who spread the movement throughout southern France and beyond.

Although **the Augustinian Prior of Brescia, Arnold**, was never accused of heresy, his criticism of the Roman Catholic Church's temporal powers, his opposition to Bernard of Clairvaux, and his support of the short-lived Commune of Rome led to his condemnation as a rebel, despite his popular participation in the mid-twelfth-century awakening. His summoning of the clergy to "apostolic poverty" would also bear fruit in the mendicant orders of the next century.

The awakening was also marked by the unusual ministry of **the Benedictine Abbess of Bingen, Hildegard** (1098–1179), whose visionary experiences, inspirational songs, plays, and prolific writings on a wide variety of topics extended her influence far beyond the areas of Germany and France she visited on her frequent preaching tours. Renowned as a preacher, "she spoke to people of all classes and called them to repent and obey the warnings God had given her."[16] Authenticated by her contemporaries, she was finally canonized in 2012 by Pope Benedict XVI and recognized as a *Doctor of the Church,* one of only four females to be so honored.

The same awakening saw the rise of **Joachim of Fiore** (1135–1202), Abbot of Curazzo and founder of the Order of San Giovanni in Fiore (1192), whose mystical interpretation of the inner meaning of history was to provide inspiration to many of the revival preachers in the next century. Dividing history into three epochs of forty-two generations of thirty years each, i.e., the Age of the Father (1260 BC—the Coming of Christ), which was the period of Law, followed by the Age of the Son (the period of Grace), Joachim foretold the Age of the Spirit would begin in 1260 AD with a powerful awakening which would herald "new religious orders that would convert the world."[17] Although Joachim may not have intended his teachings to undermine the ecclesiastical authorities, his followers did, leading to their partial condemnation in 1256.[18]

Albigenses. Inheritors of the legacy of the Paulician faith moved westward into the Piedmont valleys of northern Italy and across the Alps into southern France, particularly around Albi, whence they acquired the name *Albigenses,* used interchangeably with the term *Cathari* (the Pure Ones), from the strictness of their lives. The rapidity with which the movement spread during the revival periods of the eleventh and twelfth centuries may be ascertained from the succession of Roman Catholic ecclesiastical conferences in which it was the prime topic for condemnation, i.e., the Synod of Orleans (1022), the Councils of Arras (1025), Charroux (1028), Reims (1049), Beauvais (1114), Soissons (1114), Toulouse (1119), Languedoc (1145), Reims (1148), Tours (1163), and Lombez (1165), culminating in the Third General Council of the Lateran (1179), which issued a call to use force to repress the growing movement.[19]

Taylor summarized the spread of the work in southern France:

The Albigenses were ardent missionaries and evangelists. Their following reached such proportions that a council was held near Toulouse, France, in 1167. Various reports indicated that their numbers could be compared to the sand of the sea. By the close of the twelfth century they claimed to have followers in about one thousand cities. At the same time, it was estimated that they had several hundred thousand in their ranks.[20]

With the conversion of the new Count of Toulouse, Raymond VI (reigned 1194–1222), the Albigenses not only gained their most influential ally, but also the wrath of the new Pope Innocent III (1198–1216), under whose leadership papal authority reached its zenith. Within a decade he had proclaimed a crusade against the movement, under the leadership of Simon of Montfort, Earl of Leicester. By 1211 the crusade had degenerated into a war of conquest marked by such dreadful carnage as to appall even its instigator, Pope Innocent.[21]

Waldenses. During the awakening in the latter third of the twelfth century a wealthy merchant named Waldo of Lyons (c. 1140–1218) heard a sermon on the life of St. Alexius (fifth century) and subsequently witnessed the unexpected death of a close friend during supper, which events inspired him to enquire of a master of theology as to the best and surest way of salvation. The answer was given in the words of Christ to the rich young ruler: "If you want to be perfect, go, sell your possessions and give to the poor, and you will have treasure in heaven. Then come, follow me."[22] After making adequate provision for his wife and two daughters, he distributed his considerable wealth to the poor and began calling others to do the same. His growing band of followers, known as the Poor of Lyons, eagerly propagated his teachings, especially his criticism of the opulence and worldliness of medieval Catholicism. He also commissioned two local priests to translate the New Testament from Latin into the vernacular Arpitan (French-Provencal) language, the first translation of the Bible into a "modern" European language. Initially, in 1179, Pope Alexander III gave them approval to preach where permitted by the local bishop, but their insistence on preaching even when forbidden led to their being excommunicated and persecuted as heretics by Pope Lucius III at the Synod of Verona in 1184 and condemned by the Fourth Lateran Council in 1215, when they were referred to as *Waldenses* for the first time.[23]

Included in the crusade against the Albigenses, many of the Waldenses took refuge in the valleys of western Piedmont, others fled north into Germany, Bavaria, Austria, and Bohemia, contributing to and benefitting from successive pre-Reformation revival movements.

Endnotes

1 Latourette: *History of the Expansion*, II.110–111.

2 R. V. Pierard: art. "Otto I (the Great)" in NIDCC, 737.

3 Latourette: *History of the Expansion*, II.121.

4 Steeves: *Eerdman's Handbook,* op. cit.,246; J. G. G. Norman: art "Paulicians" in NIDCC, 755.

5 G. B. Hebraeus: *Ecclesiastical Chronicles* (trans. J. B. Abbeloos & T. J. Lamy, Paris: Maisonneuve, 1877), III.279–282.

6 S. Neill, op. cit., 93.

7 R. V. Pierard: art. "Henry II" in NIDCC, 460.

8 R. G. Clouse: art. "Flowering: the Western Church" in Eerdman's Handbook, op. cit., 252.

9 L. B. Brooks: *This Thousand Years* (South Plainfield, NJ: Bridge, 1994), 26.

10 R. G. Clouse: art. "The Crusades" in NIDCC, 273–274.

11 C. G. Thorne, Jr.: art. "Cluniacs" in NIDCC, 237.

12 M. Taylor: *Exploring Evangelism* (Kansas, MO: Beacon Hill,1964), 112–113.

13 R. V. Pierard: art. "Bernard of Clairvaux" in NIDCC, 123–124.

14 N. Cohn: *The Pursuit of the Millennium* (Oxford, UK: Oxford U. P., 1970), 50.

15 C. P. Williams: art. "Peter De Bruys" in NIDCC, 767.

16 R. G. Clouse: art. "Hildegard" in NIDCC, 470.

17 R. G. Clouse: art. "Joachim of Fiore" in NIDCC, 536.

18 G. S. M. Walker: *The Growing Storm* (London, UK: Paternoster, 1961), 147.

19 N. Weber: art. "Albigenses" in *The Catholic Encyclopedia,* vol. 1 (New York, NY: Robert Appleton, 1907).

20 M. Taylor: op. cit., 81–82.

21 N. Weber: art. "Albigenses," op. cit..

22 Matthew 19:21.

23 N. Weber: art. "Waldenses," op. cit., vol. 15.

Chapter 9

Medieval Period

1250–1350 AD

O ften negatively characterized by the opulent worldliness of both the
Roman Catholic and Orthodox churches, the medieval period was
not lacking in significant movements of spiritual renewal. Many of the
stirrings that arose at the end of the twelfth century continued unabated
and in some instances with greater power in the following years. New
movements emerged, drawing inspiration from earlier awakenings. Also
notable were the development of the preaching orders, the Friars, devoted
to the proclamation of the gospel to the common people; the enhancing of
the earlier Cathedral and Monastic schools into the medieval universities
as the scholastic movement sought to make Christian theology relevant to
the intellectuals of society; and the flowering of mysticism and the popular
devotional movement, which sought "to unite a life of inner devotion with
a life of active service in and to the world."[1] This was also the time of the
construction of the great cathedrals of Europe with spires reaching up to
God representing the prayers of the people and their desire to reach and
know God personally.

Although "the Crusades reflected the new dynamism in Western Christianity,"[2] by the fall of Acre in 1291, that dynamism had been almost totally
exhausted. Regrettably, the medieval church was also marked by intense

conflict between the religious leaders and the civic leaders. The religious leaders claimed suzerainty and authority over the nations of Western Europe; the civil leaders contrariwise resisted those claims and sought to establish their own authority over the church and its bishops in their realms.

The Thirteenth-Century Awakenings. The new century opened with a great ferment of anticipation in much of Western Europe arising in part from the prophecies of the respected Cistercian Abbot, Joachim of Fiore, foretelling of the coming Age of the Holy Spirit about 1260 when a great revival would begin and continue until the return of Christ to set up his millennial kingdom. This awakening would be marked by the rise of new religious orders leading to the greatest period of evangelism and spiritual power ever known. This may account for the papal approval of the Franciscan and Dominican Friars, when the strikingly similar followers of Waldo of Lyons had been repudiated shortly before. Despite the enthusiasm inculcated by the new orders of preachers, the widespread revival was not to be.

The Franciscans. Francis of Assisi (1181–1226), born Giovanni Bernardone, son of a wealthy cloth merchant, dreamt of becoming a knight, and served as a mercenary, a debonair soldier of fortune, until a dynamic encounter with God in 1204 near Spoleto, began a process that refocused his life. In the ruined chapel of St. Damian, near Assisi, he heard God's call to rebuild his house and renouncing his former wealth and family, he devoted himself to seeking and serving the Lord. Taken before the local magistrates and Bishop Guido by his enraged and humiliated father, he declared:

> Listen, all of you, and understand it well; Until this time I have called Pietro Bernardone my father; but now I wish to obey God. I return him the money about which he is so anxious, and my garments, and all that he has ever given me. From this moment I will say nothing but "Our Father in heaven.'[3]

Clad only in a cast-off old gardener's cloak, Francis went to the ruined sanctuary of St. Damian to rebuild it as a center where weary souls could come and seek the Lord. The effect was that over the next several days one after another of those, who had observed him at his trial, came to see what he was doing, were convinced by his life, and were converted to his way of thinking. On February 24, 1206,[4] or 1208,[5] or 1209,[6] while repairing the ancient church of St. Mary of the Angels at Portiuncula he heard the commission of the Lord Jesus:

> As you go, preach this message: "The kingdom of heaven is near." Heal the sick, raise the dead, cleanse those who have leprosy, drive out demons. Freely you have received, freely give. Do not take along any gold or silver or copper in your belts; take no bag for the journey, or extra tunic, or sandals or a staff; for the worker is worthy of his keep.[7]

Interpreting this as a divine call to apostolic evangelism and poverty, Francis began calling rich and poor alike to repentance. Within a year he had gained eleven followers, whom he gathered together in a fraternity *The Penitents of Assisi* [8] or *Frati Minores* [9] (the lesser brothers) bound by a simple rule *the Regula Primitiva*. As in the Gospels, they went out in pairs spreading the message throughout Umbria by word and joyful song. In 1209, Francis visited Rome, seeking permission from Pope Innocent III to preach and form a new religious order. With the support of Bishop Guido of Assisi and his friend, the pope's confessor, Giovanni de San Paolo, Cardinal Bishop of Sabina, he not only gained an audience with the pope, but also informal admittance for his followers as a fraternity, with the cardinal as protector. The following year on April 16, 1210, following a dream of Francis holding up the Basilica of St. John Lateran, the papal bishopric and mother church of Roman Catholicism, the pope officially endorsed the Franciscan order, centered upon Portiuncula, with a vocation for street preaching, first in Umbria and then throughout Italy and the world. A year later in 1211, an early convert, Clare of Assisi (1194–1253), established *the Order of Poor Ladies*, later called *the Poor Clares*, based upon the church of St. Damian. Following the Fourth Lateran Council of 1215, a lay fraternity *The Third Order of Brothers and Sisters of Penitence* was begun, dedicated to living out Franciscan ideals in society:

> Through the influence of Francis a new enthusiasm for spiritual things invaded Italy. Multitudes were awakened to live higher and better lives. Many wanted to forsake their homes and jobs to join the ranks of traveling preachers. Francis discouraged those who had home responsibilities from such excessive action by encouraging them to . . . find ways of serving the Lord in their neighborhoods. This action multiplied the influence of vital Christianity in awakened areas.[10]

Francis's vision to take the gospel out to the world inspired an attempt to visit Jerusalem in 1212, which was frustrated by a shipwreck of the Dalmatian coast. The next year his attempt to reach Morocco was interrupted by illness, resulting in his spending time in Spain, where he gathered many more followers. Undeterred, in the year 1219 he set forth for the Middle East with the Crusaders, determined to preach the gospel to the Muslims. In Egypt, he unsuccessfully attempted to convert Sultan Melek-el-Kamil (1180–1238) to faith in Christ.[11] The sultan, impressed with his godliness, gave him permission to preach, even though Francis' Christian message was unacceptable to his hosts. Before long Francis was expelled from their territory but subsequently, he made repeated forays into Muslim lands continuing his gospel preaching. The unique Treaty of 1229, which provided the Latin Kingdom of Jerusalem access to the Mediterranean and a decade of peace, was an indirect result of Francis' influence.

On his return to Portiuncula in 1220 the main thrust of the awakening had passed and he found that his rapidly growing order had long outgrown the primitive organization that he had established. Its now deceased protector, Cardinal Giovanni, had been replaced by Cardinal Ugolino of Segni (1170–1241), later in 1227 to be elected Pope Gregory IX, who promoted a reorganization of the order that would radically change the Grey Friars, as they were commonly known, into a clergy reform vehicle. Initially, in 1220, Francis delegated governance of the order to Peter Catani, as Vicar-General, who, upon the latter's death five months later, was succeeded by a lay-brother, Elias of Cortona (1180–1253), the provincial-minister of Syria (1217–1220), probably the most controversial of the early Franciscans. Within two years, Francis resigned as leader of the order "and henceforward he devoted himself to showing by personal example what he conceived to be the Christian ideal."[12] Shortly thereafter, the order divided, some, the Observants and their later development the Spirituals, sought to maintain his vision of a simple order of preachers reaching out in missions to the lost, especially in Muslim lands, and the others, the Conventuals preferred to observe the new ecclesiastical rules that had prompted Francis's departure. The last two years of Francis's life, in failing health, were spent in almost total isolation in the monastery at Portiuncula, during which time the stigmata or marks of the crucifixion of Christ are reputed to have appeared on his hands, his feet, and his brow.[13]

The Dominicans. Among those influenced by Francis's example was the Castilian, Dominic de Guzman (1170–1221), founder of another order of preachers, the Dominicans, or Black Friars. Initially, a Benedictine Canon and chaplain to the Bishop of Osma, Diego de Acebo (d.1207), Dominic accompanied his bishop on a diplomatic mission to Denmark in 1203. While traveling through southern France, they encountered the Cathars (Albigenses), whom Bishop Diego unsuccessfully attempted to convert to the Catholic faith. On their return the bishop and Dominic received papal permission in 1206 for another attempt to reclaim the sectarians (Cathars and Waldenses) with support of the newly appointed Cistercian Bishop Fulk of Toulouse (1150–1231), a renowned ex-Troubadour, who had experienced a profound conversion in 1195. These and other futile efforts by the Cistercians and other papal legates brought Dominic to the realization that:

It is not by the display of power and pomp, cavalcades of retainers, and richly-houseled palfreys, or by gorgeous apparel, that the heretics win proselytes; it is by zealous preaching, by apostolic humility, by austerity, by seeming, it is true, but by seeming holiness. Zeal must be met by zeal, humility by humility, false sanctity by real sanctity, preaching falsehood by preaching truth.[14]

The only success from this period was the establishing of what would become the first Dominican convent, a home for female converts of the awakening in Prouille in 1207, which served as a refuge under the protection of Bishop Fulk from the appalling slaughter of the Albigensian Crusade, launched by Pope Innocent III the next year. Although Dominic's initial attempts to gather like-minded preachers about him were frustrated, "at the Fourth Lateran Council in 1215, Dominic laid before Innocent his scheme for an order of well-educated preaching friars, directly subject to the papacy."[15] Initially sanctioned as Augustinian Canons, his Order of Preachers was established in a donated house in Toulouse under the sponsorship of Bishop Fulk. The following year Honorius III legalized them as "a mendicant order, devoted to preaching and the conversion of heretics."[16] Dominic's zeal for preaching and education eventually led him to establish in 1218 the main center of his order in Bologna, home to a flourishing university. That same year he met Francis of Assisi, confirming his conviction that a life of apostolic austerity and humility would lend credibility to the ministry of the Dominicans. By this time, however, the awakening that had brought forth his ministry was virtually at an end and despite his example of passionate devotion to winning the lost, the Dominicans would be noted historically for their participation in the infamous Inquisition, established in 1231 by Pope Gregory IX.

Also impacted by both the Franciscans and the struggle against the sectarians was Fernando Martins de Bulhoes, better known as Antony of Padua (1195–1231), who began his ministry as an Augustinian Canon in Coimbra, Portugal, was radically challenged by the heroism of the five Franciscans martyred in Morocco (1219), joined the Franciscan order himself, and was appointed the first official teacher of the order by Francis in 1221:

His gifts as a preacher were extraordinary, in addition to a clear voice and compelling manner, prophetic powers and miracles.... His Lenten series in Padua in 1231 reached the proportions of a revival, with 30,000 reported auditors at one time in an open field. The response was massive reconciliations and restitutions, such that the clergy were insufficient for the needs of the people.[17]

The Bogomils. From their western settlements in Serbia at the end of the twelfth century, the Bogomils were expelled by Stefan Nemanja, the Great Zupan, to Bosnia, where they were known as *Patarenes* or *Patareni*. Their arrival precipitated an awakening in which the ruler, Kulin Ban (reigned 1180–1204), was converted to the Bogomil faith in 1199, followed by some ten thousand of his subjects, including the Roman Catholic bishop of Bosnia and the ruler of neighboring Herzegovina.[18] Despite persecution by both the Roman Catholic Church through the kings of Hungary, and the Orthodox Church through the Byzantine emperors and their Serbian subordinates, a form of Bogomilism, known as the Bosnian Church, would remain the major faith of the country until its fall to the Ottoman Empire in 1463.

The Mongols. Outside the Byzantine Empire were also signs of awakening in the early thirteenth century, often obscured by subsequent political events. The dominant power in the east was undoubtedly the Mongol tribes from central Asia that threatened the older empires around. At the beginning of the thirteenth century, when Temujin (Genghis Khan) (1162–1227) united the Mongol tribes as the Golden Horde, a substantial proportion of his followers were actually Nestorian Christians and his sons were all married to Christian Kerait princesses, who apparently wielded considerable influence at court. Although the majority was shamanistic, the Mongols generally were tolerant of other religions until their conversion to Islam a century later. The Golden Horde's conquest of much of Russia to the north and Persia to the west did not deter the advance of the Christian faith in those regions, leading to the establishing of new bishoprics, both Orthodox in the north and Nestorian elsewhere.

In Mongolian China, Genghis Khan's grandson, Kublai Khan (1215–1294), influenced by his mother and having come into contact with Christianity among the Chinese and some of the other conquered peoples, sent an invitation by Niccolo and Maffeo Polo in 1271 for Pope

Gregory X (1210–1276) to send one hundred teachers of science and the Christian religion to reinforce the place of Christianity throughout his empire. According to popular rumor, Pope Gregory was initially very impressed until he read Kublai Khan's statement: "And so shall there be more Christians in my realm than in yours." Infuriated, the pope then tore the letter up and consigned it to the flames. A second appeal in 1286, through Arghun, Mongol Ilkhan of Persia, sent by the hand of the Nestorian Bishop, Rabban Bar Sauma (1220–1294), was not responded to by Pope Honorius IV (1285–1287), but was finally taken up by his successor, Nicholas IV (1288–1292), the first Franciscan pope, who commissioned a fellow Franciscan, John of Montecorvino (1247–1328), as the first Roman Catholic missionary to China.

Together with the Dominican Nicholas of Pistoia and the merchant Peter of Lucalongo, John set out first to Persia and then to India, where he spent some thirteen months evangelizing and baptizing more than a hundred new converts. Following the death of Nicholas in India in 1292, he finally proceeded to Khanbaliq (Beijing) in 1294, only to learn that Kublai Khan had just died. His successor, Temur (reigned 1294–1307), despite some Nestorian opposition, did, however, give him the opportunity to evangelize, establish churches, and translate the New Testament and Psalms into the Uyghur language of the Mongol rulers of China. In the awakening that followed his arrival, some six thousand were converted, leading to his being named as archbishop in 1307 by Pope Clement V (1264–1314). The Franciscan mission continued to flourish until the Chinese overthrew the Mongolian Yuan Dynasty, replacing it with the native Chinese Ming Dynasty in 1368 and expelling all Christians, whether Roman Catholic or Nestorian.

The Early Fourteenth-Century Awakenings. Although the latter half of the thirteenth century had witnessed few signs of awakening, the stirring in China at its end continued into the new century. Among those visiting the work in China, probably in 1302, were the renowned Franciscan Thomas of Tolentino (1260–1321), whose faithful ministry in Armenia and Persia since 1289 had made a considerable impact upon those nations, and the younger French Dominican, Jordan Catalani de Severac (flourished 1320–1330). On a further journey in 1321, while passing through

Bombay, Thomas's party were seized, and most of them were martyred at Thane, Jordan alone escaping with his life. Traveling south to Gujarat, he began an extremely fruitful ministry. His two letters appealing for help, in October 1321 from Gujarat and in January 1323 from Thane to his fellow-Dominicans in Tabriz, Persia, indicated that a major spiritual awakening was underway. Credited with reviving Christianity in the region and bringing thousands into the faith, in 1330 he was appointed the first Roman Catholic Bishop of Quilon in Kerala.[19] Unfortunately, with that, history fell silent regarding him.

Europe. The end of the Medieval Warm Period in Europe (950–1250) was followed by a series of local famines, culminating in torrential rains in 1314, and the Great Famine of 1315–1317, which reduced the population of the continent by some ten percent. Devastation was widespread. The papacy sought to escape the worst of it by fleeing Rome for Avignon in France, thus beginning the Babylonian Captivity (1309–1377). The brief respite in the second quarter of the century was brought to a jarring end by the arrival of the Black Death in 1347. Originating in central Asia a decade earlier, it spread throughout India and China, until it reached Europe, where in some regions up to forty percent of the population succumbed to the plague. Cities, towns, farms, cathedrals, churches, and monasteries were largely abandoned. Even the missionary work, so integral to the preaching orders, virtually came to a halt. Godly, educated clergy were replaced by anyone willing to occupy the office, whatever their motive or character might be. Added to these was the Hundred Years War (1337–1453) between England, Scotland, and France, which contributed to the physical devastation and social instability of Western Europe.

In the face of such catastrophes earnest Christians sought refuge in various mystical and devotional movements that offered a measure of solace for the troubled times. Among the most prominent of the mystical teachers were the Dominicans, Johannes (Meister) Eckhart von Hochheim (1260–1327), Henry Suso (1300–1366), and Johann Tauler (1300–1361). This mysticism was marked by:

…its immense concern for everyone's spiritual health: no longer was mysticism only for the spiritual elite. Eckhart bridges Scholasticism and mysticism, and Tauler translated an academic approach to spirituality into a practical Christianity of high personal demands, designed for all men.[20]

Describing themselves as Friends of God, their popularity spread beyond the cloister to the pew and contributed to the development of several later devotional movements. Although the amorphous Brethren of the Free Spirit has been linked to these teachers, Eckhart in particular strenuously denied any connection. Similarly, the female lay movement of the Beguines and their male counterparts, the Beghards, were variously linked with an earlier revivalist Lambert le Begue (d.1177) from Liege, the Albigensian Cathars, and the Spiritual Franciscans because of some similar doctrines and their willingness to associate with those suspected of heresy, resulting in their condemnation at the Council of Vienne (1311–1312). Subsequently they reformed adopting the Augustinian rule, but maintaining their communal style of living and revivalistic enthusiasm.

The medieval period ended on a far different note than it had begun, especially in Europe, where spiritual rebirth was more than a pious hope; it became the dominant theme of the late medieval age—the Renaissance.

Endnotes

1 W. Walker, et. al.: *A History of the Christian Church*, 4th edn. (New York, NY: Scribner's, 1985), 359.

2 B. L. Shelley: *Church History in Plain Language*, 3rd edn. (Nashville, TN: Thomas Nelson, 2008), 186.

3 M. Taylor, op. cit., 117.

4 G. S. M. Walker, op. cit., 178.

5 W. Walker, op. cit., 314.

6 Taylor, op. cit., 117.

7 Matthew 10:7–10 NIV1984.

8 G. S. M. Walker, op. cit., 180.

9 Taylor, op. cit., 118.

10 Ibid, 119.

11 R. G. Clouse: art. "Francis of Assisi" in NIDCC, 387.

12 G. S. M. Walker, op. cit., 186.

13 Ibid., 187.

14 N. Young: *The Story of Rome* (London, UK: Dent, 1907), 210, 211.

15 J. Taylor: art. "Dominic" in NIDCC, 307.

16 Ibid.

17 M. E. Rogers: art. "Antony of Padua" in NIDCC, 51.

18 Letter from Vukan, Serbian Duke of Zeta, to Pope Innocent III in 1199; N. Weber: art. "Cathari" in *The Catholic Encyclopedia,* vol. 3 (New York, NY: Robert Appleton, 1908).

19 R. J. McMahon: art. "India" in NIDCC, 504.

20 C. G. Thorne, Jr. art "Tauler, John" in NIDCC, 953.

Chapter 10

The Renaissance Period

1350–1525 AD

The late medieval period, popularly known as the Renaissance, was not only a rebirth of the classical Greek and Roman culture in Europe, but also a rebirth of society from the devastation of the Black Death (1347–1351), in which "a slow decline of population suddenly became a disaster with the onset of attacks of epidemic disease. . . . In some areas a half or a third of the population may have died; over Europe as a whole the total loss has been calculated as a quarter."[1] Medieval society was inadequate to cope with the ruin inflicted on its economic and political life, especially in population centers. Even the church reeled before the disaster. Urban clergies were less likely to survive than their rural counterparts, who were farther removed from the plague-carrying rats infesting the towns and cities. The resulting gaps in the ranks of the clergy came to be filled by anybody who had the inclination to be a priest. Thus, some of the worst characters ended up in the priesthood and treated their charges as opportunities for satisfying themselves by acquiring wealth and prestige or being in a position to enjoy immoral and godless pursuits.

It was a time of great advances in the arts and sciences but also a time in which other influences entering into Christianity drastically affected both the church and contemporary society. The Papacy in exile, safely ensconced in Avignon since 1309, maintained some semblance of control over the church, but in much of Western Europe, Christendom entered into a serious condition of decline. In this traumatic period in the history of the Western church, penitential processions of flagellants wandered the highways. "The Flagellants believed that, because of their self-inflicted torture, they would all be saved . . . They also called for the killing of the Jews, whom they believed were the enemies of God and responsible for the plague."[2] Others responded to the appalling conditions by turning to prayer, seeking the face of God. Throughout this period a great cry for reform and revival arose.

The Late Fourteenth-Century Awakening. Among the earliest to respond was John Wycliffe (c. 1329–1384), the renowned English scholastic. Although little is known of his early life, other than his birth in North Yorkshire, from about 1345, he was associated with the University of Oxford, where he came under the influence of William of Occam (1280–1349), Thomas Bradwardine (1290–1349), and Richard Fitzralph (1300–1360). As Master of Balliol College (1360–1361), and of Canterbury Hall (1365–1366), his brilliance as a scholar, his stance on Scripture teaching against clerical corruption, and in favor of national civil government, brought him to the attention of the English Regent, John of Gaunt, Duke of Lancaster (1340–1399), probably one of the richest men in history, who became his protector.

In 1378, Wycliffe took a strong stand against practices that he felt were a corruption of the biblical standards. He began a translation of the Scriptures from the Latin Vulgate into English, the first in Middle English, which made him realize that many of the current medieval church teachings were not truly biblical. Reverting to the Bible, he "denied transubstantiation, attacked the institution of the papacy, repudiated indulgences, and wished to have religious orders abolished."[3] The abuse of auricular confession, prayers for the dead, the church's obsession with material wealth, and medieval society's obsession with war were also condemned in the light of Scripture. The inevitable conflict with the established church and the diminishing of aristocratic support, especially after the Peasants' Revolt of 1381, of which Wycliffe publicly disapproved, yet was blamed for, led to the condemnation of some twenty-four of his propositions as either heretical or erroneous at the "earthquake synod" in London in 1382. Only the continuing protection of John of Gaunt kept him from being personally condemned as a heretic during his lifetime; however, the anti-Wycliffite statute *De heretico comburendo* (1401), and *the Constitutions of Oxford* (1408), sought to limit the propagation of his teachings and translation of the Scriptures. Finally, in 1415, the Council of Constance declared him a heretic and decreed his writings be burned together with his exhumed remains.

The Lollards. Although Wycliffe himself was more a zealous reformer[4] than a revivalist preacher, the seeds he sowed bore fruit in awakenings throughout the British Isles and abroad. In Britain the Poor Priests, who carried his message to the countryside in apostolic fashion, two by two, under the leadership of his associate Bible translator, Nicholas of Hereford (d. 1420),[5] were nicknamed the Lollards from the Latin lolium (a weed),[6] or from the Dutch lollen (mumble).[7] Insultingly described as the weeds among the wheat, they gladly took the name as expressing the reality of their mission to root the weeds out of the harvest field. After the expulsion of Wycliffe's sympathizers from Oxford (November 1382), the main center of Lollard activity was Leicester, where a spiritual awakening had provided a growing group of lay supporters. Armed with hand-written pages of John Purvey's (1353–1428) vernacular revision of the Wycliffe Bible translation, they spread his message across the English countryside from East Anglia to the Welsh Marches. The completion of Purvey's revision in 1395 coincided with Parliament's action outlawing the Lollard movement. Driven underground, the Lollards were restricted to clandestine meetings under the continuing threat of martyrdom, especially after the 1401 statute, yet for the next 150 years they helped precipitate periodic awakenings throughout the British Isles until the Elizabethan Settlement (1559) brought these secret disciples out of hiding and into the newer reformation movement.

The Friends of God. In the Low Countries, the Rhineland, Bavaria, along the borders of France and Switzerland, and especially in the university cities of Basle, Strasbourg, and Cologne the medieval Friends of

God continued to breathe life into a church reeling from the impact of the Babylonian captivity and then the Great Schism (1378–1417), which witnessed two and later three rival popes claiming the supremacy. Although the Conciliar Movement sought to remedy the situation by curbing the flagrant abuse of power by the papacy, its goal of reforming the church "in head and members"[8] was not to be realized. The only hope for the needed moral and administrative reform lay in renewed devotion toward God.

The Devotio Moderna. Radically converted through the influential Flemish mystic, Jan van Ruysbroeck (1293–1381), a young Dutchman, Geert Groote (1340–1384), devoted himself to seeking God and encouraged others in the same direction. By 1380 he had gathered a sizable following in Deventer, which became the nucleus of the Brethren of the Common Life. Following Groote's death from the plague, the movement, later known as Devotio Moderna (modern devotion), spread rapidly throughout the Low Countries and Germany, calling earnest believers back to the apostolic devotion of the New Testament, to a life of total and absolute commitment to God. A further center established at Windesheim near Zwolle in 1386 by Groote's disciple, Florentius Radewijns (1350–1400), was officially approved by Pope Boniface IX (1355–1404) in 1395 as an Augustinian house and became the main center for diffusing the modern devotional movement throughout the cloisters of Europe. "The ideals incorporated in its life and presented for spiritual reform and revival"[9] gave a renewed sense of purpose to the floundering monastic movement. Writings from the modern devotional movement, such as Luther's favorite *Theologia Germanica* (the German Theology), Thomas a Kempis's *The Imitation of Christ*, and the little handbook *The Practice of the Presence of God*, by Brother Lawrence (Nicholas Herman), continue to inspire believers to a renewed life of spiritual devotion. Somewhat reminiscent of the seventh-century Saxon herdsman, Caedmon of Whitby, Brother Lawrence found even as a lay worker in a monastery kitchen, he could have the sweetest fellowship and communion with the Lord.

The Hesychasm. After the Crusades the Byzantine Empire was so weakened that its very existence seemed threatened by the advancing Muslims.

In the Orthodox, Church an older mystical movement traceable back to Simeon the New Theologian (949–1022), the abbot of the monastery of St. Mamas, became the focus of a renewed spirituality, Hesychasm, through which the participant sought a direct knowledge of God through an ecstatic experience of divine energy, the "Uncreated Light." Strongly defended by Gregory Palamas (1296–1359), Archbishop of Thessalonica, Hesychasm was officially approved by the Council of Constantinople in 1341, and continues as the primary pattern of Orthodox mysticism.[10] Despite its sometimes unusual and even aberrant aspects, at its heart was a desire to experience the power and presence of God once again.

The Russian Monastic Renewal. Although Christianity east of the Muslim lands almost disappeared from history with the disintegration of the Mongol Empire, and the subsequent conversion of the majority of the Mongol tribes to Islam, in the northeast of Asia the growth that had begun in the Mongol era continued and even accelerated subsequently. Many sought to escape the oppressive rule of the Tatars by fleeing to the northern forests, where small communities of hermits gave rise to growing towns. Latourette estimated that from the thirteenth to the sixteenth century on the frontiers of Russia were established 294 new monasteries, which served as schools in the Christian faith, converting many pagans to Christ.[11] From these monasteries, missionaries proceeded to evangelize previously unreached people. Probably the greatest of these was Stephen of Perm (1340–1396), who devised an alphabet for the unwritten language of the Zyrian Finnish tribes for translating the Scriptures, and pastured a growing flock of new converts from the folk movement that resulted.

The Fifteenth-Century Awakenings. As limited as the success of the Wycliffite movement may have been in Britain, his teaching found a more ready acceptance in the central European kingdom of Bohemia. The two kingdoms had been connected in 1382 by the marriage of King Richard II of England (1367–1400) to Anne of Bohemia (1366–1394), daughter of the Holy Roman Emperor, Charles IV (1316–1378). The interaction between the Universities of Oxford and Prague popularized the writings of Wycliffe among the student body. Jan Hus (1373–1415) encountered Wycliffe's philosophical teachings in his student days, and following his ordination in 1402, became entranced by his religious writings and the prospects of ecclesiastical reform.

The Bohemian Renewal. A reform movement had begun in Prague through the ministry of the fiery Austrian Augustinian preacher, Conrad of Waldhausen (1320–1369), who in turn inspired the evangelist, Jan Milic of Kromeriz, Moravia (d. 1374), and Matthew of Janov (c. 1355–1393). "As a result of Milic's ministry, the 'red light' district in Prague was transformed into a hostel for converted prostitutes, and renamed 'Jerusalem.'"[12] Matthew, following the same pattern of strongly biblical preaching, is credited with making the first translation of the Bible into the Czech language. By the time Hus came on the scene, the stage was set for a radical move of the Holy Spirit in reforming the church and reviving the people.

The sympathy that the advocates for reform enjoyed among the church leaders during the first decade of the century quickly soured following the ill-fated attempts of the Council of Pisa (1409) to end the Great Schism, and to combat both the spread of Wycliffe's ideas and the Bohemian reform movement.[13] As rector of Prague's Bethlehem Chapel (1402) and of the university following the expulsion of the Germans in 1409, Hus became the focal figure of the reformers and of the spiritual awakening that was spreading throughout the kingdom. Tricked into attending the Council of Constance (1414), by a guarantee of safe passage from the Holy Roman Emperor, Sigismund (1361–1437), the half-brother of the Bohemian King Wenceslas (d. 1419), Hus was seized as a heretic and martyred, declaring at his burning:

> God is my witness that the evidence against me is false. I have never thought or preached except with the one intention of winning men, if possible, from their sins. In the truth of the gospel I have written, taught, and preached; today I will gladly die.[14]

The Bohemian reform movement did not die with Hus, despite numerous attempts to eliminate it, especially after Sigismund succeeded Wenceslas. Initially the most radical of the Hussite reformers, the Taborites, united most of the nation in their rejection of the imperial power; however, following the death of their leader, Jan Zizka (1360–1424), the more moderate Utraquists eventually made peace with the Roman Catholic Church in 1433. From their mountain stronghold, Mount Tabor, the militants continued as an independent church, later known as the Unitas Fratrum, and provided a refuge for displaced Bogomiles, Albigenses, and Waldenses, while encouraging spasmodic spiritual awakenings throughout central Europe.

Southern Europe. At the same time as Hus's preaching in Bethlehem Chapel was drawing the crowds in Prague, a Spanish Dominican preacher, Vincent Ferrer (1350–1419), began a preaching itinerary across southern Europe that resulted in thousands of Jews and Muslims coming to faith in Christ, miraculous answers to prayer, and even a supernatural endowment of xenolalia, enabling him to preach in the vernacular of northern Italy, Switzerland, and France, when he knew only his native Spanish Valencian dialect, and Latin. Inspired by Vincent's example, Bernardino of Siena (1380–1444), became a Franciscan friar in 1402, and devoted himself to a preaching itinerary lasting some forty years throughout northern Italy, winning many thousands to a renewed faith in Christ and promoting the revivalistic Observant movement. By the time of his death more than four thousand convents and mendicant communities in Italy, France, Spain, and Germany had been awakened.[15]

The fall of Constantinople and the remnants of the Byzantine Empire to the Ottoman Turks in 1453 sent shockwaves throughout Christendom and lent urgency to the revivalist preaching of the Observant movement in northern Italy, lest the new masters of the Balkans continue their westward expansion. The capitulation of Greek Orthodoxy to the Muslim conquerors added weight to the emergence of Moscow as the third Rome and the Russian Orthodox inheritance of the mantle of the Byzantine Church as the defender of Christian orthodoxy.

Whatever Christian ideas may have been present in the earliest phase of the Renaissance, they were increasingly overwhelmed with secular and even pagan concepts. By the middle of the fifteenth century cultured society, especially in Italy, was marked by cruelty and corruption:

Men could no longer be trusted; beneath the velvet tunic peeped the dagger, and in the sparkling cup men expected the deadly poison. Murder and incest, lust and cruelty, haunted alike the palaces of the great and the hovels of the poor. Italy in particular was full of bravos and cut-throats, who, before they struck down their victims from behind in the quiet street, did not think it incongruous first to visit the cathedral and, kneeling down, ask God's protection.[16]

Northern Italy. Although many expected that the healing of the Great Schism would restore moral stature to the papacy, it proved to be a vain expectation. The subsequent occupants of the throne of Peter in Rome were among the worst to do so, men like Pius II (1405–1464), author of erotic poems and novels; Paul II (1417–1471), notorious for cupidity and homosexuality; Sixtus IV (1414–1484), notorious for political ambition, nepotism, and cruelty; Innocent VIII (1432–1492), who institutionalized simony; and Alexander VI (1431–1503), the most infamous Borgia pope, notorious for taking a woman and then their daughter as concubines with the blessing of his cardinals and papal staff upon the incestuous relationship. Such were the popes of this period.

In that social climate, Girolamo Savonarola (1452–1498) was born in Ferrara, northern Italy, into a family renowned for its indulgence in the finer things of life in the Renaissance. A quiet young man, destined for a career in medicine, Savonarola was challenged by an Augustinian friar to devote himself to God, and in 1475 entered the Observant Dominican monastery of San Domenico in Bologna. After seven years of intense study and seeking God, he was sent to the monastery of San Marco in Florence in 1482, but made little impression there. Five years later he returned to Bologna to continue his studies.

At the behest of Count Pico della Mirandola (1463–1494), the renowned Renaissance philosopher and author of the "Oration of the Dignity of Man" (1486), often called "The Manifesto of the Renaissance," Savonarola was recalled to Florence in 1490, where in a series of sermons from the book of Revelation, his fiery apocalyptic preaching shook the city to its core. Denouncing the sensuality and scandalous vices of the city and its leaders, the Medici family, he summoned the Florentines to repentance before judgment should fall. This had a powerful impact upon the town. Pico della Mirandola declared "that the mere sound of Savonarola's voice was like as the clap of doom; a cold shiver ran through the marrow of his bones, the hairs of his head stood on end as he listened."[17]

Savonarola's prediction of the downfall of the Medici family was confirmed first by the death of Lorenzo the Magnificent (1449–1492), the patron of the arts, and the flight of his son and successor, Piero the Unfortunate (1472–1503) less than two years later, upon the invasion of the French king, Charles VIII (1470–1498). The arrival of the French was accompanied by a new plague, the French pox (syphilis), which devastated the occupied areas (1494–1495), as Savonarola prophesied. Upon the flight of Piero in 1494 Savonarola was appointed tribune of the now "Christian and religious Republic of Florence." "Under this administration he held the city in moral tension and initiated tax reform, aided the poor, reformed the courts, changing Florence from a lax, corrupt, pleasure-loving city into an ascetic, monastic-type community."[18] The immediate criminalizing of sodomy and subsequent flight of the city's large homosexual community brought down on Savonarola the wrath of Pope Alexander and the Duke of Milan, Ludovico Sforza (1452–1508), patron of Leonardo da Vinci (1452–1519), who had faced a sodomy charge while in Florence in 1476. During the carnival of 1496, Savonarola inspired the "burning of the vanities" when the citizens made in the Piazza della Signoria a bonfire of their lewd books, pictures, and sculptures, their gambling equipment, pagan relics, and even women's cosmetics, provocative dresses, hats, and false hair.

With the change in Savonarola's role from revival preacher to tribune or civic leader of Florence came a discernible change in the awakening itself. The tide that had swept him to power, began to turn. A public demonstration of the ancient ordeal of trial by fire to vindicate his integrity was forestalled by a sudden rainstorm to the frustration of the vast throng of Florentines, who proceeded to riot, giving Savonarola's opponents the opportunity of seizing power. Finally, his enemies arrested him and two of his closest disciples, Fra Domenico da Pescia and Fra Silvestro putting them on trial before two papal commissioners, whose task it was to ensure their condemnation and execution by burning in the same public square as the burning of the vanities two years before.

Despite the fact that no group of followers remained to continue Savonarola's work and the majority of Florentines returned to their old ways, many individuals like Botticelli (1445–1510), Fra Bartolommeo (1475–1517), and Michelangelo (1475–1564) were transformed and expressed their lively Christian faith to the enrichment of countless generations to come.

Spain. The quest for church renewal was not confined to northern Italy at the end of this century but the Spanish cardinal Ximenez De Cisneros (1436–1517), an Observant Franciscan, had a major impact upon the Spanish church of which he became the titular head in 1495 as Archbishop of Toledo. While court chaplain to Queen Isabella of Spain, he became a renowned reformer of the church, setting some of the most stringent standards of righteousness and godly living for the clergy there, and renewing the movement begun a century earlier under Vincent Ferrer. Both Ximenez and the renowned humanist scholar Desiderius Erasmus (1466–1536), began working on a critical edition of the Greek New Testament, based upon the early Greek manuscripts, brought to the West by Byzantine refugees. Erasmus's version was published first and became foundational to much of the New Testament studies in the West. Ximenez's Greek New Testament was published somewhat later. Despite being a very fine piece of work, it made little impact upon biblical studies outside Roman Catholicism, but contributed greatly to the Catholic Reformation. His reforming activities at the turn of the century forestalled any efforts to impact his nation by the northern reformers a generation later.

Endnotes

1   J. M. Roberts: *The Penguin History of the World*, 3rd edn. (London, UK: Penguin, 1995), 499, 500.

2   J. Taylor: art. "Flagellants" in NIDCC, 379.

3   R. G. Clouse: art. "Wycliffe, John" in NIDCC, 1064.

4   G. H. W. Parker: *The Morning Star* (Exeter, Devon: Paternoster, 1965), 56, 57.

5   R. G. Clouse: art. "Lollards" in NIDCC, 601.

6   M. Taylor, op. cit., 86.

7   W. Walker, op. cit., 380.

8   Ibid., 386.

9   Parker, op. cit., 145.

10 G. Giacumakis, Jr.: art. "Hesychasm" in NIDCC, 467.

11 Latourette: *History of the Expansion*, 259.

12 Davies, op. cit., 61.

13 J. Taylor: art. "Pisa, Council of" in NIDCC, 783.

14 B. L. Shelley, op. cit., 232.

15 Parker, op. cit., 115.

16 J. Burns: *Revivals, their Laws and Leaders* (Grand Rapids, MI: Baker, 1960), 123.

17 Ibid., 139.

18 R. G. Clouse: art. "Savonarola, Girolamo" in NIDCC, 880.

Part III

Early Evangelical
Awakenings

Chapter 11

The Reformation Period

1525–1575

This section begins a new area of investigation, namely that of the Evangelical Awakenings, which are characterized by first, the renewing of the spiritual life of the congregation as has already been apparent in the pre-reformation revivals; and second, a restoration of biblical teaching to the church. Each of the major awakenings occurring over the next five centuries was marked by a particular doctrinal emphasis. Not every awakening had the same emphasis, but every awakening highlighted a particular point of doctrine that became the main thrust of the preaching and teaching.

The major emphasis of the Reformation period was righteousness by faith. In the Puritan period, there was a strong emphasis on purifying the church from extraneous additions. In the Great Awakening of the eighteenth century, the major emphasis was on a personal relationship with God. At the beginning of the nineteenth century, the emphasis was on the Great Commission; and then a generation later the dominant note was the second coming of Christ. In the mid-nineteenth century, the major emphasis was on personal holiness, entire sanctification, then from the end of the nineteenth to the beginning of the twentieth century, the teachings regarding the baptism in the Holy Spirit and the manifestations of spiritual gifts that characterize the modern-day Pentecostal movement dominated.

Throughout the twentieth century the revivals that have swept across the land have also brought renewed emphases: the mid-century awakening was marked by evangelism and divine healing; in the second half of the century came a fresh emphasis on the body life of the church, a sense of community, and currently there is emerging an awareness of personal responsibility and accountability. It is possible that this is simply part of the preparation, and the major emphasis has yet to be revealed. The major emphasis may not always become apparent at the outset of the revival, but every evangelical awakening does have such a major and significant point of emphasis.

The flow of Christian history shows three distinct phases: in the first seven centuries the movement was from diversity toward uniformity; the next phase from the eighth to the fifteenth centuries brought variety within that uniformity; and then from the sixteenth century onward, the third phase was a movement back from uniformity to diversity. It seems as though the church is coming full circle in its progress. Since the reformation period there has emerged a greater sense of diversity among the Christians.

Protestantism started as a division from the Roman Catholic Church. Protestantism itself in a very short time divided into the Lutheran, the Zwinglian, the Anabaptist, the Anglican, and later the Calvinistic movements. Calvinism divided into various types of Calvinism and the Arminian movement, which later in turn divided into remonstrant Arminianism and Wesleyan Arminianism. Wesleyan Arminianism divided into the Wesleyan movement, the primitive Methodist movement, the Methodist connectional movement, and the holiness movement. The holiness movement divided into numerous churches including the Pentecostal movement, which itself divided into the Apostolic Faith, the Assemblies of God, the Church of God, the Pentecostal Holiness Church, the Church of God in Christ, and numerous other Pentecostal denominations in the United States of America plus many other groups around the world, each of which has gone through its own splits and divisions. Even attempts to unite

Christian groups have simply produced a greater diversity and a plethora of independent fellowships.

The Background to the Awakening. The events of the sixteenth century may be viewed historically as the culmination of the social, intellectual, and ecclesiastical currents that produced the Protestant Reformation. "Although conditioned by political, economic, social, and intellectual factors, the course of events and the writings of the Reformers themselves reveal that it was above all else a religious revival which had as its goal Christian renewal."[1] This was one of the major revival periods of history, not localized to a particular area but widespread, affecting much of established Christianity within a short time.

There were three parts to the revival movement: in **northern and western Europe** the awakening became the Reformation, which subsequently developed into Protestantism; in **southern Europe**, the renewal, often called the Counter-reformation or Catholic Reformation, was not simply a reaction to the Protestant Reformation but an outpouring of the Spirit of God; and in **the East**, especially in southern and central Russia, in areas not directly affected by the other European renewals, there was a similar spiritual awakening in the latter half of the century.

Several factors prepared the way for the great awakening of the sixteenth century, especially in western Europe. **First,** on the borders of the Christian nations was the threat posed by the Islamic Ottoman Empire, which had so recently in 1453 overthrown the remnant of the Byzantine Empire and was pressing on the doors of Western Christendom. It looked as though this empire was about to sweep everything before it. Understandably, many people were fearful as to what the future would hold for them.

Second, there was a considerable amount of dissatisfaction with the papacy in the west. The Babylonian captivity and the subsequent Great Schism with two or even three popes competing for the leadership of Western Christendom caused people to lose confidence in established religion. This was exacerbated by the profligacy of the Renaissance popes. Christendom was not functioning the way that it should and many both within the Catholic Church and outside expressed their dissatisfaction.

Third, the feudalism of medieval society was transformed by the development of the *bourgeoisie*. Although the Black Death and subsequent plagues had slowed the flow of displaced serfs to the towns, the development of the merchant class gave the poor prospects of employment unimaginable to earlier generations. Skills scattered among the villages were increasingly concentrated and developed in the growing towns. Ideas formerly mulled over in relative isolation were publicly discussed and at times acted upon.

Fourth, the invention of the printing press (1436–1450) enabled ideas to be propagated quickly and economically, especially in comparison with hand-copying. The first attempts in the West utilized woodcuts, but Johannes Gutenberg's (1395–1468) development of the movable type press made it possible to produce cheaply large amounts of literature. Martin Luther (1483–1546), like Gutenberg, was German, and the proliferation of movable type presses gave his supporters a distinct advantage over their southern opponents. By 1480, there were 110 presses in Germany, and some 270 at the beginning of the sixteenth century. It may be said that if there had been no printing press, there would have been no Reformation, because Luther's pamphlets and manuscripts would have died on the scholarly tables of copyists who would not have wasted their time copying multiple versions of Luther's writings.

Fifth, beginning at the end of fifteenth century there was a return to the actual study of the Bible. With the fall of the Byzantine Empire many of the Eastern Church leaders and the monks fled to the West bringing with them early manuscripts of the Scriptures that reawakened interest in biblical translation and interpretation. Regarding the Hebrew Scriptures, the work of the great scholar Johannes Reuchlin (1455–1522), a member of the Brethren of the Common Life, prompted a renewal of Hebrew studies that had been generally ignored since the days of Jerome, more than 1,100 years before. Reuchlin also promoted Greek studies, but it was his younger contemporary, Desiderius Erasmus (1466–1536), also educated by the Brethren of the Common Life, who was noted for his production of a Greek New Testament, based upon copies of very early Greek manuscripts of the New Testament. Biblical studies had been based almost exclusively on Jerome's Latin Vulgate text, which after more than a millennium of transcriptional errors was no longer entirely reliable. Erasmus and Reuchlin were described as the twin eyes of Europe, through which Europe was made to see the truth of the Scriptures.

Sixth, another major factor in creating a climate open to transformation was the discovery of the new world. Men's horizons were expanded. This new world with abundant wealth awaited whoever was bold enough to make the journey. Even the later Renaissance popes, seeking to refurbish the Lateran Palace and complete the building of St. Peter's Basilica in Rome, realized that the new world was a source of unlimited riches that more than replaced the loss of a few northern countries.

This new world opened new vistas; men could no longer be satisfied with the way things were. A new age had dawned, and new ideas began to develop. The old dogmas were shaken by the simple fact that instead of the earth being, as the medieval theologians had insisted, a flat disc spinning in space, Copernicus and his colleagues, who had put forward the idea of a spherical earth, were demonstrated to be correct. The new ideas of the Renaissance prompted a rethinking of more than geography and astronomy, but began to impact every area of scholarship and investigation, including the interpretation of Scripture.

With such factors affecting the thinking of the age it is not surprising that within a short time an upheaval took place in western Europe, which would have immense repercussions.

The Beginning of the Awakening. The Reformation is often dated from Luther's posting of the Ninety-Five Theses for debate upon the door of the Wittenberg Castle church (October 31, 1517), in protest against the sale of papal indulgences by the Dominican Johann Tetzler (c. 1465–1519).[2] In reality the radical changes in Luther began somewhat earlier, probably in the summer of 1511, when "wrestling with the problem of his personal salvation."[3] Guided by Johann von Staupitz, vicar-general of the Augustinian Order to which he belonged, he came to realize that his salvation depended entirely upon the justifying grace of God.[4] As a doctor of theology (1512), Luther was appointed to the lectureship in Bible at the University of Wittenberg, where his studies in the Psalms (1513–1515), and Paul's letters to the Romans (1515–1516) and Galatians (1516–1517) brought him to a life-transforming experience and understanding of justification by faith. He was also strongly influenced by the writings of Augustine of Hippo, Tauler of the Friends of God, and especially Jacques Lefevre d'Etaples (1455–1536), whose commentary on the Pauline Epistles (1512) clearly enunciated the same doctrine of justification by faith espoused by the Reformers.[5]

This teaching was a common theme in the preaching and writings of several contemporary Christian Humanist and Catholic devotional scholars, such as Erasmus, von Staupitz, his mentor, and even Giovanni Pietro Caraffa (1476–1559) later to become Pope Paul IV (1555). The fact that others had similarly discovered this truth meant that Luther was not standing alone in his proclamation. Some, like Erasmus and Ulrich Zwingli (1484–1531), the Swiss Reformer, came to this realization through the study of the Scriptures under the influence of Christian Humanism. Luther had come to this truth largely through the influence of the monastic orders. Whether from a Protestant or a Catholic perspective, it was the same truth that was realized, that a man is not justified (made righteous) on the basis of his good works or his self-deprivations or asceticism, but he is justified on the basis of simple trust in Almighty God.

Luther's protest against the sale of indulgences undoubtedly arose from his conviction that this diminished the value of Christ's death and even tended to "induce complacency and thereby imperil salvation."[6] Although Pope Leo X (Giovanni de'Medici) (1475–1521) was at first disposed to let the leadership of the Augustinian Friars deal with Luther quietly, when Luther attended the chapter meeting in Heidelberg (April 1518), "he was surprised to find that many of his fellow friars favored his teachings, and that some of the younger ones were even enthusiastic about it."[7] Among those enthused by his teachings were Martin Bucer (1491–1551) and Johann Brenz (1499–1570), who would later become leaders of the movement in Strasbourg and Stuttgart, respectively. Despite the opposition of the aging Holy Roman Emperor, Maximilian (d. 1519), and his successor Charles V (1500–1558), the support of the Saxon Elector Frederick III (the Wise) (1463–1525) ensured Luther's protection even when the pope excommunicated the incalcitrant monk, following the historic debate with Johann Eck of Ingolstadt (1486–1543) in Leipzig (1519). "In 1518 (Luther's) theology of the Cross was thoroughly Pauline, and Luther was the champion of *sola fide* (faith alone), *sola gratia* (grace alone), (and) *sola Scriptura* (the Bible alone)."[8] By 1520, his reforming theology was complete, as demonstrated by his *Sermon on the Mass* (April), *The Treatise on Good Works* (May), *On the Papacy at Rome* (June), *The Address to the German Nobility* (August), *The Babylonian Captivity of the Church* (October), and *The Freedom of the Christian Man* (November).[9]

Taken to Wartburg Castle under the protection of Elector Frederick, following the Diet of Worms in 1521, Luther had the opportunity both to continue his writings and to begin his translation of the Bible into German, probably his greatest achievement. In his year-long absence from Wittenberg, others emerged as leaders of the movement, Andreas von Carlstadt (c.1477–1541), Gabriel Zwilling (c.1487–1558), and Philip Melancthon (1497-1560), the great-nephew of Reuchlin. "Carlstadt and Zwilling gave a more radical turn to the Reformation, encouraged by the Zwickau Prophets who joined forces with them."[10]

A fiery preacher, Zwilling soon spread the revival enthusiasm to a growing following of monks and Wittenberg townspeople, who, encouraged by Carlstadt, went on an iconoclastic rampage through the city. Seeking to temper the burgeoning movement, the town council appealed to Luther to restore order by returning from the seclusion of Wartburg. By Easter 1522 Luther was back in Wittenberg, Zwilling had been appointed to a pastorate in Altenburg, near Zwickau, and Carlstadt to nearby Orlamunde.

Prior to the Diet of Worms, Luther had encouraged his ardently evangelical colleague Thomas Munzer (c. 1488–1525) to carry the message to Zwickau; however, when the Zwickau Prophets, Nicholas Storch, Thomas Drechsel, and Marcus Stubner, were expelled by the town council, Munzer fled to Prague, Bohemia, hoping to link up with the remnants of the Hussite movement. Frustrated in his quest, he moved to Allstedt in Thuringia, where over the next two years (1522–1524) he developed his parish into a more thoroughly Reformed church. When the rulers united against him, he fled south, eventually making his way to Muhlhausen, where his ardent preaching added fuel to the smoldering fires of discontent among the dispossessed peasants, which quickly erupted in the Peasants' War (1524–1525). Luther, realizing that his work depended upon the support of the German nobility, vehemently attacked his more radical colleagues, like Munzer and Carlstadt, and issued his uncompromising condemnation *Against the Murderous and Thieving Hordes of Peasants* (May 1525), inciting the rulers to use every possible means to crush the revolt. Munzer, who Luther claimed to be responsible for the whole affair, was captured at the Battle of Frankenhausen (May 1525), tortured, and beheaded:

> The Peasants' War was a watershed in reformation history, marking the end of its period of uncontrolled growth. From then on, the movement became subject to ever closer supervision by the civil authorities, who were obliged either to suppress it or to establish new evangelical church orders in their territories. The reformation, however, though it certainly lost some of its appeal to the masses, did not cease to be a spontaneous popular movement.[11]

Northern Germany and Scandinavia. As Luther was facing the Diet of Worms, the evangelical message was rapidly spreading throughout Germany. A former student from Wittenberg, Hermann Tast (1490–1551) boldly proclaimed a message of renewal in the Marienkirche in Husum, Schleswig (1522), resulting in an awakening in which the crowds exceeded the capacity of the largest buildings in the town, and filled the local cemetery. In 1526, the awakening crossed the border into Danish Flensburg, beginning the evangelical awakening in Scandinavia. About the same time Hans Tausen (1494–1561), who had been radically converted during a visit to Wittenberg, began preaching the evangelical message publicly in Viborg with notable results. When the churches became too small for the crowds thronging them, they assembled in the marketplace and Tausen used the clock tower as his pulpit. Protected by King Frederick I (reigned 1523–1533), the reformists were tolerated and under the reign of Christian III (reigned 1536–1559) and the country became officially Lutheran, as did the then Danish subordinate kingdom of Norway. Although the prime motivation for the spread of the Reformation in Sweden was more political than the result of an evangelical awakening, especially during the reign of Gustavus Vasa (1523–1560), the separation from Roman control did give the opportunity for evangelically inclined preachers like Olaf (1493–1552) and Lars Petersson (1499–1573) to lay the groundwork for a future renewal movement.

Britain. Despite a brief revival of Lollardy during the early reign of King Henry VIII (reigned 1509–1547)[12] the prime motive behind the Reformation movement in England was the king's growing estrangement from the papacy, not sympathy for the evangelical message. Independence from Rome did, however, give the opportunity for evangelical preachers like Thomas Bilney (c. 1495–1531) and his renowned associate Hugh Latimer (1485–1555) to promote spiritual awakening in the country:

> At times, Latimer preached in the open-air to 6,000 people at a time. Murray notes an entry in the records of St. Margaret's Church, Westminster, where one shilling and sixpence was expended "for mending diverse pews that were broken when Doctor Latimer did preach," presumably as a result of the great numbers crowding into the building to hear him![13]

Switzerland. As the Reformation awakening was spreading rapidly throughout Germany, it was also growing in German-speaking Switzerland. Ulrich Zwingli, while a student at the University of Vienna, had been introduced to Christian Humanism, but while completing his studies in Basle (1506), had been strongly influenced toward biblical scholarship by Thomas Wyttenbach (1472–1526), who also encouraged him to an evangelical faith in Christ's death as the price of forgiveness of sins.[14] Upon Zwingli's appointment as people's priest at the Great Minster in Zurich (December 1518), he began a systematic exposition of the Bible, beginning with Matthew's Gospel, which was only interrupted by his near-death experience from the bubonic plague (September 1519). Awakened to an intense sense of divine mission, he pursued his Bible exposition more fervently, began to carefully study Luther's writings from Germany, and initiated a reformist program in Zurich, despite the reluctance of the reform-minded Bishop of Constance, Hugo von Hohenlandenberg (1457–1532).

Some of his more radically-minded followers, like Conrad Grebel (c. 1498–1526), Georg Blaurock (c. 1492–1529), and Felix Manz (c. 1498–1527), separated from Zwingli to form the first Anabaptist congregation in nearby Zollikon (1525). Despite the death of Grebel from abuse while imprisoned and the public execution of Manz with Zwingli's approval, the radical Anabaptist wing of the revival movement could not be stopped. "Exiled from Zurich in 1527, Blaurock became an itinerant evangelist, winning several thousand to Christ and planting the Anabaptist faith over much of central Europe."[15] Many of the peasants disillusioned with Luther's magisterial reformation readily allied themselves with the Anabaptist and Radical reformation.

The Radical Reformation. The Anabaptists did not represent the entire Radical reformation movement. However, after a group of the militant apocalyptic-oriented Melchiorites, named after Melchior Hoffman (c. 1495–1543), attempted to establish a permanent city of refuge for Anabaptists in Munster under Jan Mattheys (1500–1534) and John of Leyden (1509–1536), the term "Anabaptist" became a common epithet for the whole Radical movement, and conjured up fears of the most extreme fanaticism and social disorder. The more pacifist Hutterites, Mennonites, and their related descendants sought to maintain their original vision of the church as a covenantal community of true believers.

The Catholic Reformation. Even as the movement was foundering in the north, advocates of reform and revival in the Roman Catholic dominated areas were experiencing a quickening that would renew or reform some of the existing monastic orders and give birth to new orders. "The two main centers from which the Catholic revival radiated were Spain and Italy, though spiritual renewal in both countries owed not a little to older traditions of spirituality in the Netherlands and Germany."[16]

Although in the Protestant wing the emphasis was on the individual relationship with God, in the Roman Catholic Church typically the revival movements expressed themselves through sodalities. A sodality is a community that takes vows of poverty, chastity, and obedience, i.e., monastic type orders. The revived within the Catholic Church tended to gather together into some kind of community life; to pursue the goals of the revival. Earlier renewal movements had tended to foster the contemplative life, however, the new awakening tended more toward activism, i.e., purposeful involvement in the life of people. Among the new and reformed orders were: the Theatines (1524), founded by Gaetano di Tienna (1480–1540) and Caraffa, to combat heresy and improve the morals of the clergy; the Capuchins (1525), founded by Matteo da Bascio (1495–1552), an observant Franciscan, to call his order back to their founder's simplicity of life and evangelistic preaching; the Somaschi (1532), founded by Girolamo Aemiliani (d. 1537), and the Paulines (1533), founded by Antonio Zaccaria (d.1539), and later known as the Barnabites, both devoted to the reform of the priesthood, the instruction of the young and charitable work among the victims of the Italian wars; the Brethren of Charity (1534), emerged from the work of John of Avila (1499–1569), caring for the sick; the Ursulines (1535), founded by Angela Merici (1474–1540) to combat immorality and to provide a basic education for young women and girls; and the Company of Jesus (1539), founded by Ignatius Loyola (1491–1556), and better known as the Society of Jesus (1540), a militaristic order dedicated to the service of the pope and the instruction of children and illiterates in the law of God. "By the latter half of the sixteenth century, it had become the single most powerful force in the Catholic revival and the advance guard of the Counter-Reformation."[17] Together with the reforming Council of Trent (1545–1563), it helped institutionalize much of the renewal movement within Roman Catholicism.

Five Characteristics of the Awakening. The renewal in Europe shared several distinct characteristics.

First was an emphasis on **individual spiritual responsibility**. Some of the philosophical changes that had begun during the Renaissance undoubtedly influenced this. Man was seen not so much as part of a composite whole, but as being individually responsible before God. This emerged in Lutheranism as the priesthood of all believers. In Catholicism it was expressed in an upsurge of Roman Catholic orders, especially the opening of new orders, some of which recruited from among the lower classes of society, in contrast with the existing orders, which recruited mainly from the aristocracy and the wealthier part of society.

Part of the reason for this may be seen in the *second* characteristic, **a greater accessibility to Scripture**. As noted in the background to the awakening there had been a return to the Bible but this was not confined to the scholars. Luther himself was a scholar but he devoted himself to translating the Scriptures into the language of the common man. It was unusual for most people to own personal copies of the Scriptures, because even with the increased availability through printing, they were still very expensive and also few felt qualified to rightly interpret them. It did, however, become common for a Bible to be placed upon a lectern in the church open to a particular daily reading and for literate people to go and read the set portion for personal benefit. Within the Roman Catholic Church the lectionary was developed, which contained readings from the Scriptures, and also the missal, which also provided set readings. This gave all people access to the Scriptures, thus influencing much of the spiritual life and devotion of the Catholic laity, not just the priests.

A *third* characteristic was **the developing practice of plain and earnest preaching**. In the medieval period the schoolmen had developed an intricate set of rules governing preaching, which was generally in Latin and very difficult for the ordinary person to follow. This new style of preaching in the vernacular, which ignored many of the schoolmen's rules, simply taught the people in a way they could understand. The practice may be traced back to the early Franciscans in Italy, and Wycliffe and his Lollard followers in Britain. Some of the new orders such as the Capuchins and the Paulines (Barnabites) used open-air missions when preaching to the villagers in the communities that they visited.

These combined to produce a *fourth* characteristic, **a reassessment of dogma**. No longer would thinking people accept doctrines just because the preacher said it was so. They began to check the Scriptures themselves. As they read the Scriptures and found things that did not agree with what the preacher was saying, it was not uncommon for them to challenge the preacher and to ask for an explanation or to let him know of their reservations about what he was saying.

The reforming Council of Trent carefully examined the doctrines that were being taught; setting aside some of the medieval dogmas and reassessing or rewording others so as to fit together more readily; and yet others were given an official imprimatur and were largely accepted by the Catholic church of the day. The idea that a council would attempt to deal with doctrine was foreign to the medieval papacy. Even the Council of Constance in its condemnation of heresy, did not assess true doctrine because that was a papal prerogative alone. The Council of Trent, however, rigorously examined the doctrines of the Catholic faith.

Alongside this was a *fifth* characteristic, **the quest for a devotional life** such as had distinguished the early Christians. A comparison of the devotional book beloved by Luther and his followers, the *Theologica Germanica,* with Ignatius of Loyola's *Spiritual Exercises,* foundational to Jesuit spirituality, shows a common thread of spiritual quest running through them, summoning the devout to the same level of commitment to and faith in God.

Three Notable Differences. There were, however, notable differences between the two aspects of the awakening.

First, the Protestant revival initially affected the lower classes far more than the Catholic revival did. Luther was of peasant stock, and the son of a miner; Melancthon's parents were artisans; Zwingli was of peasant ancestry. Few belonged to the nobility. The Catholic reformation, on the other side, was mainly led by aristocrats, people of a very wealthy and noble background. Ignatius of Loyola was of the nobility of the Basque region of Spain, whose parents had been strongly influenced by Cardinal Ximenez; di Tienna and Caraffa were also nobility. Aemiliani, Zaccaria, and John of Avila were from a wealthy background. Only de Bascio and his fellow Capuchins were drawn mainly from the humbler ranks of society. The awakening in the Protestant area then tended to begin at a grassroots level and spread upward, whereas in the Catholic region it began among the upper echelons of society and permeated downward, eventually reaching the masses. The aristocracy tended to be conservative, whereas common people were more open to change.

Second, the Lutheran stress on the priesthood of all believers and the direct access of every Christian to God contrasted with the Catholic emphasis on the clerical priesthood and the ecclesiastical hierarchy that mediated between God and man in matters essential to salvation.

Third, Protestant emphasis on the individual's relationship with God contrasted with Catholicism's stress on the corporate aspect of Christianity, whence came the Catholic tendency to gather the revived into sodalities, both contemplative and activist, and through that community life to pursue the goals of the revival. The Protestant, on the other hand, moved toward greater diversity, denominationalism, and individualism, fostering personal activism through direct involvement.

Three Repercussions of the Awakening. Emerging from this particular period of revival were several areas of concern in addition to the beneficial effects.

The *first* area of concern was **the alliance of the revival with political power**. The political support of Elector Frederick helped protect Luther from both pope and emperor; however, when Luther repaid the favor in speaking out against "the murderous rabble" of the Peasants' Revolt and in support of the nobility, he both alienated the common people and made the success of the Lutheran movement totally dependent upon the inclinations of the German political hierarchy. The wisdom of his decision seemed obvious when at the Diet of Speyer (1526) the princes staged their protest from which Protestantism took its name. As a result, each prince could determine the recognized faith, whether Catholic or Lutheran, within the realm.[18]

When a revival movement becomes associated with political rather than spiritual forces, it embraces a relationship that is temporal rather than eternal in its orientation. The goal of political power is to establish authority upon earth, and tragically human power has a tendency to corrupt. Even the highest aspirations and the best motives can be distorted by the political reality of the current situation, as became apparent when Landgrave Philip of Hesse (1504–1567) received Luther's approval for a "secret" bigamous marriage to Margarethe von der Saale in 1540. The ensuing scandal marred the final years of Luther's life and the future of the Reformation movement.

A *second* area of concern arises from **the emergence of strong leadership**. As important as this may be, that leadership needs to be under God. He alone is finally the Lord of the church. The Lord Jesus said: "I will build my church."[19] It was God who used Luther, not Luther who used God.

Both Luther and Zwingli were equally strong personalities; both had a radical conversion experience; both were leaders of the Awakening in their countries; and both preached substantially the same message, except regarding the Lord's Supper. After the Marburg Colloquy (1529), despite agreement on fourteen of the fifteen articles presented, the German and the Swiss movements were not to be united. This intolerance for other views emerged even more strongly in the persecution of the Anabaptists and other Radicals, and later at Geneva under Calvin, during the next awakening period. Luther and the other reforming leaders were as bitterly opposed to the Radical movement as they were to the Papists and the bitterness of their opposition gave rise to some of the most appalling examples of religious intolerance that ever encountered. The Radicals' crime was that they believed that believers should be free to worship as their conscience dictated and not as decreed by the prince of the realm in which they lived. Strength of leadership cannot be at the expense of the work of God. God's work comes first. Leaders are leaders because God has raised them up and God can set them down again.

Along with these is a *third*, **the problem of institutionalization**. In any revival an awakened community can readily institutionalize revival patterns. Ignatius Loyola's *Spiritual Exercises*, which were intended to bring a person into an awareness of God's presence and to develop his sensitivity to the Holy Spirit, eventually became simply a ritual to be followed and the purpose was forgotten. Although Protestants tended to form denominations rather than sodalities, they faced the same challenge, that of simply continuing revival practices because that was the way the early leaders did things and therefore that is the only way to do them. The leader's practices become institutionalized as part of the church's way of doing things even if they have little spiritual significance for later generations.

In his book on personal renewal Lovelace gives a graphic illustration about the Rio Grande in the area where he was raised, how in the wintertime the river shrinks down to a narrow stream, on both sides of which are the mud flats that were shaped and formed by the swirling waters of spring and summer. They remain as stark reminders of the once rushing waters.[20] That happens in revivals and the denominations they have given rise to. The patterns, forms, and shapes are there bearing testimony to what once was, how the water of the Spirit flowed through the midst. The form and ritual remain but the flow of the Spirit may be simply a memory until the next revival comes. Then perhaps the Spirit of God will not just flow around those areas but reshape them.

Four Legacies of the Reformation Awakening. Despite the problem areas that brought the Reformation Awakening to a somewhat embarrassing halt, the movement left a legacy for future generations.

In the *first* place, **the doctrine of justification by faith** was reestablished as foundational to the Christian's ongoing relationship with God.

Second, **the fundamental role of the Bible in establishing Christian doctrine** became dominant. Luther's *sola Scriptura,* the Scripture alone as a basis, was to become the theme for successive revivals in the centuries that followed.

Third, **the individual's personal responsibility before God** was to have considerable influence in the future. The individual's relationship with God could not be left in the hands of others, but all are summoned to a personal relationship with the Almighty.

Fourth, **the concept of the church as a gathered community of believers** had its foundation in Luther's doctrine of the priesthood of all believers, and although it did not come to full fruition until the next revival, the Puritan Awakening, its roots were planted in the Reformation. A path was begun that would lead back to a purified church on fire for God as the next major revival period revealed. The Reformation Awakening, despite its faults, set the church on the right path, a true apostolic relationship with its Lord.

Endnotes

1 R. D. Linder: art. "The Reformation" in NIDCC, 830.

2 Ibid.

3 C. S. Meyer: art. "Luther, Martin" in NIDCC, 609.

4 J. Atkinson: *The Great Light* (Exeter, UK: Paternoster, 1968), 18ff.

5 J. G. G. Norman: art. "Lefevre d'Etaples, Jacques" in NIDCC, 589.

6 R.H. Bainton: *Here I Stand* (Nashville, TN: Abingdon, 1978 edn.), 63.

7 J. L. Gonzalez: *The Story of Christianity*, vol. 2 (San Francisco, CA: Harper & Row, 1985), 23.

8 Meyer, op. cit., 609.

9 Ibid., 610.

10 J. G. G. Norman: art. "Zwilling, Gabriel" in NIDCC, 1073.

11 W. Walker, op. cit., 438.

12 Ibid., 481.

13 Davies, op. cit., 63.

14 J. G. G. Norman: art. "Wyttenbach, Thomas" in NIDCC, 1065.

15 R. D. Linder: art. "Blaurock, Georg" in NIDCC, 137.

16 W. Walker, op. cit., 502.

17 Ibid., 509.

18 Atkinson, op. cit., 101.

19 Matthew 16:18.

20 R. F. Lovelace: *Renewal as a Way of Life* (Downers Grove, IL: InterVarsity Press, 1985), 193.

Chapter 12

Puritan Awakenings

1575–1715

The evangelical awakening that inspired the magisterial reformation began to dissipate in the aftermath of the Peasants' War and Protestantism began to emerge in Germany. Meanwhile, the Swiss branch of the movement under the moderating leadership of Johann Heinrich Bullinger (1504–1575) was seeking to reestablish itself following the separation of the radical Anabaptists and the death of Zwingli in the Battle of Kappel (1531). The Roman Catholic Church prepared for its own reformation through the new orders culminating in the Council of Trent. The political divisions within France and between it and the mainly Germanic Holy Roman Empire ensured that whatever influence the earlier awakening may have engendered there, it would not result in a widespread movement into Protestantism. Nevertheless, the fruit of France was to have a major impact on subsequent awakenings throughout the Western world, beginning with the Puritan awakenings, which came in three phases.

First was **the early Puritan awakening**, the main phase of which ran from about 1550 to 1590. During this time several prominent individuals and movements emerged, such as John Calvin (1509–1564) and his successors in Switzerland, John Knox (c. 1510–1572) in Scotland, James Arminius (1560–1609) and the conflict with hyper-Calvinism in Holland, the Huguenots in France, and the Anglican reestablishment in the days of Queen Elizabeth I (1533–1603), after the devastating attempt of Queen Mary I (1516–1558) to return England to Roman Catholicism.

The middle Puritan awakening largely occupied the period from 1630 to 1655 and included the early days of the American colonies and the subsequent stirrings in New England; the commonwealth period in England and the emergence of the Quakers and the Baptist movement; and the later Remonstrance movement in Holland.

The later Puritan awakening lasted from about 1675 through to 1715 and was marked in Scotland by the Covenanters' resistance to the later Stuarts; the English independents' stance against the church establishment; and the Camisard movement in France among the remnants of the Huguenots who, following the revocation of the Edict of Nantes (1685) had fled into the Cevennes Mountains and experienced a remarkable outpouring of God's Spirit. Pietism emerged in Germany with P. J. Spener (1635–1705) and A. H. Francke (1663–1727), and rapidly spread to Scandinavia and beyond. In New England the ministry of people like Solomon Stoddard (1643–1729) and Cotton Mather (1663–1728) from the end of the seventeenth to the beginning of the eighteenth century helped prepare the way for the next great revival known as the Great Awakening.

While these may be considered as three different revivals, because of the substantial time period involved, and the individual characteristics of each awakening, those involved in each of the awakenings were basically Puritans, and there were common features throughout:

  a. Return to Biblical Faith
  b. Restored Place for Preaching and Teaching
  c. Emphasis on Experiential Faith
  d. Increasing Role for Laity
  e. Recognition of the Ministry of the Holy Spirit.

The Early Puritan Awakening. French-speaking Europe. Inspired by the earlier ministry of Jacques Lefevre d'Etaples, the young Frenchman Guillaume Farel (1489–1565), made an abortive attempt at reforming the church in his homeland. Despite the sympathy and protection of the brilliant Marguerite of Angeloume (1492–1549), the older sister of King Francis I (1494–1547), Farel was expelled from France (1523), together with other advocates of reform. Subsequently, "he became the leader of a peripatetic band of evangelists preaching mainly in French-speaking Switzerland. His own fiery preaching often led to rough handling by mobs of opponents."[1] A powerful move of the Holy Spirit in Berne in 1528 provided Farel with a base from which to spread renewal throughout the area, reaching as far as Lausanne and Geneva. Although his initial attempt (1532) to preach in Geneva, a city renowned for its cosmopolitan libertarianism, was met with great resistance, on his return the following year the climate had begun to change as an evangelical awakening began.

Among those enthused by Luther's exposition at Heidelberg (1518) was a young Dominican, Martin Bucer, who after a moderately successful attempt to bring renewal to Wissembourg (1522), moved on to the free imperial city of Strasbourg, where his leadership and diplomacy proved invaluable to the movement. A tireless champion of unity among the reformers, Bucer made Strasbourg the center for Reformation teaching and organization, and a refuge for exiles.

About 1532, a young humanist law student, Jean Cauvin (John Calvin), at the University of Paris was suddenly and radically converted. Changing his focus to biblical studies, he quickly became embroiled in the reforming undercurrent; however, when the new rector, Nicholas Cop (1501?–1540), gave an inaugural address calling for evangelical reform (1533), there was "an explosion of anti-Protestant feeling which forced both Cop and Calvin to leave Paris."[2] Eventually settling in Basle, Calvin published the first edition of *Institutes of the Christian Religion* (1536), as an apologetic for the evangelical faith. Learning of Bucer's work in Strasbourg, he decided to head there with his siblings, Antoine and Marie, by way of Geneva. When Farel heard of the young scholar's presence, he persuaded his fellow-countrymen to remain to help consolidate the work. Unfortunately, Calvin's obduracy provoked such a backlash from the townspeople that Farel and Calvin had to flee, Farel to Neuchatel and Calvin to Strasbourg. There (1538–1541), under the beneficent influence of Bucer, he developed his theology, particularly regarding the church and salvation, enlarged his *Institutes*, prepared his *Commentary on Romans*, pastored a congregation of French refugees, and married Idelette de Bure (d.1549), widow of Anabaptist John Storder (d.1539).

When Cardinal Jacopo Sadoleto (1477–1547) attempted to woo Geneva back to the Catholic fold, the newly appointed pro-reform city government appealed to Calvin to return. On his return in 1541 he began to establish a system of courts "to bring every citizen under the moral discipline of the church."[3] His goal, following the Augustinian model, was to remold Geneva into a City of God established on earth with both temporal and spiritual power. Like his temporary asylum of Strasbourg, he also made it "a city of refuge, welcoming within its gates the depressed, the persecuted, and the down-trodden. (I)t became soon, to the whole of Europe, the city of light."[4] Unfortunately, those who did not conform to Calvin's theological and moral standards found that there was a harsher side to this "city of light." During his first five years (1542–1546) "fifty-eight persons in Geneva were condemned to death and seventy-six to banishment."[5] This pattern continued throughout his rule there. He also made Geneva the center for theological training that set a stamp on the early Puritan awakening.

Britain. The accession to the throne in 1553 of Mary Tudor (1516–1558), the English king Henry VIII's oldest daughter by Catharine of Aragon (1485–1536), brought severe persecution to those who had supported Henry's rejection of papal authority and the aborted reforms of King Edward VI (1537–1553). Nearly three hundred were martyred for their faith, including Hugh Latimer, Nicholas Ridley, and Thomas Cranmer. About eight hundred British reformers fled to Europe.[6] Unwelcome in the Lutheran-controlled areas because of Henry's repudiation of the reformer's views, for which Pope Leo X had designated him Defender of the Faith (1521), most ended up in Calvin's Geneva, where they were strongly influenced by his life and teaching. John Knox, the Scottish reformer, described it as "the most perfect school of Christ that ever was since the days of the Apostles. In other places I confess Christ to be truly preached: but manners and religion to be so sincerely reformed I have not yet seen in any place besides."[7]

Calvin. Although caricatured in old age as a dark and dismal character with a black hat, long cloak, and a beard, the younger Calvin was a powerful preacher with a significant ministry, who won the people to a wholehearted commitment to the Lord by his fervent evangelical piety and love for God. As is evident from his commentaries, Calvin had some perceptive insights into God's truth, a genuine experience with God, and a desire to propagate that experience and that faith to the whole world. Through the Genevan Academy, which opened in 1559 under the direction of Theodore Beza (1519–1605), Calvin's successor, his theology came to dominate reformation thinking throughout much of Europe and thence to the New World. Some, like Jerome Bolsec (d.1585), in Calvin's lifetime, and James Arminius, subsequently, took issue with aspects of his theology, especially a concept of absolute divine sovereignty that made God the author of sin, and the pre-creation arbitrary selection of some to salvation and others to damnation, irrespective of their individual relationship to Christ. Calvin's successor, Beza, proved to be even more obdurate than the reformer, taking Calvin's teachings to an extreme later known as hyper-Calvinism, ending any remaining impulse of renewal and beginning "Reformed Scholasticism."[8]

The Reformation Awakening despite its faults set the church on the right path, a true apostolic relationship with its Lord. From the Imperial Church for more than a millennium, the church and the state had been involved in a struggle as to which was the dominant partner. Luther's dependence on the German princes decided the pattern for much of the magisterial Reformation as expressed in the formula *cuius regio, eius religio* arising from the Peace of Augsburg (1555). Those born into a Lutheran area automatically became Lutheran. The original biblical concept of the church as a fellowshipping body of like-minded believers brought together through a personal relationship with Christ was unimaginable to any but a minority of radical reformers.

Out of Geneva a reformed concept of the church emerged. Instead of viewing the church as combining spiritual with temporal power there was a movement toward the more biblical concept of the church as a spiritual body with spiritual powers and its main focus being upon the conversion of the individual. Only among the Anglicans of England and the Presbyterians of Scotland was there a continuation of something approaching a magisterial or Landeskirche approach. For the rest of the reformed movement in Holland, and later in North America, the emphasis was upon the individual's commitment to Christ as primary.

The Puritan movement focused on a renewed and more biblical understanding of the church. The true Puritan took a stand against that extreme teaching of the gathered church concept and endeavored to establish a concept of the church that retained the best of Calvinism along with the best of the old Augustinian vision of the church's role. From this new perspective the Puritan preachers, preaching for conversion, saw people converted and joining the church of their choice, which is much more in keeping with modern evangelicalism than the Lutheran understanding of evangelicalism. The end result was that in the next time period, the middle Puritan period, further division began to take place among the people who were touched by the revival.

The Middle Puritan Awakening. Out of the reaction to the accession of the Scottish Stuarts to the English throne came a religious movement seeking to purify the church in England by returning to earlier Puritan principles, and a political movement seeking to curb the excesses of the Stuart monarchy with its assertion of "the divine right of kings." The religious movement resulted in the middle Puritan Awakening and in the political impetus in the civil war that ushered in the commonwealth period in England. The extent to which the two aspects coincided has been debated. According to Toon:

> In 1640, Puritans were united in their desire to purify the national church and remove prelacy. Thus they were the religious force behind Parliament in the civil wars. They preached and fought for the opportunity to create a godly nation before the last days of the age dawned.[9]

Among the outstanding preachers were people like **Richard Baxter** (1615–1691), who ministered in the city of Kidderminster, England, from

1641 to 1660. His ministry largely covers this middle Puritan Awakening period. When Baxter arrived at Kidderminster, a city of about 2,000, he described the people as an ignorant, rude rabble, who hardly ever had any serious preaching among them, but as he began to labor there and preach, some radical changes began to take place. Baxter was one of the outstanding preachers of that day but also a very humble man of God. He labored long hours, visiting with his congregation. He would preach every morning before his congregation went about their daily business on Mondays, Tuesdays, Wednesdays, and Fridays; Thursday mornings were devoted to the catechizing of the young people; Saturdays were devoted to family affairs and he would visit the people in their homes, etc., and then Sunday he would preach twice to his congregation. God began to move in a most remarkable fashion. When he arrived, there was hardly a street in Kidderminster where a believing family was to be found. By 1660 there was no street in Kidderminster that had more than one unsaved family in it.

In his church, built to accommodate about 1,000 people, they added five galleries so that the building would hold a total congregation of about 1,700 people, and that in a town of approximately 2,000 adults. He is reputed to have said that on any given day you could walk down the streets of Kidderminster and hear a hundred families singing psalms and repeating the sermons from the previous Sunday among themselves. The inns and the alehouses were almost abandoned. Baxter made a practice of meeting with each family in the town and interviewing them about their spiritual life and their relationship with God. He would meet with seven or eight such families a day, spending about an hour with each family, and so every year he would visit all eight hundred families of the community. First, he would hear them recite the Westminster Shorter Catechism and then he would examine them about their sins to make sure that they understood it, urging them, as he said, with all possible engaging reason and vehemence to live by the doctrines that they espoused. His book *The Reformed Pastor* became the handbook of Puritanism and of the evangelical faith. It had a truly powerful influence on the developments taking place in this Puritan period.

People like Richard Baxter were outstanding in the extreme. But there were others who adopted different approaches to the faith. One of the more remarkable was **George Fox** (1624–1691) and his "Quaker" movement. About the year of 1650, Fox, having had a radical conversion experience some seven years before, began a ministry that was to have an immense impact on the development of the Christian faith during this middle Puritan period. Fox fell under great conviction of sin and consulted with the religious leaders of the day, seeking an answer to his soul's search. Some of the advice he was given was quite irrelevant to his search for spiritual things. One minister advised him to try tobacco and sing psalms. Another advised him to get married. A third suggested that bloodletting and the use of leeches might help him a lot with his spiritual problems. Finally, one day as he was traveling from place to place looking for someone who could give him an answer, he heard a voice say: "There is one even Christ Jesus who can speak to thy condition." As he sought the face of God, Christ was revealed to him in an immediate experience and his life was radically transformed. He continued attending the churches, but when the preacher had finished preaching, then Fox would share his testimony of the radical change that Christ had made in his life.

This did not go down well with the established clergy. They had very strong views about an unordained person preaching. One preacher was very upset that Fox knew the Bible so well and declared: "Well, if you know the Bible that well then take it!" and hit him over the head with a brassbound Bible. Consequently, Fox began to do most of his preaching outside the churches and great crowds gathered to hear him in the open air. His open-air preaching was so effective, that, for example, it is said that many thousands came to Christ through his preaching on Pendle Hill in Derbyshire in the English Midlands. Many of those early converts gathered around him as evangelists, calling themselves *the Friends of Truth,* whence the later name *the Society of Friends.* The origin of the epithet "Quaker" dates from 1650 when Fox was arrested in Derby for unauthorized preaching. Judge Bennett, in sentencing him to six months in jail for this offense, remarked that Fox was such a self-opinionated young man that he would not even tremble at the presence of the august judge. Whereupon, Fox responded that he only trembled in the presence of Almighty God and that the magistrates should themselves tremble at the word of the Lord. The judge told him: "Then you are Quakers and I will make you quake when I have finished with you." The term "Quaker," given in derision, they gladly adopted as a name for the movement of those who quake in the presence of Almighty God. Undoubtedly through the ministry of Fox many quaked under the Spirit of God as he preached.[10]

Those early evangelists traveled wherever they could get a hearing for the gospel, speaking to the servants of the great houses and speaking to the nobility. They refused to bow the knee to worldly and earthly rulers and insisted that they would only doff the hat to those who were of equal status with them before the Lord. When they were dealing with the ungodly, they kept their hats on, which did not please their noble contemporaries in England. Their rationale was that as far as they were concerned, they stood before God, and God alone was the one to whom they were responsible. Furthermore, since the King James and earlier versions of the Scriptures used the old popular pronouns "thee" and "thou" for addressing Almighty God, they refused to use the more formal "you" when addressing other people, persisting with this older peculiarity of speech lest they appear to exalt others above God.

Another peculiarity of the Quaker movement, which did not endear them to the population in general, was the fact that initially they allowed women to preach. Later, however, in the nineteenth century when the fire of the Holy Spirit burning in Quakerism had long since diminished, they moved away from the practice. Their early openness to women preachers caused them a lot of problems because although the Puritans generally were open to allowing any spiritual man in the congregation to speak, they would not accept the participation of women, as Fox permitted. In Elizabethan times, Edmund Grindal (c. 1519–1583), Archbishop of Canterbury, was suspended from office in 1577 for allowing prophesyings to take place in the Church of England. *Prophesyings* were meetings for Bible exposition, in which any man, but not woman, present could expound the Scriptures and speak under the direct inspiration of the Holy Spirit.

One notable Quaker practice was their reliance upon the moving of the Holy Spirit for messages to communicate to the congregation at large. During the period when the revival was burning strongly these messages showed every characteristic of being an operation of the gifts of the Holy Spirit. They would speak words of knowledge and words of wisdom: some of the recorded utterances by Quakers brought a powerful sense of God's presence upon the congregations. Later, however, as the revival fire diminished the practice became just a formality.

From their beginning the Quakers were committed to being a peace movement; they believed it unscriptural to defend themselves, and therefore they were opposed to war and physical conflict. Even in modern times they are renowned for their pacifism.

The Later Puritan Awakenings. The Puritan revival in the middle of the seventeenth century began to grind to a halt after the Commonwealth period in England. In the aftermath of the Stuart restoration there was a serious decline in public morals and a great sense of frustration on the part of those godly Puritans and nonconformists, who were ejected from their churches because of their unwillingness to support the restoration monarchy and the Anglican episcopacy. By the Five Mile Act (1665), such ministers were forbidden to come within five miles of incorporated towns or of their former parishes. They had to flee into the countryside where presumably they would be unable to gather together a congregation to hear their vigorous style of preaching. Their former pulpits and charges were generally filled by unworthy men who were willing to compromise their faith and to fit in with the restoration monarchy and the current moral decline. That period of declension was to continue in England for some time. Spiritual religion was confined to a few godly men like Philip Henry (1631–1696), his son Matthew Henry (1662–1714), the renowned Bible expositor, and Isaac Watts (1674–1748), the poet and hymn-writer, whose Christian paraphrases of the Psalms inspired generations of believers.

The first stirrings of renewal in this period were on the European continent, especially through the Pietist movement, which contributed to the transformation of European Protestantism and even spilled over into the Roman Catholic Church through the Jansenist movement. From continental Europe the renewal spread into England and into America, helping lay the foundation for the great revival of evangelical religion of the eighteenth century.

Out of this later Puritan period came some of the patterns and streams that were later to emerge and merge together in a powerful flow of the Spirit of God, for example, between 1650 and 1750 there were many factors that influenced the famous revivalists of the early eigteenth century. Fox and his Quakers had a considerable impact upon Wesley in inspiring **the class meetings** that became the basis of Wesleyanism. The Puritans also with their pious classes provided a further influence upon Wesley and upon Whitfield, and through the New England Awakening, upon Jonathan Edwards, especially through his grandfather Solomon Stoddard, renowned for his preaching ministry and for the seasons of harvest that came during his time as the leader of the Church in Northampton.

Also, the ministry of Spener, Francke, and the Pietists not only influenced Zinzendorf and the Moravians, who in turn had a great influence upon Wesley and upon his conversion, but also Theodore Jacobus Frelinghuysen (1691–1747), the Dutch Pietist preacher, who is credited with starting the revival in the Americas. He came to minister among the Dutch colonists in the area of New Amsterdam, later acquired by the British and renamed New York, and among their compatriots in the Raritan Valley area of New Jersey. His ministry had a great impact and contributed to the conversion of the Tennants and ultimately of Jonathan Edwards himself, who was mightily used subsequently. These various streams all flowed together to finally come into that river of blessing known as the Great Awakening, the topic of the next chapter.

The Pietist movement may be traced back to Philipp Jacob Spener, who was actually awakened in the earlier revival in the middle of the seventeenth century. When he was sixteen years of age in 1651, he enrolled at Strasbourg University where he was greatly influenced by Johann Schmidt (1594–1658), the prominent professor of theology and one of the major revivalist preachers in German-speaking Europe during the middle Puritan period. Schmidt was described by contemporaries as a Christian of the purest character and as the agent of spiritual awakening in many young men who came under his influence at that university.[11] One such young man was Spener, who arrived at Strasbourg intent upon an education and left two years later with his master's degree and a fire in his heart kindled by the Spirit of God.

Another influence upon Spener was the devotional classic *True Christianity* by Johann Arndt (1555–1621), which focused on the fact that union with God through Christ was only possible through the new birth. Arndt's writing combined together a religious mysticism with practical ethical elements. This type of writing, describing the committed life, was quite prominent in Puritanism. The similar writings of people like Anglican Bishop Jeremy Taylor (1613–1667), author of *Holy Living* (1650) and *Holy Dying* (1651), set a high standard of godly living before the believer and especially before the young people of the middle Puritan period. Most of these writings had a strong mystical element to them.

On leaving Strasbourg University Spener traveled to Switzerland, where he imbibed some of the spirit of Calvin and of the Geneva movement, the birthplace of the earliest evangelical Puritanism. Staying in Basel, and Geneva he came under the influence of a powerful Puritan preacher named Jean de Labadie (1610–1674), from the middle Puritan period in the French-speaking area. His book *Manual of Prayer* was translated by Spener into German and was one of the handbooks to be used by the later Pietist movement. Upon his return to Germany in 1661, Spener began a powerful ministry in Strasbourg, from where was called to be the senior pastor of the Lutheran church in the imperial city of Frankfurt on the Main River. On his arrival he discovered the spiritual life and discipline of the church was at a low ebb and so began to preach from his own experience the strong demands of God in relation to the prayer life, to a life of commitment, and to the new birth. Much of his preaching reflects not so much Lutheranism as a reformed Puritan type of teaching.

Most of his ministry, however, in relation to revival, was not done from the pulpit but in the catechizing of the families of his congregation in their own homes, like the model English Puritan, Richard Baxter. Spener would visit in turn the home of each family in the congregation and, as the Scots

Covenanters were wont to do, would greet them with: "How is it with your soul?" After questioning them most intensely on their spiritual life and walk with God, he would then pray through with them until they were changed, revolutionized, and set on fire for God. Thus, in turn each family in the church was subjected to this as the pastor's visits brought them face-to-face with spiritual reality.

That approach to pastoral ministry is not common today except in those churches that have adopted the small group or cell group approach. Among the Puritans and Pietists, however, it was just one family at a time that was dealt with, not people from several families. There was a greater focus on the family during the Puritan period. In fact, every Puritan man was the priest of his own family, and the pattern of Puritan family life is one that lent itself well to this kind of approach that Spener adopted in his Lutheran church in Frankfurt on Main.

In the typical Puritan family, the whole family would go to church on a Sunday morning, when the only public services were held. On return from the church the husband would after lunch question the family on the spiritual message that had been delivered by the pastor that Sunday morning. Then the children would be handed over to the care of the mother, who would teach them writing or rereading the portions of Scripture related to the Sunday morning ministry in the church. Most families were quite large, some as many as twenty children. The mother would treat them much as a Sunday school class and she would devise means of reinforcing the message for them. While she was doing that, the husband would repeat the church service for the household servants, who were not able to go to church on Sunday morning. They would sing the same songs and he would repeat the pastor's sermon. Then Monday through Friday the husband would go around in the community meeting with his friends, etc., and over a glass of ale at the local inn would talk over some of the spiritual lessons that they had learned from the previous Sunday's sermons and so through interaction with fellow household leaders from the other homes in the community, would reinforce the messages that they had heard from the pastor. In many instances the pastor himself would join them at the inn where they would engage in spiritual conversation, discussing the message of the Word and how they could translate it into action. Every evening during the week they had a family altar time in which the whole family met together. Father led the family devotions, would read the Scriptures, give an exposition, and lead the whole family in prayer.

Saturday was preparation day for going to church. On the Saturday evening the children would be bathed and then would be assigned the portion of Scripture to read that was going to be dealt with in church the next day. Because the preachers generally tended to follow a prepared schedule in preaching, when they went to church Sunday morning everybody knew what the theme of the Sunday services was going to be. With that kind of structure already in place among the Puritan families it was easy for someone like Spener to perform his ministerial duties in visiting these families, engaging in catechizing them, ensuring that they knew what the previous Sunday's message had been, and thus could advance in their spiritual life.

Spener realized that if he was to see the spiritual life of his congregation awakened then he would have to focus on both these aspects, the public proclamation of the Word and the private catechizing of the members of the congregation. He decided to take it one step further in lifting the spiritual life of the people by conducting *collegia pietatis,* gatherings for mutual edification in which pastors and laymen could study the Bible and pray together. These classes in holy living, which began in 1670, were to be the hallmark of this revival and the next. Nominal Christians, whose faith was less fervent, found that as they began to attend these special classes, the Spirit of God began to touch their hearts and their awareness of the things of God began to increase. In 1675 Spener wrote *Pia Desideria* (Earnest Desire), from which the name Pietist was derived, as a preface to Arndt's *True Christianity,* which had made a great impact on his own devotional life. His preface contained propositions for overcoming the current perceived weakness of the church, which became:

...the essence of his Pietistic doctrines—the central importance of
Bible study, restoration of the priesthood of all believers, true faith

expressed not in knowing but in deeds of love to one's neighbor, avoidance of theological disputation, emphasis upon spiritual life and devotional literature in the training of ministers, and preaching that should awaken in the hearers faith and its fruits.[12]

Later that year he "joyfully observed that in several places students are aroused. Such movements of hearts seen in many at the same time are a clear proof of the divine presence, and show that a time is at hand in which God will have pity upon his church."[13] His expectations were soon realized; by 1683 revival was burning throughout most of German-speaking Europe and beyond.

His ministry was not generally accepted by his Lutheran colleagues. His twice-weekly meetings for Bible study and prayer he intended to be *ecclesiolae in ecclesia* (churches within the church), "which would aid the pastor in his spiritual duties and return the church to the spiritual level of the early Christian communities."[14] To some, these meetings were divisive, encouraged pride on the part of the "super-spirituals," and took the pastor's attention away from the rest of the congregation, which was totally contrary to Spener's intention.

The strongest attack came from Albrecht Christian Rothe (1651–1701), pastor of St. Ulrich's Church, whose book *A Portrait of Pietism* (1691) was filled with unsupported accusations of substantial errors in relation to Lutheranism, to the Scriptures, and to a variety of practical issues, including the suggestion that the small group meetings were hotbeds of immorality, in which women were being seduced from their relationship to their family and instead of submitting to the leadership of their own husband were brought under the undue influence of the pastor and other men involved in the classes. While admittedly possible, there was no historical evidence to support such accusations. Nevertheless, for the rest of his life until his death in 1705, Spener's personal life and work was under the unrelenting attack of this strong and well-organized opposition.

The main banner of Pietism was taken up by one of the professors at Halle University, the great preacher **August Herman Francke** (1663–1727). Francke at the age of sixteen was a student at the University of Erfurt, and transferred from there to Kiel University, where he remained for the next five years before going on to the University of Leipzig. From there in 1684 he matriculated among the highest in his class in the area of theology. He was one of the few to receive a doctor of theology degree, even though he was only twenty-one years of age at the time, which was no small achievement since that placed him on a par with some of the great leaders of the Christian church of the past. He obviously had a bright future as a preacher and as a teacher.

In 1687, while professor of Hebrew at the University of Leipzig, he came into a living and vital faith as he was preparing a theological lecture on the subject of faith. He said while preparing his lecture suddenly God's presence came upon him and the Lord began to wrestle with him:

> At one time I was crying, at another pacing the floor with great unrest, then falling on my knees implored Him whom I knew not to release me from this wrestling. And God answered my prayer suddenly by changing my heart and my mind and my life so that when I rose like Jacob of old I knew that I had wrestled with God.[15]

That God had done a transforming work in his life was obvious from his later comments. "Casting away despair and doubt, I entered into a life of assurance and joy and the sudden transition was so wonderful that I lived in an ecstasy for many a day afterwards."[16]

Francke's life was transformed in a matter of moments in the kind of radical conversion experience that was to become quite common in the Great Awakening of the next century. That transformation in his own life led him "to conduct Bible classes at Leipzig which led to a revival among both students and townspeople."[17] He began to preach what was described as an accelerated program of experiential religion; that people could be radically transformed by a simple encounter with Almighty God. Although he did not give altar calls in the modern way, the whole thrust of his preaching and of his teaching was that there did not need to be a lengthy period of conviction and soul searching before conversion could take place. Such a crisis experience was certainly not common among the

Puritans. They would go for six months under an intense conviction of sin before finally arriving at some sense of deliverance. True conversion could take place in a moment. He likened conversion to natural birth in which although there may be a gestation period of some nine months the actual birth may be relatively brief and not an extended time period.

Francke, from his base as the professor of theology at Halle (1698–1727), devoted himself untiringly to promoting a revival of genuine Christianity. Although in his earlier days at Erfurt he had encountered opposition, at Halle he faced the virulent opposition of Rothe. When, however, Rothe saw that the tide began to turn against him, he left Halle for Leipzig to continue his opposition to Spener and the work the latter was involved in there. This left the way free for Francke to make Halle one of the major centers of Pietism among Lutherans and beyond, opening the university to non-Lutherans and Reformed students, most of whom came from German-speaking areas such as Switzerland, Strasbourg area, and Holland.

Missionary Activity. Through Francke's ministry a revolutionizing development within Protestantism began. The Catholic Reformation had resulted in extensive missionary activity by the Roman Catholic Church. However, at the time of the Reformation and immediately afterward, no Protestant domains impinged upon non-Christian lands. The Protestant lands were bordered either by the sea, or by Roman Catholicism, or by the Orthodox lands of Eastern Europe and the Russian Empire. The development of the colonial system that began in the late Elizabethan period, first in New England and then in other lands, brought Protestants for the first time into direct contact with the heathen. Other Protestant monarchs followed Elizabeth's example. Colonies were established in the midst of non-Christian cultures and communities. It would only be a matter of time before somebody had a vision for evangelizing the heathen. There may have been some unorganized efforts by early American settlers at Jamestown, Virginia, under Admiral John Smith (1580–1631), many of whom were Puritans, to evangelize some of the Indians they encountered, which would have been the first direct attempt by the English to engage in some kind of missionary activity, but it was not strictly organized as a mission society.

The king of Denmark and Norway, Frederick IV (1671–1730), who came to the throne in 1699, became a convinced Pietist in 1721, after a life of debauchery, and sought to promote Pietism throughout his realm and around the world. Denmark had colonies in India, and King Frederick, even before his personal conversion, had a strong interest in the conversion of the Indian nationals to the Christian faith. Approaching Halle University, he asked if there were students there who would be willing to travel to his colonies and to engage in evangelization activities. Bartholomaeus Ziegenbalg (1682–1719) and Heinrich Pluetschau (1678–1747) volunteered and have the distinction of being the first Protestant missionaries to travel in the service of the gospel. Setting sail for India (November 29, 1705), they arrived in the Danish colony at Tranquebar on July 19, 1706, signaling the birth of organized Protestant missionary activity. The Danish government furnished the money, Halle University furnished the missionaries, and Pietism inspired the Danish Halle mission, the first Protestant missionary society.

Endnotes

1 N. S. Pollard: art "Farel, Guillaume" in NIDCC, 369.

2 W. S. Reid: art. "Calvin, John" in NIDCC, 177.

3 A. Lindt: art. "John Calvin" in *Eerdman's Handbook to the History of Christianity*, op. cit., 381.

4 J. Burns, op. cit., 227.

5 G. Harkness: *John Calvin: The Man and His Ethics* (Nashville, TN: Abingdon, 1948), 29–30.

6 Cairns, op. cit., 332.

7 Ibid.

8 R. Schnucker: art. "Beza, Theodore" in NIDCC, 126.

9 P. Toon: art. "Puritans; Puritanism" in NIDCC, 815.

10 Arthur O. Roberts: art. "George Fox and the Quakers" in *Eerdmans' Handbook to the History of Christianity*, 480 ff.

11 F. A. G. Tholuck: *Philip Jacob Spener* (New York, NY: F. M. Barton, 1861), 449.

12 R. V. Pierard: art. "Spener, Philipp Jakob" in NIDCC, 925.

13 Tholuck, op. cit., 453.

14 Pierard, op. cit., 925.

15 A. W. Nagler: *Pietism and Methodism* (Nashville: Publishing House of the Methodist Episcopal Church, South, 1918), 58.

16 Ibid., 59.

17 R. G. Clouse: art. "Francke, August Hermann" in NIDCC, 388.

Chapter 13

The Great Awakening

1715–1770

The major revival period of the eighteenth century has often been called the Great Awakening.[1] This particular move of God, associated with the ministry of Jonathan Edwards (1703–1758) and others in New England and throughout the American colonies; the ministry of the Wesley brothers and George Whitefield (1714–1770) throughout the British Isles; and the Moravian movement in Germany, is seen as the birth of Evangelicalism and as a model for subsequent modern evangelical awakenings.

This awakening was not the first outpouring of God's Spirit during the eighteenth century. The successive waves of revival throughout the later Puritan period continued into the early years of the new century. For example, in the community of Northampton in the Connecticut Valley of Massachusetts where Solomon Stoddard (1643–1729), the grandfather of Jonathan Edwards, ministered for almost sixty years, there were "seasons of harvest," in 1679, then again in 1683, yet again in 1696, then in 1712, and finally shortly before Stoddard's death in 1718. When Jonathan Edwards came into the leadership of that church after the death of his grandfather, he was coming into an area that had been mightily blessed over the years by a succession of revivals.

Preparation for the Great Awakening. Several notable factors prepared the way for the Great Awakening. First of all, from the Puritan period came the concept of the gathered church, which gave rise to small group ministry. In England, they were called religious societies. These religious societies were intended to quicken the spiritual life of the individual believer by bringing him into a relationship with fellow believers who had experienced the power of God and shared a similar desire for the things of God. Wesley's Holy Club at the University of Oxford that actually preceded the Great Awakening was a typical religious society. It was also at a typical Puritan Anglican Society meeting in Aldersgate, London, that John Wesley (1703–1791) himself was converted to Christ.

Through this concept of the gathered church and the gathering together of these small groups of like-minded believers with a shared experience of God and a great intensity for seeking God, the Puritan awakening would prepare the way for many of the things that would happen in the Great Awakening of the eighteenth century.

Also, coming out of the independent movements of the middle Puritan awakening there was the practice of open-air meetings and an openness to the move of the Holy Spirit, a strong emphasis from the Quakers, particularly on the inner witness. Samuel Wesley (1662–1735) on his deathbed declared to his son, John Wesley: "The inner witness, that is the strongest proof of Christianity." Although he himself was an Episcopalian clergyman, his wife's father, Dr. Samuel Annesley (1620?–1696), had been a Puritan of the old school and very much an independent clergyman after the commonwealth period was over, with a ministry outside of the Church of England as was the ministry of Samuel Wesley's own father, John Westley (1636–1678) and that of his grandfather, Bartholomew Westley (1596–1680). Samuel himself came back into the Church of England under the influence of the Archbishop of Canterbury John Tillotson (1630–1694), who had devoted himself at the behest of King William and Queen Mary to seek the reconciliation of dissenting clergy. However, he, like many other former dissenters, brought back with him into the Church of England some of the concepts and ideas of the commonwealth period's independence movement.

From the Pietist branch of Puritanism came the emphasis on the class meeting, which was a small group meeting within a church that was geared for the edification of the believers. The difference between that and the Puritan society concept is that the latter was much more interdenominational or inter-church, whereas the Pietist class was within the local church itself. As primarily a gathering of true believers, it was intended to promote revival within the church itself and to promote Christian piety and edification among believers. Wesley's class meetings, influenced by both Pietistic Moravianism and the Anglican Puritan society meetings, were a continuation of this particular type of practice.

From the Moravians came the emphasis on personal spiritual experience, especially the emphasis on a transformed life. To the Moravians sanctification took place at the point of conversion. Like the Lutheran Church, they laid great stress upon a radical conversion experience that brought deliverance from the past life and a new life in Christ. Because this was not apparent in every person's life, and some people apparently did not come into the full deliverance, the Moravians concluded that such a person was not truly converted. To the Wesleyan, there was a second stage to the Christian's experience, which he called entire sanctification or perfection in love. Later, in the middle of the nineteenth century, this experience was renamed the baptism in the Holy Spirit, which prepared the way for the coming of the Pentecostal movement. However, the Moravian stress upon the victorious life greatly influenced Wesley. His own spiritual experience came from the witness of Moravians, first through Bishop August Spangenberg (1704–1792) and the party that was traveling on the same ship as Wesley, out to the colony in Georgia. Later, on Wesley's return to England, still in an unconverted condition, from his missionary activity in Georgia, through his meeting with Peter Boehler (1712–1775), the leader of the Moravians in the UK, he was introduced to the concept of faith. Boehler told him to preach faith until he had it and then to preach faith because he had it. That was enough to inspire his thinking. While lying ill in the home of John Bray in Little Britain, John Wesley's brother, Charles, came to Christ through the efforts of another Moravian, William Holland, who gave him a copy of Luther's *Commentary on Galatians*.[2] These elements all helped prepare the way for what was about to happen and flowed into the Great Awakening.

In investigating the cause of the awakening itself, it is common to focus attention on the period in the American colonies from 1740, and in Britain from about 1739 onward. In reality the revival began earlier. So often when God is going to send a major spiritual awakening, he prepares the way with a stirring and a quickening of some individuals' hearts.

In the revival cycle it was noted that not only is there a period of decline, but then comes the irruption of a prophetic ministry, in which though only a small number might participate, there is the preparation for a general outpouring of God's Spirit. Sometimes this preparation period goes unnoticed, but it is always there. There was such an observable preparation period, in some instances a considerable time, prior to this Great Awakening.

Wales. In 1711 in Wales, there came the first signs of the coming awakening, when God began to pour out his Spirit and brought to Christ, first of all, the great Welsh preacher, Griffith Jones (1683–1761) of Llanddowror in Carmarthenshire. Griffith Jones was a powerful preacher of the Word of God. Not only was he touched, but also Pryce Davies of Talgarth (c. 1675–1740), another renowned Welsh preacher, was touched by the Spirit of God about the same time and continued a very strong evangelistic ministry for some considerable time. Griffith Jones was strongly involved in the preaching ministry both in his home parish in Wales and later in the Anglican Society meetings. In fact, as early as 1713 John Dalton (1680–1724) of Clog-y-Fran, Carmarthenshire, wrote a letter to the Society for the Propagation of Christian Knowledge, declaring:

> When Mr. Jones is invited to preach anywhere and also when he preaches in his own church, to which there doesn't belong any more than 10 or 12 small families, it is to be admired what a numerous congregation he eventually ministers to. Sometimes as many as 500 or 600 hearers, sometimes even 1,000, a number that is not to be found in any other church in Wales on any other occasion. And it seems as though his sermon consists mostly of plain and familiar dialect of their native language. Undoubtedly Mr. Jones is one of the greatest masters of the Welsh tongue that ever Wales was blessed with both in respect of fluency of speech and eminently in scriptural

and Christian knowledge. When he preaches it is as though a light were turned on in the church.[3]

Griffith Jones's ministry was to have a powerful effect. Daniel Rowlands (1713–1790), one of the early Welsh revivalists, was converted through the ministry of Griffith Jones in 1735. Not only he but also George Whitefield came to Christ through the ministry of Griffith Jones. He has been rightly called "the morning star of the Great Awakening," because to a large degree he prepared the way for much that was going to happen in the future.

Alongside his ministry, which was that of a firebrand, was also the quite different ministry of Pryce Davies, who was very much the clergyman. A very austere and unemotional type of Welshman, he was the pastor of the parish church in Talgarth. He addressed his congregation, we are told, in solemn tones, that such an awful sense of the presence of God would come, especially when he spoke as he did on Palm Sunday in preparation for the communion service that was to be celebrated on Easter Sunday, and pleaded with those people to prepare to celebrate the Lord's Supper. He said:

> You plead your unfitness to come to the Holy Communion. Let me tell you that if you are not fit to come to the Lord's Supper you are not fit to come to church. You are not fit to live; you are not fit to die.[4]

Sitting in his congregation was the local schoolmaster, Howell Harris (1714–1771). The young man attended church because it was the right thing for schoolmasters to do in that community. As Pryce Davies in solemn tones spoke of fitness to take the Lord's Supper, those words went right home to Harris's heart and he resolved to prepare himself to receive the communion on Easter day no matter what it took. He spent the next week living as he felt in an exemplary fashion and quite satisfied with his own righteousness, turned up to take communion. A common practice among the Welsh and Scots was "to build the fence" around the communion table, i.e., to preach the Word of God and the demands of God so stringently that when the invitation was given for those who felt their hearts to be right with God to come forward to receive the communion, at times the whole congregation would stay in their seats. The spiritual fence had been built so high that they felt unable to get over it to come to the communion table.

As Pryce Davies began to build the fence that Sunday morning, Harris, full of self-righteousness, began to realize that apart from the grace of God, it was not possible for him to take the bread and the wine in remembrance of the death of our Lord. As Pryce Davies laid the foundation of the grace of God in the gospel, he opened his heart, accepted Christ as his Savior, and was radically transformed, as were many others in that church that day. The conversion of Howell Harris was notable because he was a schoolmaster, not a clergyman, and yet his ministry was to make a phenomenal impact on Wales from 1735 onward. The Spirit of God flowed through him in a powerful way. As he went around and preached, he was on fire, so he felt, with the love of God. Although naturally he was inclined to reticence, when the Spirit of God came upon him, he could not resist.

The situation in Wales at the time was not promising; in fact he described the area where he lived as a universal deluge of swearing, lying, reviling, drunkenness, fighting and gaming which had overspread the country and no one seemed to care for their souls. Harris traveled from church to church appealing to the clergy to raise their voices and stand against the wickedness and sin that was taking place in the community, but none would respond, so he began preaching himself. First, it was simply the reading of the Scriptures in public and then expounding those Scriptures, and then he would visit the sick in their homes and his former companions, urging them to forsake their evil ways and turn to God. When it became obvious that the clergy were not flowing with the Spirit of God, he would go to the churches. After the clergy had finished their service, he would then stand on one of the gravestones outside the parish church and as the parishioners left, he would address them from the Scriptures, giving his own invitations. Amazing things happened in the peoples' lives because as they came out, they were met with the Word of God.

In 1736, Harris was introduced to Griffith Jones and the two wings of the revival in Wales, that stemming from Griffith Jones's ministry and that stemming to a lesser degree from Pryce Davies' ministry flowed together, and from 1736 onward he began a ministry of itinerant evangelism, traveling from town to town, even at times facing the violence of mobs that were set upon him by the parish clergy who resented this unordained schoolmaster coming in and preaching the gospel of Christ. George Whitefield described him:

> A burning and shining light has been in those parts; a barrier against profaneness and immorality, an indefatigable promoter of the true gospel of Jesus Christ. . . . He is of a most catholic spirit, loves all that love our Lord Jesus Christ, and, therefore, he is slighted by bigots and dissenters. He is condemned by all that are lovers of pleasure rather than lovers of God: but God has greatly blessed his pious endeavors. Many call and own him as their spiritual father; and, I believe, would lay down their lives for his sake. He discourses generally in a field, from a wall, a table, anything else, but at other times in a house. He has established near thirty societies in South Wales and still his sphere of action is enlarged daily. He is full of faith and the Holy Ghost.[5]

Daniel Rowlands was also converted through Griffith Jones about the same time as Harris. It is interesting to see the comparison. Daniel Rowlands was in fact a lot like Pryce Davies, an ordained clergyman, pastor of a parish church, pompous, stiff, rigid, but when Griffith Jones visited Rowlands' parish and prevailed upon Rowlands to allow him to preach in his church, at first Rowlands was skeptical about allowing this traveling clergyman to preach for him. Jones, therefore, seeing the skeptical look on Rowlands' face, stuck to praying. As he prayed, he said that in a split second between his ending that prayer and announcing his sermon text the Spirit of God like an arrow pierced the consciousness of Daniel Rowlands and he was radically saved before he ever heard a sermon from Griffith Jones. The Spirit of God simply broke into his life in such a radical way that Howell Harris later described Daniel Rowlands as "a second St. Paul in his own pulpit"[6] and in the immediate area. His preaching gained unusual power. We are told that multitudes trembled at his presence. The church sometimes rang with the shouts and shrieks of those with whom the Spirit of God was deeply dealing. His fame spread throughout Wales and so that other clergy invited him to visit their churches to minister the Word of God and to bring spiritual awakening to their churches. This was a man who in his youth was a stiff and starchy character, skeptical of enthusiasm, and of the fire of the Holy Spirit as evidenced in the ministry of people like Griffith Jones, but God was going to use him and turned him right around.

Continental Europe. Alongside the preparation in Wales, God was also moving in the European continent. The Moravians in the seventeenth century had been subjected to intense persecution and had been driven from one place to another until finally at the beginning of the eighteenth entury, the Pietist convert Count Nicolaus Ludwig von Zinzendorf (1700–1760) opened his estate to a settlement of Moravians at a place which they called Herrnhut (the Lord's watchtower). That became the main center for the Moravians to take refuge from persecution in both the Roman Catholic-dominated area and the Protestant-dominated area.

Many of the members of what was to be known as the Moravian movement, also called the United Brethren (Unitas Fratrum), were descendants of the converts of Hus, the great revivalist of pre-reformation days. Many had been absorbed into the radical wing of the great Reformation period and as a result had been subjected to severe persecution just as the other radicals were. Some of these radicals moved on to Holland and became Mennonites, later establishing their home in the American colonies. Others took refuge on the estates of this Pietistic count in South-eastern Germany, where he gladly granted them a plot of land to live on. From June 17, 1722, they began to establish their settlements on Zinzendorf's land, but at first, because of their differing backgrounds, Socinian, Mennonite, other independent movements, there was much conflict between the disparate groups. Lutheran clergyman pastor Johann Roethe, from the nearby Berthelsdorf Lutheran parish church, was deeply concerned that this community was going to disintegrate and undertook to be the spiritual advisor to the community. Pastor Roethe's ministry at first was not well accepted because they wanted to manage their own spiritual affairs as a distinct society within the local Lutheran parish. Roethe, however, considered that would mean a continuation of the divisiveness and conflicts between the various factions at Herrnhut.

On August 12, 1727, he summoned together all the members of the Herrnhut community and placed before them some statutes, injunctions, and prohibitions to regulate the affairs of this community. After agreeing with these they were then to celebrate their agreement by a breaking of bread service that would lead into the service of Holy Communion; and in this breaking of bread they each were given a small loaf of bread and were to go and be reconciled to their neighbor by offering the loaf to him or her. By sharing each other's bread, they would hopefully bury their differences and at least get along with each other. The Spirit of God broke into that meeting in a phenomenal way. As Skevington Wood described it:

> They experienced a veritable Pentecost of spiritual power. The fire of the Lord fell and they were lost in wonder, love and praise. They left the house of God hardly knowing whether they belonged on earth or had already gone to Heaven.[7]

That began a prayer meeting that was to last for thirty years nonstop, seeking the face of God and praying for revival. Many of the events of the revival that followed stemmed from the fact that this community devoted itself to praying through for a spiritual awakening. The final dissolution of the prayer meeting did not come about until the very last of these Moravians had left the community to go forth as missionaries to reach the unevangelized.

Some of the first to leave the community went to evangelize the slaves of the British Caribbean, selling themselves into slavery so that they could get near the slaves in St. Thomas, Jamaica, and other Caribbean islands. God so worked in their lives that they counted even their own personal freedom to be worth nothing compared with the task of preaching the gospel to the lost. It takes a revival to bring people to that level of commitment. God certainly did great things.

The Origins of the Great Awakening. These origins are often traced back to the ministry of Theodore Frelinghuysen (1691–1747) in the American colonies and through him to Gilbert Tennent (1703–1764), his brothers William (1705–1777), and John (1707–1732), and others in the New York area and New Jersey, who were greatly used by God in those early days.

Frelinghuysen was a Pietist minister who was called to leave Westphalia in Germany and after studying in Holland, was called to minister among the Dutch Reformed settlers in New Amsterdam. He arrived in the American colonies in 1720 and began a ministry in the Raritan Valley, through which some powerful things began to happen. The four small churches that he served steadily began to diminish in size because as some were converted, others left, until finally after three years, things came to a crisis when the four heads of the leading families of each church agreed together to appeal to the superintendent minister to have Frelinghuysen removed from the pastorate of their churches because he preached people out of the church.

In a typical early sermon, he challenged his congregation:

What do you think of my hearers? Are you poor, contrite in spirit, those who tremble at the word of God? If you have given your honest attention you will, you have been able to learn how it is with you in this respect. Calmly ask yourselves in the presence of the allseeing God "Am I spiritually poor?" Have I sensible knowledge of my sad and condemned state? Do I feel in myself that I am so guilty and impure and evil, so alienated from God and the life of God, so wretched, poor, miserable, blind, naked and unable to deliver myself or do anything toward my deliverance that I must perish if I remain like this? Secondly, ask yourselves "Have I a sense of my spiritual needs?" Third, ask yourself "Am I contrite in spirit through a painful sense of sin?"[8]

When he had finished his almost totally negative sermon, a few fell under conviction of sin but most decided that that was not the kind of ministry they wanted. First, they made charges against him and tried to get him dismissed. They even went to New York to see if they could enlist the help of some of the other clergy, and finally went to see Bernard Freeman in Long Island, the superintendent minister of that whole area. As far as Freeman was concerned, he knew that their reaction was prompted by the fact that they were uncomfortable with the pastor's preaching, not because of any sin or failure on the part of the pastor. So, he sent them away with a very clear message:

> Be careful you do not unjustly accuse your pastor for he has been abundantly certified by the synod in Holland and also by the Synod of Amsterdam which declared him to be orthodox and sent him to you. It is not heresy or soul-destroying doctrine that he is preaching but it is a clear presentation of the truth of Christ. I see that you are all affected by the spirit of hatred and revenge. Because he sharply exposes sin, you try to help the Devil! You should love your spiritual father, who earnestly reproves you and accepting it in love, apply it to your improvement.[9]

Although Freeman dismissed the charges, it did not stop the opposition and eventually he became involved, going so far as in 1725 to publish a book called *The Complaint Against Frelinghuysen*, which he circulated widely in the whole area. In 1726, however, God began to pour out his Spirit so powerfully that even the most virulent opponents of his preaching fell under such an awareness of their lost condition and of their sin that many came to Christ and were radically converted.

Instead of the church continuing to empty, sinners began to flock to the churches to seek spiritual help and advice from Frelinghuysen. Jonathan Edwards looked back on the ministry of Frelinghuysen when talking of the revival that had come later under his own ministry said:

The shower of divine blessing has been yet more extensive: there was no small degree of it in some parts of the Jerseys; as I was informed when I was in New York. Especially the Rev. William Tennent, a minister who seemed to have such things much at heart, told me of a very great awakening of many in a place called The Mountains, under the ministry of one Mr. Cross; and of a very considerable revival of religion in another place under the ministry of his brother the Rev. Gilbert Tennent; and also at another place, under the ministry of a very pious young gentleman, a Dutch minister, whose name as I remember was Freelinghousa (sic.).[10]

Gilbert Tennent and his father, William, entered the ministry in New York following the emigration of his parents to that area from Ireland where, as Presbyterians, they were greatly used by God in ministry and in a stirring, that preceded the main revival. When Gilbert Tennent was ordained into the ministry, he came into contact with Frelinghuysen and was set on fire for God, beginning a very powerful revival ministry among the Presbyterians in the area around New Brunswick. Tennent felt that the ministry of Frelinghuysen was one of the most important elements in his own personal life. In a letter, more than twenty years later, he recounted:

> The labors of the Reverend Mr. Frelinghousa (sic.), a Dutch Calvinist minister, were much blessed to the people of New Brunswick and places adjacent, especially about the time of his coming among them, which was about twenty-four years ago. When I came there, which was about seven years after, I had the pleasure of seeing much of the fruits of his ministry.[11]

Many of his hearers appeared to be converted people. Christian experience and pious practice were the normal pattern of life in that community. There was such a move of God that not only affected the Tennents but also years later, when George Whitefield came from England to visit the American colonies and met the Tennents and Frelinghuysen, he himself was set on fire for God. He came ostensibly to set up orphanages and to help with the newly arrived colonists from England, but was converted from a born again Anglican preacher into a firebrand for revival through meeting these men. Later he himself was to meet that other American firebrand, Jonathan Edwards.

Jonathan Edwards had been brought into a vital relationship through the ministry of his grandfather, Solomon Stoddard. Upon his grandfather's death, he was elected to be his successor at the church in Northampton in Connecticut. His call to ministry at Northampton Church was to be one of the most difficult periods of Jonathan Edwards' life. He began his ministry there in 1724 and discovered that, despite the succession of revivals that had come through the ministry of Solomon Stoddard, at the time that he, Jonathan Edwards, took over the leadership of the church, he was distressed by the licentiousness of the townspeople. Many were apparently addicted to "night walking," a common practice at that time whereby young people would walk out into the countryside around the town and the young men and young women would engage in immorality with whoever they happened to meet. Because it was dark, they would not know who they had been with, and so they would consider themselves not responsible for their actions. Often, they frequented the taverns and somewhat inebriated, they would engage in lewd practices, and would even hold conventions for both sexes for mirth and jollity, which they called "The Frolics," spending the greater part of the night engaging in all manner of immorality, as part of those frolics.[12] Although Edwards tried to awaken them from their complacency for several years, they were resistant to his every effort to make them aware of the peril that they were facing, until in 1734 something remarkable began to happen. Edwards recalls:

> The Spirit of God began extraordinarily to set in, and wonderfully to work among us; and there were, very suddenly and wonderfully, one after another, five or six persons who were to all appearances savingly converted, and some of them wrought upon in a very remarkable manner.[13]

Although the numbers converted under Edwards appear small, five or six, not thousands, it should be noted that Northampton was not a large, heavily populated community, but had only about a thousand inhabitants, so the conversion of five or six people could make a powerful impact, especially when the people had been so insensible and even resistant to the things of God. He later recounted:

> This work of God, as it was carried on, and the number of true saints multiplied, soon made a glorious alteration in the town; so that in the spring and summer following, in the year 1735, the town seemed to be full of the presence of God; it was never so full of love, nor of joy, and yet so full of distress, as it was then. There were remarkable tokens of God's presence in almost every house. It was a time of joy in families on account of salvation being brought unto them.[14]

This first "harvest" under Edwards' ministry lasted more than a year and was the equal of anything that Stoddard had experienced during the many harvests that had taken place in his ministry. In total, more than 300 souls, out of a total population of slightly more than 1,000, were brought into a saving relationship with Christ in the space of about six months during that revival, about equal a number of males as females. Thus the greater part of the persons in the town above sixteen years of age had come to the saving knowledge of Christ. He did not count the conversion of children, only those of mature years, sixteen years of age and above. Probably three to four hundred would be under the age of sixteen and the rest over sixteen. Since some would already be believers, a substantial part of the population was in fact born again. That made a great impact on that community.

Once this powerful move of God's Spirit was over, the people in the town resented much of the teachings of Edwards and he did face some very strong opposition. However, following the visit of George Whitefield to the American colonies in 1740 and the quickening that brought about in Whitefield's own life and his visit to New England where Edwards was ministering, a further move of revival took place. This became the main thrust of revival, from about 1740 onward.

The main movement of revival began to take place throughout almost the whole of New England and the eastern seaboard of America. There was a great sense of the convicting power of God. Edwards himself preached his famous sermon, *Sinners in the Hands of an Angry God* at Enfield, Connecticut, on July 8, 1741. In that sermon, Edwards denounced, scathingly, the sinfulness of his hearers, but the style of delivery was very cold, very calm, very unmoved. He was not a flaming firebrand of a preacher, like the Tennents, and certainly not like George Whitefield. He was very stiff and starchy, much more like Theodore Frelinghuysen, who was himself a very stiff Dutchman with little emotion. One of the townspeople, looking back upon that event, that proclamation, said Mr. Edwards in preaching used no gestures, but looked straight forward. Gideon Clark said: "He looked on the bell rope until he looked it off its hook."[15] He looked neither to the right nor to the left but in slow and unemotional tones spoke of the justice of God. But the impact on his congregation was enormous as he declared:

> There is nothing that keeps wicked men at any one moment out of Hell but the mere pleasure of God, oh sinner consider the fearful danger you are in. It is a great furnace of wrath, the wide and bottomless pit full of the fire of wrath that you are held over in the hand of that God whose wrath is provoked and incensed as much against you as against many of the damned in hell. You hang by a slender thread with the flames of divine wrath flashing about it and ready every moment to singe it and burn it asunder.[16]

People began to realize the awfulness of their situation. It is said that some of his hearers began to cling to the doorposts and the pillars in the church lest they fall into this awful hell that Edwards was describing before them in such unemotional tones. Perhaps that monotone contributed toward the impact of that sermon. It is said that the tones of Edwards' voice were like the clanging of the bell at the funeral and every sinner present saw himself ready to plunge into a lost eternity. No wonder revival came and spread across New England and for the next four years moved in great power throughout the American colonies.

The Methodist Awakening. Revival was already burning in the UK, particularly in England. The main people associated with this were John and Charles Wesley and George Whitefield. They stand out because of the way in which God used them during this time. Some, like Professor Norman Sykes (1897–1961), claim that there were in fact two different evangelical revivals taking place at the same time, one Calvinistic and one Arminian: the Calvinistic, led by people like George Whitefield and Selina Hastings (1707–1791), the Countess of Huntingdon, who was a great revivalist in her own right and the last of the major revivalists to die, and the Arminian, led by John and Charles Wesley and their associates and which also included the Moravian movement in England. It is a false dichotomy to separate these two evangelical revivals because in the first place, John and Charles Wesley were Anglican clergymen, as was George Whitefield. Initially they worked together very closely. It was not until the revival was well underway and indeed in a waning condition that the separation between the former associates took place. The Wesleys developed their distinctive theology of Wesleyan Arminianism, and Whitefield, following his visit to America in the early 1740s adopted a more Calvinistic approach to the Christian faith.

The doctrinal division came upon the heels of the revival rather than preceding or accompanying it. The progress of the revival was unhindered by doctrinal division, but went forward with equal power and indeed under the Wesleys was renewed about 1760. The first phase of the revival, that we trace back to the conversion of the Wesleys and Whitefield in the 1730s, came to a country that was morally and spiritually almost bankrupt. The situation in England was quite appalling. Wesley himself in 1745 looked back on those days and described them in these terms:

> Now what can an impartial person think concerning the present state of religion in England? Is there a nation under the sun which has so deeply fallen from the very first principles of all religion? Where is the country in which is found so utter a disregard to even heathen morality, such a thorough contempt of justice and truth and all that should be dear and honorable to rational creatures?

What species of vice can possibly be named even of those that nature itself abhors, of which we have not had for many years a plentiful and still increasing harvest? What sin remains either in Rome or Constantinople which we have not imported long ago, if it was not of our native growth, and improved upon it ever since until now it has reached a level of refinement that would astonish the darkest ages of human history? Such a con of villainies of every kind considered with all that aggravations, such a scorn of whatever bears the face of virtue, such injustice, fraud and falsehood, above all such perjury and such a method of law we may defy the whole world to produce? What multitudes are found throughout our land, who do not even profess any religion at all? And what numbers of those who profess much confute their profession by their practice? And perhaps by their exorbitant pride, vanity, covetousness, rapaciousness and oppression cause the very name of religion to stink in the nostrils of many otherwise reasonable men.[17]

Wesley did not have a high opinion of the state of religion in the British Isles at the time of the revival or even during the period of revival. One thing to be kept clearly in mind is that although in a period of revival there may be a great moving of God's Spirit and a widespread conversion of the lost, yet not all men are converted in most revivals. There may be an occasional revival where in a very small city such as the one in Samaria, or two cities like Lydda and Sharon,[18] everybody turns to the Lord, but generally some may be resistant to the revival and as in the revival at the beginning of the nineteenth century, will endeavor to drown by alcohol the convicting power of the Holy Spirit, resisting any efforts by God to bring them to repentance.

One of the hallmarks of revivals is initially a polarizing of the community into the truly converted, who separate themselves from the rest of the community, which in response becomes even more anti-Christian, anti-moral in their activities. As the revival continues there comes a movement toward a more moral tone in the community, as the impact of the lives of the converted and revived begins to influence sensible and rational people, who in the period of high enthusiasm may have dismissed the value of the revival, but later realize the life-changing power present in that revival.

Wesley described the situation in general terms, but, for example, it was quite common in the markets of London and rural areas, for men to hire out their wives to anyone who wanted to pay the price. The wives were paraded like cattle at a cattle market and whoever wanted to hire a wife for a day could do so.[19] Bars, or gin shops, as they were called, abounded. It is estimated that in the city of London there were five gin shops for every church and they would advertise: "Drunk for 1d. (one penny); Dead Drunk for 2d. Clean straw to lie on."[20] People would drink themselves into insensibility and in the gin shop's back room or outhouse they would be laid, or more likely, thrown on the straw to sleep it off until they were sensible enough to walk.

George Berkeley (1685–1753), the Bishop of Cloyne, in 1738, the year before the revival broke out, declared that morality and religion in Britain had collapsed to a degree that was never known before in any Christian country, and he doubted very seriously that it could survive.[21] His attempt to combat the ungodliness of that day using philosophical arguments was certainly different from that of the Wesleys. They came face-to-face with God and found that a revival of true religion, of faith in God, was enough to turn the hearts of men from their sinful ways, whereas a philosophical argument would not even reach them. The common man was interested in something that would make his life better. Wesley certainly discovered what that was, when he came to faith in Christ.

His conversion took place on a visit to an Anglican Society meeting in Aldersgate Street in London. As he heard a layman read Luther's preface to the Romans, he found his heart "strangely warmed within" him. He felt that he did trust in Christ alone for salvation from sin and was radically converted. On testifying to his brother, he discovered that his brother had had a similar conversion experience just a few days before on Pentecost Sunday, when in a state of sickness he had been taken to the home of a charcoal burner named Bray, an uneducated man who knew nothing except Christ, but proceeded to talk about what he did know all day long and every day for the rest of his life. As he spoke of

Christ to Charles Wesley, Charles' recovery from sickness went far deeper than his physical body because he recovered from this sickness of sin by a real conversion experience of the Lord Jesus Christ and was radically transformed. When John came to tell him of the change that had taken place in his life, Charles recounted back to him his own experience of the grace of God.

The term "Methodist" itself, which was applied to the Wesleys and to Whitefield, did not originate at the time of the revival, but much earlier as a contemptuous term given to the members of Wesley's Holy Club at Oxford University where he was a fellow of the University. They were called Methodists because they believed in a methodological approach to the things of God and to spirituality. They had their prayer methods and their Bible study methods and this systematic approach earned them the name of Methodist. They divided their day up into a certain number of hours for prayer, for Bible study, for good works, for preaching, for studying, for reading various types of beneficial literature, whether theological or classical like Shakespeare's plays; everything was done by method, hence the nickname Methodists. Despite not being initially a specifically religious term, it later was applied to the religious movement that the Wesleys and Whitefield were involved in. The very strength of Wesley's methodical approach was to have a phenomenal effect upon the revival.

Herein lies a parallel between Wesley and his friends with their methodological approach, and Charles Finney, who was a lawyer, was also a great methodologist, although not a Methodist. Finney believed that revival comes from the right use of the means for stimulating a revival and was very much human-oriented in his approach to revival, whereas Wesley developed a much more warmhearted and God-conscious approach to revival, because of the way the grace of God had found him out and transformed his life, because of his strong background in theology, and because of his understanding of some of the principles of Pietism as filtered through the Moravian movement especially. The theology coming out of Wesley's movement was quite different from the theology that came out of Finney's movement even though in their attitude the two men were very similar.

The main thrust of the revival began in 1739 in the Fetter Lane Society meeting in London. The Fetter Lane Society was in fact a Moravian society that met in Fetter Lane, near Fleet Street, the great newspaper center of London, not far from St. Paul's Cathedral. During the love-feast held in the night of New Year's Day 1739, Wesley later described the event:

> About three in the morning, as we were continuing instant in prayer, the power of God came mightily upon us, insomuch that many cried out for exceeding joy, and many fell to the ground. As soon as we were recovered a little from that awe and amazement at the presence of His majesty, we broke out with one voice, "We praise Thee, O God; we acknowledge Thee to be the Lord!"[22]

Following that quickening and outpouring of God's Spirit, Wesley's ministry became quite phenomenal. In fact, beginning in the open air and traveling across Britain he covered 250,000 miles between then and his death in 1791, preaching more than 40,000 sermons. At the end of those fifty-two years of ministry he left behind 140,000 members of his Methodist societies and introduced some 1,500 other preachers into the ministry to care for the flock. Few could boast such results from their period of ministry.

In 1760 came **a renewed period of visitation**. Tragically, the renewed period of visitation did not generally affect the American colonies because the French and Indian War was taking place, following which further agitation took place against the British government, resulting in conflict between the government and the American colonists from 1776 onward. Revival in the American colonies was not generally renewed until after that conflict was over. But it was renewed in Britain.

There was a powerful move of God that took place beginning from my home county of Yorkshire. Many churches built in the 1740s were extended in the 1760s, extended again in 1805, extended yet again in the 1860s, extended yet again in 1905, and then closed in the 1960s. Such examples exist throughout the region tracing the history of Christianity by the marker stones around the church walls that tell of the extensions constructed as the Spirit of God came in powerful waves and brought multitudes into the kingdom of God.

In 1781 Wesley, when writing the history of the Methodists, reported:

> Here began that glorious work of sanctification which had been nearly at a stand for 20 years; but which now, from time to time, spread, first to various parts of Yorkshire, afterwards in London, then through most parts of England, next through Dublin, Limerick, and all of the southwest of Ireland.[23]

A century later, after the potato famine, when many Irish Evangelical Protestants had emigrated to the United States of America, leaving only a small community in Ireland, the population balance changed in favor of Roman Catholicism. However, in the 1760s when multitudes in Ireland had come into an evangelical faith, in every community in southern Ireland there were to be found Methodist meeting places that were thronged with worshipers. Many of them, in small communities of just two or three thousand people, would seat over 1,000 people, and in many of them at the height of the revival there was standing room only because of the large numbers that came to God. God was doing great things.

Six Effects of the Great Awakening. Some of the effects of the awakening may be summarized under several headings.

First, *theologically*, it transformed the whole situation. Deism, as it was called, died during the Great Awakening. The Enlightenment movement was successfully answered and made little impact upon either the UK or the Americas until after the revival period was over.

Second, *orthodox doctrine* was vindicated and, in fact, by the latter half of the eighteenth century to be a Christian was to be evangelical. There were few who were not. There was a general agreement among religious people as to what a Christian was and it was expressed in terms of evangelical faith. Religious literature was also diffused widely through publishing houses like the Society for Promoting Christian Knowledge, giving rise to a more educated laity in the church.

Third, *Christian tolerance and fellowship* was broadened across denominational lines. The cleavage between the established and the dissenting churches, the free churches, was repaired as people came together in worshiping God and acknowledged the faith that each had.

Fourth, *education* was promoted. The school system had its birth in the Great Awakening. Robert Raikes (1735–1811) and his Gloucester Sunday schools were the start of a regular school system and the Sunday School movement itself. Another school system called the Ragged Schools also started to educate the urchins and street people.

Fifth, *the modern missionary movement* received its impetus out of this awakening. Although the main thrust of the missionary movement came in the next revival, William Carey (1761–1834) was converted through the influence of the Wesleyan revival.

Sixth, *profound social effects* were produced. The prisons, through John Howard (1726–1790), and the hospitals all were mightily affected by this awakening. This was truly a move of God and much of what we enjoy today in the way of civilization resulted from the awakening under the Wesleys, Whitefield and Edwards in the eighteenth century. Revival converts, like William Wilberforce (1759–1833), were at the forefront of the movement to abolish slavery from 1787 until it was outlawed in all British dominions in 1833 at Wilberforce's death.

Endnotes

1   J. Tracy: *The Great Awakening: A History of the Revival of Religion in the Time of Edwards and Whitefield* (Boston, 1842).

2   A. S. Wood: *The Inextinguishable Blaze: Spiritual Renewal and Advance in the Eighteenth Century* (Exeter, Devon: Paternoster, 1960), 109.

3   Ibid., 42.

4   Ibid., 49.

5   Ibid., 51.

6   Ibid., 47.

7   Ibid., 69.

8   K. J. Hardman: *The Spiritual Awakeners* (Chicago, IL: Moody, 1983), 57, 58.

9   Ibid.

10 C. C. Goen (ed.): "The Great Awakening" in *The Works of Jonathan Edwards*, vol. 4 (New Haven, CT: Yale University Press, 1972), 155–156

11 Cited in Tracy, op. cit., 33–34.

12 Goen, op. cit., 146.

13 Ibid., 149.

14 Ibid., 151.

15 P. Miller: *Jonathan Edwards* (New York, NY: William Sloane, 1949), 51.

16 Ibid.

17 J. Wesley: *A Plain Account of Christian Perfection* (New York, NY: Lane & Scott, 1850), 336.

18 Acts 8, 9.

19 J. W. Bready: *England: Before and After Wesley* (London, UK: Hodder & Stoughton, 1939), 159.

20 Ibid., 147.

21 Ibid, 19.

22 Curnock, N. (ed.): *The Journal of the Rev. John Wesley A. M.*, vol. 2 (London, Epworth, 1938), 121–122.

23 Jackson, T. (ed.): *Works of John Wesley*, vol. XIII (London, UK, Wesleyan Methodist, 1865), 331.

Chapter 14

The Second Great Awakening

1770–1835

The Second Great Awakening is sometimes called the missionary awakening or missionary revival because it is often credited with giving birth to the modern Protestant missionary movement. The colonial expansion of the European powers had given rise to some missionary activity dedicated to transplanting the faith of the homeland to the overseas colonies; however, the success of the effort had been tempered by the fact that Christianity was then considered the religion of the conquerors. A fresh approach had begun under the Pietists, the Danish Halle mission, in 1705, which in turn inspired the Moravians in the Great Awakening a quarter century later. Of their work De Jong wrote: "Their self-sacrifice, love and total commitment to evangelization are unparalleled in the history of missions."[1] Nevertheless, the main impetus for the modern missionary movement originated in this Great Awakening.

Latourette designated the nineteenth century as *The Great Century*, and accounted for its accomplishments, especially in the realm of missions by commenting:

> The nineteenth century spread of Christianity was due primarily to a new burst of religious life. . . . It was from this abounding vigour that

there issued the missionary enterprise which during the nineteenth century so augmented the numerical strength and the influence of Christianity. The revival of Christianity showed itself primarily in Protestantism. . . . Yet Roman Catholicism also displayed renewed life and spread more widely than ever before.[2]

The Prelude to the Awakening. However, Latourette also noted: "The vigour and expansion of nineteenth century Christianity were preceded by a period when the faith appeared to be at a low ebb and when its future seemed dubious."[3] After the Great Awakening of the eighteenth century associated with the Pietists and Moravians in Europe, and the Wesley brothers, Whitfield, Jonathan Edwards, and their successors, in Britain and America, the natural expectation would have been that the spiritual sensibilities of America, Britain, and Europe would have been so elevated that nothing could have dissuaded the people from following the Lord. Tragically, especially in America and on the mainland of Europe, it was not so.

Although many of the ideas inspiring the American War of Independence (1775–1782) came from seeds sown in the Great Awakening, most of the fathers of the American Revolution were either nominal Christians, Deists, or ardently opposed to the Christian faith, and were strongly influenced by the rationalism of the European Enlightenment. Thomas Jefferson (1743–1826), "the father of the republic," was a rationalist deist who, although he believed that there was quite possibly a God who started all things, did not believe in the reality of the revelation of God in Christ nor in the Christian Scriptures. He even went so far as to compile his own version of the "scriptures" with statements from Jesus combined with statements from other popular devotional writers, all of which he considered equally inspiring. Benjamin Franklin (1706–1790) and John Adams (1735–1826) tended toward a more tolerant religious deism than did the ardent Englishman Thomas Paine (1737–1809), whose writings were immensely popular in the revolutionary period, and to a large degree sparked what was taking place. Some, like Henry Dearborn (1751–1829), Charles Lee (1732–1782), and Henry Lee (1756–1818), were totally opposed to all religious faith whatsoever. A few, like George Washington (1732–1799) and James Madison (1751–1836), made some nominal profession of Christianity, and a small number, like Patrick Henry (1736–1799) and Richard Henry Lee (1732–1794), appeared more evangelical in their faith.

Despite the noted religious inspiration of the American Revolution, the departure of many of the loyalist clergy for Canada and England and the proliferation of Enlightenment ideas marked the beginning of a major period of religious decline in much of the newly independent former colonies. Shortly after the revolution, according to contemporary accounts, from a population of five million the United States boasted 300,000 drunkards, 15,000 of whom died each year. "There was a surfeit of lawlessness, a profusion of gamblers, of gangs of robbers and slave stealers. Drunkenness was common and profanity prevalent. Immorality had increased, as honesty and veracity declined."[4]

According to Ashbel Green (1762–1848), president of Princeton, in the year 1782 there was no more than two students enrolled at Princeton who professed religion and "only five or six who scrupled the use of profane language in conversation, and sometimes it was of a very shocking kind."[5] In most of the universities and colleges there were infidel clubs, indulging in all kinds of immorality and lasciviousness. In the Infidel Club at Yale during the presidency of the Congregationalist, Ezra Stiles (1727–1795, president from 1778), of the twenty men and seven women who were the leaders of that club, several were shot for murder or robbery; others were hanged for horse stealing or murder; yet others drank themselves to death; two men and a woman, engaged in immorality and drunkenness, while sleeping off the effects of their antics, were set upon by wild dogs and eaten. The seven female leaders of that club had a total of thirty-four illegitimate children between them, and had no idea as to the father of any of them.[6] The moral decline plummeted to its very depths by the 1790s. Lyman Beecher's (1775–1863) description of the Yale of 1795 prior to the presidency of Timothy Dwight (1752–1817) was typical of college campuses:

College was in a most ungodly state. The college church was almost extinct. Most of the students were skeptical and rowdies were plenty. Wine and liquors were kept in many rooms; intemperance, profanity, gambling and licentiousness were common.[7]

Timothy Dwight, the grandson of Jonathan Edwards, who was so powerfully used in the Great Awakening, succeeded Stiles as president of Yale in 1795, and lamented: "The dregs of infidelity from France, Germany and Britain have been vomited upon the American states. The whole mass of pollution from those countries has been emptied upon this country and who knows what the end will be."[8] Orr noted that at the beginning of the last decade of the century:

Bishop James Madison in the diocese of Virginia agreed with the conviction of Chief Justice John Marshall, a devout layman, who wrote that the Church was too far gone ever to be revived; while Bishop Samuel Provoost of New York felt that the situation was hopeless, and simply ceased functioning.[9]

To some it looked as though Christianity was finished in the new republic, with no possibility of remedy. In 1798, the Presbyterian General Assembly condemned the profaneness, pride, luxury, injustice, intemperance, and lewdness abounding in the nation. They noted that every species of debauchery and loose indulgence was prevalent. They also lamented the growth of Unitarianism and Universalism in the previously Puritan New England to the loss of orthodox Christianity. During that time, some of the most strategic parishes of New England of the Congregational Church turned Unitarian. The renowned Harvard University, founded for the training of young men for the Christian ministry, became a Unitarian establishment and remains so to this day more than two hundred years later. Even the Virginia Baptists lamented: "We are going through a very wintry season in which the love of many has grown cold." Similarly, the Methodists along the eastern seaboard were losing 4,000 members per year for much of the 1780s and 1790s, although some of that loss could be accounted for by the massive westward immigration across the Allegheny Mountains. Hardman appropriately noted: "Multitudes were leaving, lured by the opening frontier. Nearly 1 million people had deserted the East by 1800, seeking a new life and hoping for riches in the Ohio and Allegheny River valleys."[10]

In the early days of colonial Methodism, an Anglican Rector in Bath, Virginia, Devereux Jarratt (1733–1801) had welcomed in 1772 one of Wesley's first emissaries to America, Robert Williams (d.1775). His ministry prepared the way for a spiritual awakening from 1775–1777, that spread from the southern counties of Virginia into North Carolina, even as the revolutionary fervor was convulsing the rest of the American colonies. Within a year of Williams' arrival in southern Virginia two Methodist circuits were established, which in 1774 embraced some 291 members; the next year (1775) there were three circuits with 935 members; two years later six circuits with 4,379 members, two-thirds of the total Methodist membership in America.[11] Wesley's withdrawal of the Methodist preachers in 1775 had left the independently minded Francis Asbury (1745–1816) as the lone representative from Britain of that fellowship in the infant republic. What some thought would be disastrous for the movement turned out instead to be a blessing as it forced Asbury to develop local leadership for the remaining functioning churches. "Largely due to his work, the membership roughly doubled during the war years."[12] Immediately after the end of the war Wesley appointed as the Superintendent of the American Methodist work Dr. Thomas Coke (1747–1814), an ordained Anglican clergyman, who together with Asbury, summoned the American preachers to the historic "Christmas Conference" in 1784 at which the Methodist Episcopal Church was born with Coke and Asbury the first Superintendents (later in 1787 the title was changed to *Bishop*).

Despite the separation between the American colonies and British North America, until the War of 1812 the Methodists of both Upper and Lower Canada were organizationally linked to the Methodist Episcopal Church and shared in the same outpouring of the Spirit. The major move of the Spirit in Canada, however, occurred in the Maritime Provinces through the ministry of Henry Alline (1748–1784), "the Apostle to Nova Scotia."

Born in Rhode Island, to a traditional Congregationalist family, he moved north with his parents to farm land vacated during the "Acadian Expulsion" (1755–1764). His powerful conversion experience in 1775 launched his itinerant ministry as a "New Light" evangelist, which, although rejected by the more formal Congregational Church, resulted in the founding of many Independent and, indirectly, Baptist Churches in Nova Scotia and throughout the Maritimes.[13]

The Concert of Prayer for Revival. In an attempt to advance the Great Awakening in Scotland in the wake of the Cambuslang and the Kilsyth Revivals (1742), John Erskine (1721–1803) of Greyfriars, Edinburgh, in 1744 circulated an appeal to the evangelical clergymen of England and Scotland to unite in prayer for revival. Copies were also forwarded to the clergy of New England, where Jonathan Edwards used Erskine's appeal as the basis of his influential book *A Humble Attempt to Promote Explicit Agreement and Visible Union of God's People in Extraordinary Prayer for the Revival of Religion and the Advancement of Christ's Kingdom* (1747). Some forty years later Andrew Fuller (1754–1815), a leader of the evangelical Particular Baptists in England, appended to his published sermon *The Nature and Importance of Walking by Faith* (1784), what turned out to be a more significant writing, based on Erskine's and Edwards' appeals, *A Few Persuasives to a General Union in Prayer For the Revival of Religion,* which provided the impetus for a general *Prayer Union*. Within a decade the Prayer Union movement had spread throughout the English-speaking world including the United States of America, where Isaac Backus (1724–1806) and his colleagues in New England, using the term *Concert of Prayer*, devoted the first Tuesday of each quarter, at first, and then each month to intercession for the revival of religion. Many congregations began to experience both an outpouring of God's Spirit and an ingathering of souls.[14]

In the First Baptist Church, Bedford, England, where John Bunyan had been the pastor about 150 years before, crowds of 800 attended afternoon and evening prayer meetings, and once a month there was a united prayer meeting with the Second Baptist Church and the town's independent congregation attended by some 2,000 participants in a town of a little more than 3,500 people.[15] At a Prayer Union meeting for Baptist ministers in

Northampton in 1786, William Carey (1761–1834) first reminded them of their responsibility for the evangelization of the heathen. Six years later at a similar meeting in Nottingham, he delivered his epochal message that resulted in the formation of what was to become the Baptist Missionary Society (1792) and his own departure for India a year later, which marked the birth of the modern missionary endeavor.[16]

Not only the Baptists, but also the Congregationalists and the Methodists, in the final years of Wesley's leadership, joined in establishing prayer meetings for the revival of the Christian faith. Even some Church of England parishes led by evangelical clergy engaged the entire parish in earnest prayer for revival two to three hours each day, five days a week. Such intensity of prayer inevitably was marked by periodic local stirrings.

The Awakening in Britain. The awakening proper, however, began the year that John Wesley died (1791) in the north of England in **Yorkshire**, with the appointment of William Bramwell (1759–1818) to take charge of the Methodist work in Dewsbury. Beginning each morning with a 5 a.m. prayer meeting, Bramwell's church soon became the epicenter of the Great Yorkshire Revival (1792–1797), in which each week for the first year at least a hundred converts were added to the church in Dewsbury and its immediate environs. Within a month of the initial outpouring the revival spread further north to the city of Halifax, where in the first month 600 people came to Christ. From there it spread eastward to Bradford and Leeds, south to Sheffield, north to York and Harrogate, and eventually westward across the Pennines into Lancashire and to other parts of the country. In Hull, near Yorkshire's east coast, between 1790 and 1793 the Methodist church more than doubled its numbers from 600 to over 1200; between 1794 and 1795 it more than doubled yet again to 2,500; and by the end of the century had topped 5,000. Testimony to the impact of the revival is marked by the extensions built to the chapels of the region to accommodate the crowds thronging them.

During the last two decades of John Wesley's life, the Methodist movement in Britain had shown steady growth from 120 preachers and 29,406 members in 1770, to 171 preachers and 44,330 members in 1780, to 291 preachers and 71,578 members in 1790. In 1800, however, the number of members escalated to 110,067 with a small increase in preachers to 364. In the next decade the number of preachers almost doubled to 726 and membership reached 165,798, and four years later in 1814 there were 842 preachers caring for 203,273 members.[17]

From the final decade of the eighteenth century until the Napoleonic Wars (1803–1815) absorbed the nation's energies and attention, periodic revival fires were kindled throughout Britain, affecting primarily the dissenting chapels and the few Evangelical Anglican parishes remaining after the final break with the Methodists. Henry Venn (1724–1797), Vicar of Yelling, drew many of the Anglican leaders touched by the revival into an evangelical action group later known as **the Clapham Sect** (1790–1830), which helped inspire William Wilberforce's anti-slavery crusade, the London Missionary Society (1795), the Religious Tract Society (1799), the Sunday School Union, and the British and Foreign Bible Society (1804). Venn also had a major influence on Charles Simeon (1759–1836), Vicar of Holy Trinity, Cambridge, whose ministry not only saw spiritual awakening in the church and university, but also, while accompanying James Haldane (1768–1851) in Perthshire, Scotland, saw a remarkable outpouring of the Spirit there (1796), that was to inspire Haldane and others in their future ministries.

The 1805 visit of Lorenzo Dow (1777–1834) to England, in which he promoted the American novelty of **camp meetings**, sparked renewed revival among the increasingly staid Wesleyan Methodists. The description of the camp meetings so inspired Hugh Bourne (1772–1852) that he and others who had been touched by the Potteries Revival (1797–1804) decided to hold a day-long prayer meeting at Mow Cop (1807), which both rekindled the revival fire to the chagrin of the Wesleyans and caused the withdrawal of the revivalists to form the Primitive Methodist Connexion (1811), under the leadership of Bourne and William Clowes (1780–1851). A similar outpouring of the Spirit in the extreme southwest of England under the ministry of William Bryant (later O'Bryan) (1778–1868) resulted in the Bible Christians (1815) separating from the Wesleyans as a revivalistic alternative:

By the eve of Waterloo, the progress of the Awakening had taken on such proportions in England that observers reported "great multitudes of Evangelical ministers in the Established churches" and "vast accessions recently made to the number of chapels and meeting houses among various classes of Dissenters."[18]

The principality of **Wales** was similarly blessed by repeated outpourings of the Spirit throughout the final decades of the eighteenth century, affecting every Protestant denomination. The Congregational Churches were particularly stirred through the ministries of clergy such as Isaac Price (1735–1805) at Crug-y-bar (1781), Richard Tibbott (1719–1798) at Llanbryn-mawr (1787), and William Williams (1781–1840) of Wern. The Baptist churches also were revived by the fiery preaching of the evangelist, Christmas Evans (1766–1838). The ministry of the Calvinistic Methodist minister Thomas Charles (1755–1814) of Bala initiated the school system in Wales in 1784, inspired "a great revival of true religion in North Wales"[19] in 1791, and helped members of the Clapham Sect found the British and Foreign Bible Society in 1804, to provide Welsh language Bibles for the multitudes of new converts thronging the churches there.

As in England and Wales, **Scotland** enjoyed spasmodic local stirrings throughout the last two decades of the eighteenth century; however, the major outpourings of the Spirit there were not to come until the post-Napoleonic period. Among those raised up through the early stirrings were two brothers, Robert (1764–1842) and James Haldane, whose ministries were to have a powerful impact in their homeland, in Ireland, and in much of continental Europe. The latter influenced by Simeon's revival preaching in 1796 embarked on several evangelistic tours in the Scottish Highlands (1797), Islands (1800), and Lowlands (1800–1801), which prompted notable spiritual awakenings, even though his lack of fluency in Gaelic limited his personal influence in some areas. The revival flame, however, was quickly taken up by local Gaelic-speaking preachers like John MacDonald (1779–1849) of Ferintosh, whom Orr described as "the greatest revival preacher that the Highlands ever produced."[20] Similarly influenced by Simeon's ministry was Alexander Stewart (1764–1821), whose pastorate in Moulin was marked by repeated spiritual awakenings in 1798 and 1800.[21]

Despite the political turmoil in **Ireland** inspired by the American and French Revolutions, the final decades of the eighteenth century were marked by periodic awakenings in various areas such as County Fermanagh (1783–1784), County Down (1791), and throughout the rural North, West, and South beginning in 1799. A general evangelical awakening among the younger clergy of the Church of Ireland (1798–1805), resulting in hundreds of converts each month, was reinforced by the visits of James Haldane to Ulster (1801) and the American evangelist Lorenzo Dow (1804).[22]

The Impact upon Europe. From the American Revolution came much of the impetus for the French Revolution of 1789, which in turn brought a rising tide of infidelity, idolatry, and immorality that threatened to engulf the whole of Europe in a modern version of ancient paganism. That, together with the subsequent Napoleonic conquests of most of Europe south of the Baltic Sea and much of Russia, brought a great sense of foreboding across the continent, which severely hindered the work of God. After the revolutionary period was over and Napoleon had been defeated, many areas affected by the turmoil did experience spiritual awakening from 1815 onward.

The Revival in Scandinavia. In Scandinavia, however, the fear of what was happening in the rest of Europe drove people to prayer and God answered by pouring out his Spirit there as in other parts of the Western world. The fact that they did turn to God also contributed to their spiritual and moral strength in resisting the French armies.

Among prominent persons participating in the Scandinavian revival was the Norwegian lay preacher **Hans Nielsen Hauge** (1771–1824). Hauge was born to a peasant family, and confirmed in the Lutheran church in 1786. While studying Luther's catechism just two days before his twenty-fifth birthday in 1796, he experienced a strange warming of his heart comparable to John Wesley's experience of some sixty years earlier. He said later: "My soul was in that instance so uplifted to God that I was no longer conscious of myself."[23]

He began to share his experience of a personal assurance of salvation with others and found that among the peasant farmers of Scandinavia there was an openness to his message that was not shared by the upper classes, despite the fact that both the upper classes and the farmers for several years prior had been experiencing periodic stirrings from the Spirit. Hauge, however, became the main promoter of revival in Scandinavia as he tramped throughout Norway and into other parts of Scandinavia, proclaiming the gospel and sharing his testimony. Although the Lutheran bishops Ole Irgens (1724–1803) and Johan Nordal Brun (1745–1816) of Bergen were sympathetic, having been revived themselves, other bishops were very hostile. Between 1797 and 1804 he was arrested ten times for preaching the gospel illegally to the peasant farmers without the approval of the parish priest. In 1804, Hauge was arrested yet again and remained in prison until 1809 when he was tried and sentenced to a further five years in prison for the crime of being an unauthorized preacher of the gospel.[24] Amazingly, however, even within the prisons the Spirit of God moved and many prisoners came to Christ. Their transformed lives prompted the king of Norway to release them, and send them overseas as part of the Scandinavian immigration into the United States of America, where many of them settled along the Mississippi and Minnesota rivers in modern Minnesota and Wisconsin.

Hauge and his followers, "the readers," had a radical influence on Norwegian society as a whole, but the movement's most powerful impact was on the laity of the Lutheran church and its ethos, transforming it from the external and formal to the personal and spiritual. The roots of modern Scandinavian Evangelicalism reach back to the Haugean revival of two centuries ago.

In **Sweden**, the peasant farmers had been already impacted by Hauge but now it was the clergy's turn, and a great movement began at a clergy level that was to transform the Lutheran church in Sweden into a strong and virile evangelical movement. The awakening began through the ministry of a Swedish Lutheran pastor, Jakob Otto Hoof (1768–1839). In Hoof's church it was customary after the communion service for the pastor to consume the leftover communion wine. On the day in 1808 set aside to commemorate the patron saint of that church there was a communion service every hour. Waking the next morning from a drunken stupor, Hoof resolved never to drink again until the next saint's day. Then the Spirit of God began to speak to his heart and there in his parsonage he turned to the Lord, was soundly converted, thoroughly revived, and began to proclaim that God wanted revival in his community. The impact of his ministry was amazing. Not only did the Spirit of God begin to fall on his church but everywhere he traveled throughout southwest Sweden, beginning in Goeteborg and Svenljunga, and heading northward to Stockholm, revival accompanied his ministry. Others, like Peter Lorenz Sellergren (1768–1843), who had been touched by Hauge's ministry, also began to spread the revival fire throughout Sweden. By end of the first decade of the nineteenth century, Sweden was ablaze with the Spirit of God and almost 90 percent of the clergy of the Lutheran church in Sweden had been revived, and become themselves promoters of revival.[25]

Across the border in **Finland**, where one tenth of the population was of Swedish descent, many were strongly affected by the revival under Hoof. Hearing of the revival in the rest of Scandinavia, Finnish-speaking believers began to seek God for a revival in Finland. At first the movement was very low key confined to the laity but then with the further impact of the revival under Hoof, revival began to spread among the clergy also. The most significant awakening came in 1796 in Telppasniitty through Juhana Lustig. The same year, the young Paavo Ruotsalainen (1777–1852) came to Christ and was to have a significant role in the later phases of the revival movement. At the revival's peak more than one third of the total population of Finland had come to Christ. This general revival throughout Scandinavia to a large degree enabled the region to remain free from the Napoleonic invasions and the wars that were devastating much of the rest of Europe.

The Awakening in North America. The revival in North America started somewhat later than the revival in Britain. The stirrings of revival in the early 1770s had been effectively brought to an end by the Revolutionary War, which ultimately was to convulse the whole of the colonies and bring with it a period of decline. As the Concert of Prayer movement began to spread, a new awareness of God began to permeate the nation until by 1798 the awakening had become a general revival of religion. Every state in New England and every evangelical denomination were affected by the revival. Congregations were crowded; conviction ran deep; many thoroughgoing conversions were reported. Although the revival in the western states gained notoriety for some of the extravagant manifestations attributed to it, in its New England and mid-Atlantic phases there was no mention of emotional extravagance whatsoever, but rather it was a quiet, thorough, deep work of Almighty God transforming the hearts of the people.

The Eastern States. There were two major aspects to the Eastern states awakening: first of all, among the **churches**, and second, in the **colleges,** notorious as hotbeds of infidelity and immorality. Some of the early local revivals began in Massachusetts, especially around the area of Plainfield. The evangelistic ministry of Moses Hallock (1760–1837), a veteran of the Revolutionary War, was blessed by the Spirit of God moving upon his congregation in 1791, despite his ignorance and his uncouth sermons. Quickly the awakening spread to the Baptist churches of Boston, First Baptist Church, then Second Baptist Church, and then to the last remaining bastion of New England Congregationalism in Boston, the old South Church, where there was a notable movement of God's Spirit, which substantially emptied the former Congregational now Unitarian churches in Boston. The Congregational work in Boston, despite the fact that the old churches did not return to the fold, ended up much stronger that it had been before the loss of most of its churches to the Unitarians.

As the news of the awakening spread over the border into Connecticut the young people of the churches, especially around New Hartford, began to seek God for a move of his Spirit. The first Sunday in November, 1798, the Spirit of God swept over all the congregations in New Hartford simultaneously. More than fifty families were affected and brought to a saving knowledge of Christ. The awakening in Massachusetts was primarily among older people, whereas the awakening in Connecticut was primarily among the young people.

The third major center was in the town of Norfolk at the other side of Connecticut. In January 1799, despite the fact that this area had not yet been affected by the revival movement, a group of God-fearing people in the town, hearing of the awakening in other towns, sent a delegation to visit the places that had experienced revival, with instructions to stay wherever they found revival burning until they themselves were revived, and then to return as firebrands to kindle revival in their town. The return of the delegates did exactly as expected, and revival ensued. As the revived delegates divided into small groups of two or three and shared their testimonies of the revival that was burning in the other towns in Massachusetts and in Connecticut, the Spirit of God was poured out powerfully. By the summer of 1799 it is recorded that "displays of divine power and grace" had become conspicuous beyond anything previously witnessed even at the height of the Great Awakening of the eighteenth century.[26] There was a sense of the Spirit of God sweeping over the whole town. Not only were the Christians revived in the outpouring of the Holy Spirit, but more than 150 townspeople confessed conversion and parts of the town that had been largely untouched by the churches previously were profoundly affected.

By the end of the summer, revival was burning powerfully throughout New England and as far south as Maryland. Fresh waves of the Spirit swept through both the larger towns and the smallest hamlets from the late 1790s until the War of 1812 once again distracted the attention of the young nation, by which time the whole eastern seaboard had experienced a remarkable revival of religion.

Dr. Philip Milledoler (1775–1852), a serious future college president, experienced outpourings of the Spirit in his Pine Street Dutch Reformed Church in Philadelphia from the turn of the century, until 1805. He then "served as minister of the Rutgers Street Dutch Reformed Church in New York between 1807 and 1812, and witnessed an awakening that lasted three years and increased his congregation from eighty to more than seven hundred . . . through ministration of the Word and regular communion."[27]

As a result of the awakening in New York City came an innovation to evangelical services. In the earlier revivals, people literally *fell* under conviction where they were in the congregation. Then either the Holy Spirit dealt with them directly or if the preacher wanted to help them, he had to push his way through the crowd in order to minister to them. When numbers were small that was feasible but when churches were crowded with people wall-to-wall, it was almost impossible. From December 1806 to January 1807 during the revival in New York City, in the Methodist Episcopal Church pastored by Aaron Hunt (1768–1858), the Spirit of God began to move powerfully as the evangelist Seth Crowell (1781–1826) was ministering. The place was so crowded that it was impossible for the ministers to reach those needing prayer. So, Hunt cleared an area in front of the pulpit, which he called the altar. Then, when people in the congregation fell under conviction, others could pick them up, pass them over the heads of the congregation and lay them there. The pastor or the evangelist could come from the high pulpit, and minister to them at the altar until they had recovered their senses and experienced the joy of their salvation. They could then rejoin the congregation. Alternatively, the convicted could come forward to the area voluntarily or by invitation, from which came the evangelical practice of the altar call.

By the year 1810, the practice had been taken up in the camp meetings. Instead of those who were "slain in the Spirit" or who fell under conviction, being taken outside of the circle of the preachers and the congregation and laid among the trees and the bushes until they had recovered their senses, as in the early camp meetings, now they cleared a place in front of the platform, where those affected could be placed. This was safer, more convenient, and made the platform and altar the focal point for ministry.

Not only among the Presbyterians and Congregationalists, but also among the newer Methodist churches, there was a significant outpouring of God's Spirit. Jonathan Crowther (1759–1824), the Wesleyan Methodist historian, writing in 1814, noted: "The prosperity of Methodism in the United States, has, for the last ten or twelve years, somewhat eclipsed the glory at home."[28] By 1813 the movement there recorded 214,327 members.

The earliest awakenings on **the college campuses** actually preceded the general outpouring of the Spirit on the churches, beginning in 1787:

At Hampden-Sydney College in Virginia, a few students, none of them an active Christian but all of them concerned about the moral state of the college met for prayer. They locked themselves in a room, for fear of the other students. . . . The ungodly students created a disturbance, and the President came to investigate. He rebuked the rowdies and invited the intercessors to his study for continued prayer. This continued in power, until an awakening was felt at last. Within a short space of time, more than half the number of students professed conversion in a movement which stirred the local churches also.[29]

Similarly, small groups of students, sometimes only two or three, at other colleges, such as Harvard, Bowdoin, Brown, Dartmouth, Middlebury, Williams, and Andover, committed themselves to prayer for their fellow students who were typically profligate, and as a result considerable numbers were powerfully converted. When, in 1795, Timothy Dwight took on the presidency of Yale College, as it then was, the college was notorious for its profligacy. Dwight invited the students to freely attack the truth of the Scriptures and to ask him any question that they desired about the Scriptures, or about theology, and in chapel he would answer their questions. He began a sermon series simply called *Lectures in Systematic Theology*, which prompted several students to seek to improve the moral conditions of the college.[30] A substantial number of the students each year were converted but the powerful awakening finally came in 1802 when a full half of the student body made a profession of faith in Christ. Further revivals came in 1808, 1813, and 1815 resulting in the majority of the students being soundly converted to Christ and many entering the Christian ministry.

Some who transferred from Yale to other colleges took the revival with them; a few transferred because they did not want to be converted. One group of five students, who were members of the filthy speech movement, transferred to Amherst College because they did not want to be caught by the revival. When asked at Amherst why they had transferred, they told of what was occurring at Yale. Their account made such an impact upon their fellow students that their hearers fell under the convicting power of the Holy Spirit and were soundly converted to God. Then they began to pray for the five from Yale who had transferred in. There was nowhere else to transfer to and so they ended up becoming converted to Christ. Even unbelievers prompted spiritual awakening because God was moving. The same could be told of Andover, Princeton, Washington, and other university colleges, through the study of theology, which was the chief means of spiritual awakening of young people of the student age group. Through the theological lectures of Dwight, the Great Awakening of 1800 was sparked at Yale College, and spread throughout the college campuses.[31]

New colleges were founded in the general area that continued to represent the evangelical faith; new seminaries were established in Hartford, Connecticut, not far from the Massachusetts border, and in Andover, that were to provide the need for a converted pastorate. For the next fifty years student awakenings became the norm along the eastern seaboard. The Spirit of God was moving in power and reaching young people.

The Missionary Movement. Arising from this general period of revival among the colleges and universities was a ministry that was to have worldwide repercussions. Among those who were touched was a group of students at Williams College. They formed the Confidential Society, recording their activity in code, because many in the college were opposed to their evangelical fervor. One summer afternoon, five of these students were out in a maple grove, meeting for prayer, when a thunderstorm came through. Fleeing to a nearby farm, they burrowed their way into a haystack and in the sticky warmth there continued their prayer meeting. One of the young men, Samuel Mills (1783–1818), had fled the revivals in Connecticut to Williams College, trying to escape the revival fervor, but there had come under spiritual conviction and been soundly converted. As they were praying for the needs of the lost, Mills had a revelation that God would evangelize the world through their ministry if they were willing, and together they resolved: "We can evangelize the world if we are willing." This "Haystack Compact" was the beginning of the American missionary enterprise.[32] In 1810 at Andover he and his friends went to the home of an interested professor to see if it was possible for the American churches to sponsor foreign missions themselves, which meeting prompted the formation of the American Board of Commissioners for Foreign Missions.

From that group of students Adoniram Judson (1788–1850) was the first one to go forth, initially under the auspices of the London Missionary Society. In 1812, the Judsons set sail for India and began the work of evangelism in that nation. Sadly, their reception in India was not good and so they traveled on to Burma, beginning a lifelong missionary work there. This marked the beginning of the great inroads that were to be made into the rest of the world by American missionaries. In quick succession missionary societies were formed in all the denominations in the United States of America. By the middle of the nineteenth century, American missionaries were active on most of the continents of the world and were being powerfully used by God to reach the unevangelized. This awakening then provided a powerful and lasting impetus to modern foreign missions.

The Western States. Beyond that was the revival that was taking place in the western states. The move of God's Spirit in the eastern states had caused a great ingathering into the church but west of the Allegheny Mountains the population was largely beyond the reach of the traditional churches. Many, who were converted in the East, went over the mountains and established farms in the west between the Allegheny Mountains and the Ohio River, the area comprising the modern states of Ohio, Indiana, Kentucky, Tennessee, and Mississippi. The small cells of Christian witness they established there were preyed upon by the criminals, ruffians, and rogues of the East who had also fled westward to escape the just punishment of their crimes and established refuges in the same region.

Peter Cartwright, one of the Methodist circuit riders, described the situation in Kentucky in the area around Logan County:

Logan County, when my father moved into it, was called "Rogue's Harbor." Here many refugees from all parts of the Union fled to escape punishment or justice; for although there was law, it could not be executed, and it was a desperate state of society. Murderers, horse thieves, highway robbers and counterfeiters fled there, until they combined and actually formed a majority. Those who favored a better state of morals were called "Regulators." But they encountered fierce opposition from the "Rogues," and a battle was fought with guns, pistols, dirks, knives, and clubs, in which battle the Regulators were defeated and the Rogues established their authority over the whole county. Any man's wife was fair game for the Rogues. Any man's property was fair game. The Rogues would go in and hold up the decent folks and take off their wives and daughters, confiscate their property because there was no effective law in that whole area.[33]

One man, who had been involved in several revivals in North Carolina in the late 1780s and early 1790s, was James McGready (1763–1817), a Presbyterian preacher. Unfortunately, he was described as a man whose "appearance was unprepossessing, his voice tremulous and coarse, his gestures uncouth, and his manner inelegant."[34] Some described him as so ugly that he attracted attention on the street. Among the genteel inhabitants of North Carolina, apart from the times when the Spirit of God was moving powerfully, his ministry was not widely accepted or effective. He decided to go west and establish a ministry among people who would not find his appearance such a deterrent. So, he went, or was sent, to Rogue's Harbor, Logan County, in Kentucky, where it was felt he could do little harm. He accepted the pastorate in 1796 of three small Kentucky churches, with a combined membership of less than a hundred believers. Intensely committed to the concert of prayer, he signed up those believers to guarantee to spend at least thirty minutes every day in prayer for an outpouring of God's Spirit. After three years, God began to move. McGready called the three churches to a united communion service at a place called Red River, during which the Spirit of God moved in great power. The most bold and daring sinners, who dared to attend that meeting, were reduced to tearful conviction. He decided to have another one in August and again the Spirit of God moved. The winter of 1799 was spent in weeping and mourning, and seeking God in fasting and prayer. They decided that during the summer of 1800, they would have not just a communion service, but also a time for preaching and for ministering the Word of God. In July of 1800, families of settlers came together for a great camp meeting, the very first such meeting to be held in the United States of America.

Barton Stone (1772–1844), another Presbyterian minister, decided to observe what was going on in this meeting. He reported:

> The scene was new to me and passing strange. It baffled description. Many, very many, fell down as men slain in battle and continued for hours together in an apparently breathless and motionless state, sometimes for a few minutes reviving and exhibiting symptoms of life by a deep groan or a piercing shriek, or by a prayer for mercy, fervently uttered. After lying there for hours, they obtained deliverance. The gloomy cloud that had covered their faces seemed gradually and visibly to disappear, and hope in smiles brightened into joy. They would rise shouting deliverance, and then would address the surrounding multitudes in language truly eloquent and impressive. With astonishment did I hear men, women and children declaring the wonderful works of God and the glorious mysteries of the Gospel.[35]

A great move of God took place, but the climax of the revival was not to come until the next year at Cane Ridge, Kentucky, when in August a camp meeting was called and, according to the militia that was brought out to control the crowd, at least 25,000 people assembled for it. Just five years before, when McGready went to that area, there were three churches amounting to less than a hundred believers, and now 25,000 people gathered in Cane Ridge for the greatest camp meeting of them all. Five ministers simultaneously preached to the crowd in different parts of the encampment. The way they arranged the camp was in the form of a circle. The center was cleared, and round the edge of the circle they cut down pairs of trees, one just a few inches above the ground and one about chest high with a slight slope to it. The preacher would then stand on the smaller stump and put his Bible on the taller stump and proceed to address the crowd. Each of the preachers looked inward, and the people all gathered in the center clearing. When each man had finished his sermon and those, who had fallen down under conviction, had been carried out and laid in the woods outside of the circle, another preacher would take over the preaching, followed by another in turn. There were usually about five preaching simultaneously. Each of them had a crowd of approximately 5,000 looking in his direction. If a person heard another preacher that he liked the sound of better than the one he was listening to, he worked his way through the crowd until he was facing him and could hear his sermon better. The congregation simply stood or sat there as the Spirit of God swept across the whole group, bringing people to Christ and transforming lives.

Leonard Woolsey Bacon, the historian, said that the people who assembled were sober and cautious, not enthusiastic or weakly credulous. Many suffered prostration, or physical collapse, under the power of the Spirit of God and under a sense of great conviction. Some, as conviction fell upon them, would hold on to tree trunks and saplings trembling under the power of the Spirit of God as they attempted to resist. This gave rise to mocking stories of people "treeing the Devil," or barking like dogs, most of which were distortions propagated by later critics of revival.[36]

Dr. John Boles concluded: "These grossly exaggerated revival exercises, which have been cited widely to discredit the revival, were probably restricted to a comparative few. . . . Except at the very start, they were never a significant factor in the camp meetings."[37] In 1803 during the Presbyterian Church's Kentucky synod in Lexington some had raised the question of the rumored excesses at the camp meetings and proposed a motion of censure. David Rice responded:

Is it worse to be repenting, forsaking sin, flying from the wrath to come, crying for mercy, hearing sermons, praying and singing praises to God and even spending whole days and nights at these things? Is it worse to be doing that than to be involved in debauchery, cursing and swearing, drinking and reveling, gaming and cheating, quarreling and fighting or even fiddling and dancing? Which is worse?[38]

The attempted motion of censure was lost and the Presbyterian Church wholeheartedly supported the work, which quickly spread across the state and throughout the Baptist and Methodist denominations also. Years later, George Baxter recorded:

On my way, I was informed by settlers on the road that the character of Kentucky was entirely changed, and that they were as remarkable for sobriety as they formerly had been for dissoluteness and immorality. And indeed I found Kentucky to appearances the most moral place I had ever seen. A profane expression was hardly ever heard. A religious awe seemed to pervade the country. Upon the whole, I think the revival in Kentucky the most extraordinary that has ever visited the church of Christ.[39]

God did a great work in turning that whole area around. What was said about Kentucky to a large extent characterized the American frontier. Names can be multiplied but the fact is that God was moving, bringing about a great revival. Voltaire's boast that Christianity would be forgotten within a century was certainly not going to come true. If anything, it would be Voltaire's teachings that would be forgotten within the century and his home was later acquired by the Bible Society in France and became their headquarters for printing and promoting the Bible and Christian literature throughout the French speaking world.

Endnotes

1 J. A. De Jong: art. "Expansion World-wide" in *Eerdmans' Handbook*, 476.

2 K. S. Latourette: *History of the Expansion*, IV, 4.

3 Ibid.

4 J. E. Orr: *The Eager Feet: Evangelical Awakenings, 1790–1830* (Chicago: Moody, 1975), 8.

5 Quoted in K. J. Hardman: *Seasons of Refreshing* (Eugene, OR: Wipf & Stock, 1994), 106.

6 Orr, op. cit., 8.

7 Quoted in Orr, ibid., 9.

8 Ibid., 9.

9 Ibid., 10.

10 Hardman, op. cit., 107.

11 W. W. Sweet: *The Story of Religion in America* (New York, NY: Harper & Row, 1950 edn.),153–154.

12 Ibid.,120.

13 H. Skilton: art "Alline Henry" in NIDCC, 29.

14 Orr, op. cit., 52.

15 Ibid.,16.

16 Ibid., 90, 91.

17 J. Crowther: *The History of the Wesleyan Methodists* (London, UK: Edwards, 1814), 168.

18 Orr, op. cit., 24.

19 Ibid., 29.

20 Ibid., 33.

21 R. E. Davies: *I Will Pour Out My Spirit* (Tunbridge Wells, UK: Monarch, 1992), 117.

22 Orr, op. cit., 40–45.

23 Quoted in Orr, ibid., 47.

24 Ibid., 47, 48.

25 Ibid., 49.

26 Ibid., 54.

27 Ibid., 56, 57.

28 Crowther, op. cit., 168.

29 J. E. Orr: *Campus Aflame* (Glendale, CA: Regal, 1971), 25.

30 Hardman, op. cit., 113.

31 Orr, op. cit., 25–28.

32 Orr, *Eager Feet*, op. cit., 94.

33 P. Cartwright, C.L. Wallis (ed.): *The Autobiography of Peter Cartwright*, (Nashville, TN: Abingdon, 1956), 5.

34 Orr, op. cit., 60.

35 Quoted in Orr, ibid., 61.

36 Ibid., 229.

37 Quoted in Orr, ibid., 62.

38 Ibid., 62.

39 Ibid., 63.

Part IV

Late Evangelical
Awakenings

Chapter 15

Adventist Awakenings

1835–1845

This period of evangelical awakenings in the USA lasted from about 1825 to 1842. Dr. Edwin Orr in his book *The Eager Feet: Evangelical Awakenings 1790 to 1830*[1] treats this as part of the earlier Second Great Awakening, which began at the end of the eighteenth century, and he divided into three phases: 1795–1810, 1810–1825, and finally, 1825–1835. In many parts of the world the revival did not totally stop in 1810 and then a new revival began in 1825, when the cycle repeated itself, but rather there was a diminishing, followed by a resurgence, when the full flood of revival returned the way that it had been earlier. There were, however, features in this time period that warrant it being treated separately. Many aspects of this revival were similar to the earlier revivals, but also some amazing things began to happen that would have lasting repercussions.

God in the earlier phases of the awakening was setting the scene for what he was going to do during this climactic and remarkable time. Earlier revivals prompted practices which subsequently became a regular feature of spiritual life in the evangelical churches, for example, during the Puritan and the early part of the Great Awakening revivals it was not customary to have evening church services. Normally church services were held on Sunday mornings and throughout the rest of the week there were no organized services. Among the Puritans there was a strong emphasis on the family altar, and family-oriented ministry filled the remainder of the week. The Wesleyan Methodists adopted the Pietistic practice of having class meetings. Small groups would meet at different times during the week so that the preacher or the leaders could relate more effectively to the members, since, when thousands of people are thronging the church, it is difficult to do so.

In the twentieth century, Sunday night and midweek services were virtually synonymous with evangelicalism, but they did not really become part of evangelicalism until Charles G. Finney (1792–1875), taking advantage of the development of street and home lighting systems, began such meetings. Furthermore, in the wintertime the conducting of evening services could be very dangerous, as in cities, in the days before street lighting, thieves and robbers could lurk in dark passageways, or in the doorways of houses waiting for the unsuspecting traveler, and even country roads were threatened by brigands and highwaymen. In the camp meetings of the Second Great Awakening, however, services were held in the evenings and not just on a Sunday morning, because the camp meetings usually took place in the summertime when the longer daylight hours made evening meetings more feasible.

Finney also promoted "the anxious seat" or "altar call" as part of evangelical church practices. Many churches are now constructed with a whole altar area in front of the pulpit indicating an intention to continue the same pattern popularized in the early nineteenth-century revivals. It is not surprising that people from other cultures do not have an altar area, not because they do not believe in altar calls, or in invitations or challenges going out to the congregation, but because they did not have the same history in this area so as to make it part of their culture. The practice may not be specifically biblical, although not incompatible with the Bible, and cultures where the altar call is not practiced, are not indicative of a church that is out of line with Scripture or with biblical practice.

It is not surprising that many features of this revival have already been encountered in other areas and things that once were not present within Christianity by this time have become normal. Also, this revival in fact covered more of the world's population than any previous revival. Virtually every place where Christianity was located was affected by the revival, so extensive were its dimensions. In fact, each successive revival from the Great Awakening onward was more widespread in its impact than the previous one.

Famous names of great preachers, like Daniel Baker, Charles Finney, William Miller, Asahel Nettleton, Lyman Beecher and his son, Henry Ward Beecher, all belong to this revival period in the United States of America. In Scandinavia George Scott and Carl Olof Rosenius were greatly used by God. In Britain, from Scotland, W. C. Burns, Thomas Chalmers (1780–1847), Robert Murray McCheyne, and Edward Irving, the founder of the Irvingite Catholic Apostolic Church, who had considerable influence in London; among the Wesleyan Methodists in England, James Caughey (1810–1891), the Irish-American; in Dublin, John Nelson Darby (1800–1882), the originator of the Plymouth Brethren (Christian Brethren) movement. Under the ministry of the father of the famous Bronte family, Patrick Bronte (1777–1861) a notable move of God took place in Haworth, Yorkshire, bringing many to Christ.

Europe. With the downfall of the Napoleonic empire, revival spread to the mainland of Europe from 1815 onwards. The main impetus for revival in much of Europe was the ministry of two Scottish revivalists, Robert (1764–1842) and James Haldane (1768–1851). Robert especially was extensively used by God in spreading the revival message throughout Europe. He had experienced a great touch from God through the ministry of people like Thomas Chalmers in Scotland and felt a great burden for Europe, that the continent generally should experience the kind of revival that was affecting Britain and Scandinavia. First, Robert made a visit to Germany, Switzerland, and France, and then, his brother James resigned from his ministry in Edinburgh and joined Robert in this powerful evangelistic outreach to Europe.

Alongside of the ministry of the Haldanes was the ministry of several German revivalists, whom God was pleased to use in a powerful way. George Mueller (1805–1898), renowned for his establishing of the Orphans' Homes in Bristol, England, and the Bethesda (Open) Brethren Assembly, was involved in revival in Germany before he emigrated to Britain, and later influenced several in the Dutch revival movement. But much more important for the revival movement in Germany was the ministry of Dr. Karl Friedrich Steinkopf (1773–1859), the pastor of the German church in London and one of the cofounders of the British and Foreign Bible Society, who, having been revived in London, decided to return to Germany and there to establish revival centers and organizations to promote revival and missions, including the German Bible Society and the Deutsche Christentumsgesellschaft (the German Christian Fellowship), which helped support the new London Missionary Society both financially and with workers.

Among those whom Steinkopf influenced was Baroness Barbara von Krudener (1764–1824) whose ministry, as a member of the nobility, had a powerful impact on the royal households of Europe, especially in Germany, throughout the Baltics, and into Russia. The kaiser of Germany attended the baroness's Bible classes. She led to Christ the queen of Prussia, the queen of Bavaria, the queen of Hanover (mother of Queen Victoria of England), the queen of Holland, and the queen of Sweden. She even went so far as to present the gospel of Christ to the Russian tsar and his family: Tsar Alexander I accepted Christ and opened the settlements of western Siberia for evangelization; Tsarina Elisabeth also accepted Christ and became a strong evangelical influence within the Russian Orthodox Church. Although she held her meetings among the rich in the noble palaces of Europe, she did not neglect the poor, but took the leftover food from the banquet halls of the wealthy to the poor and, while sharing the food with them, would testify of Christ. Wherever she went, however, she was harassed by opponents; yet until her death in 1824 she continued inspiring evangelists.

In Europe, France, Switzerland, and Holland, were all convulsed by the Spirit of God. *Le Reveil* movement from its beginning in Switzerland through the ministry of the Haldanes, began to affect a substantial part of the world. The West Indies were touched. Among the Pacific Islands, Tonga, Hawaii, and Fiji, all experienced great moves of God's Spirit in this same time period. Similarly, South Africa, Botswana, the Gold Coast, now known as Ghana, and Nigeria, all experienced the power of God, as the Spirit of God moved in Africa.

Around the Indian Ocean, India, Burma, and Ceylon, were all touched by the Spirit of God. Madagascar experienced a great revival that lasted for two years and resulted in an immense persecution of the Christians, who were slaughtered by the hundreds, and all the missionaries were expelled. Even though the Christians experienced such intense persecution, there was a continuing Christian presence because as they were killed so more seemed to emerge and the work of God continued. Even Indonesia, on the eastern edge of the ocean, experienced a revival, among the Dutch settlements in that country.

This revival was probably the most widespread up to that time; never since the day of Pentecost had so much of the Christian church been affected by revivals. The only reason the day of Pentecost affected a larger percentage of the Christian church was that the only Christian church in existence was there in Jerusalem and it in total experienced revival.

The intensity of the revival is well illustrated by the ministry of the American evangelist **Charles Grandison Finney**, whose name is strongly linked with the awakening. Charles Finney was raised in New England; his early life in western New York and Connecticut, among the pioneer families of that area was quite typical for children of his age. He early decided that he did not wish to become a farmer and so at the age of sixteen secured a job teaching school for four years from 1808 to 1812 in Warren, Connecticut, out in the wilds. The Second Great Awakening completely bypassed that area, leaving him unaffected during his youth. Although he returned to high school in 1812 to complete his education and he had proposed to go on to Yale, he decided against it, feeling that it would be easier to educate himself and less expensive. He continued teaching school in New Jersey for two more years and then began to look for new horizons. His decision in 1818 to study law took him to Adams, in western New York, where he joined the law firm of Judge Benjamin Wright and became an attorney under the judge's supervision.[2]

His goal was to make his fortune and live in affluence. He said of himself: "I was almost as ignorant of religion as a heathen. I'd been brought up mostly in the woods. I had little regard for the sabbath and no definite knowledge of religious truth."[3] However, when he moved to Adams, he discovered that not only was much of American law based upon scriptural teaching but also in this larger town almost everybody went to church. If he did not go to church, then he would not be accepted, and he was concerned to be accepted. So, he began attending the Presbyterian Church, pastored by George W. Gale (1789–1861). As Finney was an accomplished musician, he was asked to become the choir leader at the church, despite his acknowledged ignorance of religion in general, and Christianity in particular. That was no barrier to his serving as the choir director.

After his admission to the bar as a lawyer he established a solid law practice. However, in his association with the Presbyterian Church he came into a degree of conflict with Pastor Gale, a hyper-Calvinist. Finney said that Gale could never preach that people must repent without making sure that they understood that they could not repent. He could never call upon them to believe without being sure to inform them that unless they were born again by the Holy Spirit, they could not exercise faith. He was determined to be perfectly orthodox in his Calvinism. The result was that people did not repent, nor believe, and his church was as full of heathens as Finney himself was.

As Finney read the Scriptures, he became more and more uncomfortable, and finally he realized that he had to face up to eternal verities. Therefore, on Sunday night, October 6, 1821, he resolved that he would give special consideration to spiritual matters, as he described it, and try to settle the question of his soul's salvation once and for all. Going out into the woods, he determined that he would not leave that spot until God had revealed the truth to him. The following day, Monday, October 7, he had a lifechanging encounter with God in the woods. But complete release did not come until the Wednesday evening. After the day's business he closed his office and he said: "There was no fire and no light in the room, nevertheless it appeared to me as if it were perfectly light. As I went in and shut the door after me it seemed as if I met the Lord Jesus Christ face to face."[4] He was broken down at the feet of the Master.

Later that evening, he experienced what he described as his baptism of the Holy Spirit:

> I received a mighty baptism of the Holy Ghost. Without any expectation of it, without ever having the thought in my mind that there was any such a thing for me, without any recollection that I had ever heard the thing mentioned by any person in the world, the Holy Spirit descended upon me in a manner that seemed to go through me, body and soul. No words can express the wonderful love that was shed abroad in my heart. I wept aloud with joy and love; and I do not know, but I should say, I literally bellowed out the unutterable gushings of my heart. These waves came over me, and over me, and over me, one after another, until I recollect I cried out, "I shall die if these waves continue to pass over me." I said, "Lord, I cannot bear any more;" and yet I had no fear of death.[5]

That night a member of the choir came by Finney's office to talk of some choir business and found Finney weeping loudly. He asked if he was in pain or greatly troubled over something. Finney said: "No, but so happy that I cannot live." He immediately left and returned with one of the church elders, a dour older man, who, on hearing Finney's testimony, burst into laughter. His account was interrupted again by the visit of a young man, with whom Finney had been conversing about religion. On overhearing part of the testimony, he was so astonished that he fell on his knees, saying: "Do pray for me!" whereupon the elder, the choir member and Finney each prayed, leading the young man to faith in Christ.

The next morning, he shared his testimony with Judge Wright, leading him to faith in Christ also. Shortly afterward, a deacon from the church came to remind him that he was his attorney for a lawsuit to tried at ten o'clock that morning, to which Finney responded: "Deacon B___, I have a retainer from the Lord Jesus Christ to plead His cause and I cannot plead yours." He recommended that he engage another attorney. The deacon was so impressed with the change in this worldly and sophisticated young man that he decided to settle his lawsuit out of court and seek what Finney had for himself.[6] Finney seemingly knew from the outset that he would be called to some kind of preaching ministry. Despite his earlier reluctance to ever leave his legal profession, after receiving this baptism of the Spirit, Finney noted:

> I was quite willing to preach the Gospel. Nay, I found that I was unwilling to do anything else. I had no disposition to make money. I had no hungering and thirsting after worldly pleasures and amusement in any direction. My whole mind was taken up with Jesus and His salvation.[7]

With this great sense of mission, he went out and began to witness, sharing the gospel of Christ with all that he could meet. That first full day of his salvation he said, "I spoke with many persons that day, and I believe the Spirit of God made lasting impressions upon every one of them. I cannot remember one whom I spoke with, who was not soon after converted."[8] The news of his conversion spread. That evening the whole town was drawn to the Presbyterian Church, including the preacher, George Gale, although no service or gathering had been announced. Finney described how a mysterious hush gripped the crowd, filling the church and waiting to see what would happen. There was no program for opening the service as they waited in the presence of God. Then as one man the whole congregation looked in Finney's direction and he shared his testimony of what God had done in his life. He declared that religion, true religion, came from God alone, and was for everybody who would believe the promises.

Some considered that Finney had become mentally unhinged; others believing his testimony, were converted. Pastor Gale arose and confessed that he had discouraged the praying people of the church from praying for Finney because he saw no hope for Finney's salvation. He acknowledged that when he first heard of what had happened, he could not believe it, thinking that it was just Finney making fun of them. Then he asked Finney to lead out in public prayer for the salvation of the whole congregation, and one after another fell under conviction and was powerfully converted to Christ.

The next day, Gale had scheduled Finney, as the choir leader, to meet with the young people to talk to them about choir activities, but instead of talking about choir activities, he talked about the Lord, and was able to lead most of those young people to commit their lives to Christ. Only one young person in that group remained unconverted by the end of that meeting. Word spread throughout the whole village so that for more than a week, Finney recounted: "I didn't feel at all inclined to sleep or eat, I seemed to spend all day and all night talking to those who did not know Christ and sharing with them the glad news of salvation."

Returning to his parents' home in Henderson, he testified to them and to his friends from earlier days. Although Finney had never previously heard a prayer offered in his home, his father, Sylvester, bowed his head and asked him to lead in a prayer. There and then both father and mother were converted to Christ. For three days Finney stayed there as revival began to pulsate through the whole area.

Convinced that he should offer himself for ministry, Finney contacted the Presbyterian Church leadership and was appointed under the supervision of Mr. Gale, the hyper-Calvinist. Despite his disagreements with Gale over the interpretation of Scripture, the possibility of salvation for all, and the extent of the Holy Spirit's work, when a Universalist came to the town of Adams while Gale was sick, he asked Finney to go and repudiate his teachings, which Finney did.[9] As a result, those who had been influenced by the Universalist returned to the Christian faith and became soundly converted, including the Universalist himself. Gale was so impressed that he recommended to the St. Lawrence Presbytery that Finney should be licensed as a minister within the Presbyterian Church, despite his theological differences over Calvinism. In March 1824, Finney was licensed to preach and was appointed as the full-time missionary to the towns of Evans Mills and Antwerp in western New York under the auspices of the Female Missionary Society for the Western District of the State of New York, a missionary society among the Presbyterians that was supported by a women's organization.

Before Finney's appointment, the Baptist and Congregational churches in Evans's Mills, who shared the local schoolhouse, had been earnestly seeking the Lord for revival. From the beginning of his ministry there Finney realized that God was going to do something in that community, and within a few weeks their prayers were answered. He said:

> The Spirit of God came upon me with such power it was like opening a battery upon them. For more than an hour the Word of God came through me to them in a manner I could see was carrying all before it. It was a fire and a hammer, breaking the rock, and as the sword that was piercing to the dividing asunder of soul and spirit. I saw that a general conviction was spreading over the whole congregation.[10]

From there he went on to a community of Germans quite close to the city. They had a regular service once a year when the German pastor would visit them. Finney's ministry was so effective that not only was the whole church converted to Christ, but almost the whole town was converted.

Unfortunately, the situation in Antwerp was very different, earning the place the nickname "Sodom" locally. The enmity against other preachers by the dominant Universalists was so great that they even took the wheels off the preachers' carriages. By the year 1823 no preacher was willing to come and there had been no actual or even attempted religious services in that place for over a year. When Finney arrived there, he discovered that profanity was commonplace and the few remaining Christians were fearful for their lives should anyone attempt to begin religious services. Despite the threats, Finney began services, first in the hotel drawing room, then in the schoolhouse, and finally the long-closed Presbyterian Church was reopened. Revival had come.[11]

In October 1824, Finney returned to Adams to receive ordination and as an ordained man to marry Miss Lydia Andrews from Adams Presbyterian Church. A few days later, he returned to Evans Mills to find a house, and borrow a wagon to transport their household goods there, promising to return in a week. On his arrival in Evans Mills, he was met by a delegation from Perch River where he had preached immediately before returning to

Adams, informing him that his earlier ministry had precipitated revival, and imploring him to return. His promised one service became three and the revival spread to Brownville, where he decided to spend the winter promoting revival and supervising the spiritual awakening.[12]

In the early spring of 1825, he finally set out for Adams to bring his patiently waiting new wife and their household goods back to Evans's Mills. On the way he stopped at Le Rayville to have his horse shod. When some of the people learned that Finney was there, they came to the blacksmith shop and prevailed upon him to preach for them that day at 1:00 p.m. The schoolhouse was packed and as he preached, "the Spirit of God came down with great power." After preaching again that evening and throughout the next day, he realized that his wife was still awaiting him. So, he sent one of the converts to pick up his wife, while he "went on preaching, and there was a powerful revival."[13] After a lengthy stay in Le Rayville he went on to Gouverneur and from there to DeKalb, where there were further manifestations of revival.

The main outburst of the revival did not come, however, until October of 1825 in the city of Western, New York. At that time the eastern newspapers began to carry reprints of the revival reports from upstate New York and evidences of revival began to emerge across the eastern seaboard and even inland into some of the frontier towns west of New York, Ohio, and Indiana. It was obvious that God was doing something. The main focus of the reports was of course on Finney himself. Mr. Gale, his former pastor and tutor, had retired to Western, New York, in 1824. Finney's visit there in 1825 transformed Gale from a life-long hyper Calvinist into an ardent revivalist. Seeing the evidence of what God was doing had such an impact upon his life that Gale joined the new Oneida Evangelistic Band, the group of revivalists that followed in the footsteps of Finney and even went out in their own revival ministry. Gale began a new lease on his own personal ministry at that point from Western to Rome, New York. Finney reported on the revival in Rome:

> The town was full of prayer. Go whither you would, you heard the voice of prayer. Wherever there was a sinner unconverted, especially

if he manifested opposition you find two or three brethren or sisters agreeing to make him a particular subject of prayer.[14]

Incredible results were arising from Finney's ministry and from the general attitude of prayer that was spreading. The Oneida Presbytery began to take a dubious view of Finney's "New Measures," and so those who were revivalistic in their orientation formed their own fellowship, the Oneida Revival Fellowship, and with that accountability one to another, the work spread in a remarkable way and they were able to continue this ministry.

What were these "**New Measures**" that Finney introduced into revivalism that were the cause of so much opposition? The first new measure that created problems for Finney and his associates was his practice of having **protracted meetings**. As noted at the outset, it was not the common practice in those days to have services in evenings and services extended beyond an hour and a half were considered to be unusual except for the summer camp meetings.

A second factor that was considered problematic was Finney's **communitywide visitation of homes**. The Puritan pastors had made the practice of regularly visiting the homes of the members of the flock. Finney, however, did not limit it to the members of the flock, but he extended his visitation practice to include evangelistic visitation, following the apostolic model as described in Acts 5:42: "Day after day, in the temple courts and from house to house, they never stopped teaching and proclaiming the good news that Jesus is the Messiah." His visiting of every home in the whole community declaring the gospel of Christ to all who would admit him did not sit well with some of the organized clergy in the town, especially those who were not sympathetic to the revival.

A third element was **the use of prayer and testimonies by women**. In times of revival in the past women had been moved upon to lead out in prayer or in Bible times, even prophesy in public. Finney did not just permit it, he encouraged it, contrary to the custom of the time.

Fourth, the practice of **praying for people by name**. At Adams Presbyterian Church George Gale confessed that he had discouraged the church prayer group from praying for Finney by name because he doubted that

Finney would ever be saved. In fact, they did continue praying for Finney and Finney was saved. Finney felt that if it could happen to him, it could happen to anybody; therefore, he actively encouraged people to pray for the unconverted by name, and they were saved, as in the revival in Rome, New York, where any sinner was liable to be prayed for individually and by name. In many instances they were brought to a real knowledge of Christ. This practice was one that arose spontaneously in revival but by Finney and his followers ultimately became institutionalized as a normal pattern.

Fifth, his use of **the Anxious Seat**. In the initial phase of the revival at the beginning of the century, an altar area was cleared where those who fell under conviction could be placed in order to receive ministration, or they could come forward voluntarily and spontaneously. Subsequently, it became a regular feature in the evangelical church to have such a cleared area immediately in front of the pulpit into which those under conviction could move for ministry. Finney went a step further and encouraged people to come anyway, believing that conviction would fall upon them if they did so. The linking of the altar area with the invitation or challenge marked a new development in evangelical ministry and Finney's novelty of "the Altar Call" become standard procedure in many fellowships.

Probably the biggest problem that they had with Finney was **the use of common language**. There was great reservation over the fact that Finney addressed people in language that they could understand. He broke the canons of homiletical construction for his sermons. He used blunt and plain language, but without profanity, ofttimes intended to shock people into listening and paying heed to what he had to say. His language was not the language of the educated, though he was an educated man; nor the language of the theologian, although he did write his own very effective lectures on systematic theology; nor the language of the clergy, although he was an ordained clergyman. He used the language of the courtroom, the language of the lawyer, seeking to persuade, not a learned judge, but a panel of jurors to influence them to make the right decision, as the lawyer sees it.

The last of Finney's new measures was **unseasonable hours for meetings**. Late at night, when the day's work was done Finney would call a meeting. Early in the morning, before the day's work was begun, Finney called a meeting. During the day Finney would go and hold meetings during the lunch break. He went wherever he could get a crowd, and preached. Although some thought that inappropriate, to Finney wherever there were hungry hearts there was a responsibility to proclaim the Word of God.

From rural New York state, by 1828, his influence spread down to Wilmington, Delaware, where there was a great revival early that year, finally reaching Philadelphia, which was known as the "dead center" of Presbyterianism in the United States of America. There appeared to be little spiritual life in that whole city and when Finney arrived there, the only two churches open to him were those led by Dr. James Wilson and Thomas Skinner, who were among the most influential ministers in the Presbyterian Church. From the revival meetings held in both those churches a great awakening spread throughout the Presbyterian churches and beyond into the German church, the largest church in the city. This church had not been touched by any previous awakening, so when Finney requested permission to hold services there, all denominations were invited to attend, more in the style of the united campaign popularized by evangelists like D. L. Moody, Billy Sunday, and Billy Graham. The result was that for the next year and a half, meetings continued in the German church, which would seat three thousand, every night of the week, except Saturday, until the majority of the population of Philadelphia had been brought to Christ. The "dead center" of Presbyterianism had come alive with the gospel of Christ. That was not simply evangelism, but evangelism arising out of the moving of the Spirit of revival in the whole community, which drew people together to hear the gospel and to make the response that only the Holy Spirit can bring about.

From Philadelphia, Finney moved on to New York City, which many believed would be the graveyard of Finney's revivalism, but it was not so. In the fall of 1829, Anson Phelps, the renowned preacher, invited Finney to come to New York City, following his Philadelphia meetings. For the first three months meetings were held in a vacant church on Van Devanter Street, until it became obvious that what was happening needed a larger location, and so the old Universalist Church on Prince Street was purchased to be a permanent revival center in New York. The meetings there continued for the next eight months, producing considerable results. First, Finney decided to organize **a church** for those who did not have a church home. The population of New York City was so great that if everyone wanted to attend church, all the churches in the city would not hold the number of people, yet there were empty churches around. Finney determined that this empty church building that they were using would become a new church, the First Free Presbyterian Church, and Joel Parker became its pastor.

The church was unusual in that the pews were rent free. Customarily, in the Presbyterian Church families purchased or rented pews, which were reserved exclusively for the family's use either for the duration of their rental or if they had purchased the pew, for succeeding generations. There were usually a few free pews available for those visiting the church or without pews of their own. As most of the pews were owned by specific families, when revival came, if the pew-holders stayed away, there would be empty pews in the church, while the majority of the attendees had to stand at the back or in the aisles, unable to use the locked pews. In the Free Presbyterian Church, any seat was available to any person visiting the church.

The second product of this move in New York was **the establishment of the magazine *The New York Evangelist*** which was devoted to propagating not only testimonies about the revival, but also revival theology throughout the United States of America. It became the voice of Finney's revivalism, and the reading of this magazine often inspired people to pray and seek God for revival in their community.

In the fall of 1830, Finney received urgent requests to come to Rochester, New York. Revival had already begun in Rochester. Joel Parker was from there and had experienced a great revival in his church, but having now come to New York City, it looked as though the revival in Rochester was about to end, until Finney himself decided to go to Rochester to add fuel to the fire that Parker's ministry had begun. During that meeting a godly businessman who owned a local weaving factory invited Finney to visit the factory and hold lunchtime services for the workers. As Finney entered the factory, so the story goes, a young lady who had attended some of Finney's meetings in the city made a rather careless remark to her companion. Finney was not certain that he heard what she said but turned and looked at her. She became so embarrassed that she broke the thread on her machine and fumblingly tried to repair it. In her embarrassment everything began to go wrong, and so Finney came over and spoke to her words of encouragement and even kindness, whereupon she broke into tears and repented of her disparaging remarks. As a result, a spirit of revival swept across the factory and work ended for lunch early that day as the whole factory turned to God.

Some accounts of the incident claim that the factory owner was converted as a result of, or *in* that prayer meeting; however, he was already a born-again revival-oriented member of Joel Parker's old church, having been converted and set on fire for God long before Finney ever arrived on the scene. It was at his request that Finney came to the factory in the first place. Certainly, the revival spread even more effectively from that invitation, and Finney's six-month ministry there established his reputation as a national revivalist.

Finney's revival, as it has come to be called, from the 1830s and 1840s, is really a misnomer. Because although the fame of what happened in Rochester and later in Boston in 1830, 1831, and 1832 spread, giving the impression that the revival was truly Finney's, Finney himself in his autobiography said the very fame of the work in Rochester was an efficient instrument in the hands of the Spirit of God in promoting the greatest revival of religion that this country had ever witnessed. Finney quoted Lyman Beecher as saying:

That was the greatest work of God and the greatest revival of religion that the world has ever seen in so short a time. 100,000 were reported as having connected themselves with churches as a result of that great revival. This is unparalleled in the history of the church and of the progress of religion.[15]

Although Finney did not directly apply Beecher's comments to his own ministry, he quoted it in context of his own ministry in such a way that some people got the impression that Finney was the only one being used and that the revival under Finney's leadership alone brought 100,000 people to Christ. In fact, the Rochester revival saw about 1,000 people come to Christ, and the work in Boston, a few more. Probably over fifty years of ministry Finney did see some 100,000 individuals come to Christ, but the revival was already underway before Finney ever got to Rochester, and was apparent under the ministry of many other people than Charles Finney. Finney was not the only one. In fact, the revival was burning powerfully in some areas where Finney never visited. For instance, in Kenyon College in Ohio, an Episcopalian institution, there was a great sweeping revival. Out of that college, fifty young people volunteered for the Christian ministry and went out as preachers.

At Union College in Schenectady were early-morning and late-evening prayer meetings and the Spirit of God fell upon those attending. Even in Yale the further revival there brought over fifty young people to Christ. In fact, it spread so radically that ultimately only 100 of the more than 350 students were left unconverted through that revival, and yet Finney never even visited Yale nor did he visit the New Haven area of Connecticut. It spread enormously, not only in the universities and colleges but also in Kentucky in the town of Glasgow, where in 1830 such a powerful revival swept through the town of about 5,500 that more than 1,500 people joined the Baptist churches, and every other church reported great increase. Revival was everywhere. There were tremendous outpourings of God's Spirit taking place. There was a general revival throughout Georgia. The Spirit of God moved in great power. The peak of the revival was not in New England where Finney was ministering but in Richmond, Virginia, where it crested in July of 1831.[16] Almost every person in the city came to Christ and experienced a life-changing transformation.

Not only among the white population but also among the African Americans the 1830 awakening had a tremendous impact. Among the Methodists in South Carolina there were only about 3,700 white Methodists in the beginning of the century, and about 1,000 African Americans. By the end of the earlier revival the figure had grown to about 14,000 white Methodists and about 5,000 black Methodists, a great but not disproportionate increase of black Methodists. But in the 1830s there were 24,000 white Methodists in South Carolina and 23,500 black Methodists. The proportion had transformed enormously and a powerful work was taking place among the black community of that area. Despite the oppression and slavery that they were in, the Spirit of God moved upon their hearts and they came in their thousands to Christ. God moved in tremendous power, and the origins of the former Abyssinian Methodist Episcopal Church, later the Ethiopian Methodist Episcopal Church, were in that revival. There was a growing outreach to the black community.

At this time also began the first Baptist outreaches to the black community. Up until that time, although the Methodists had made an attempt to evangelize the black community, initially unsuccessfully, but later very successful, the Baptists had made no attempt to evangelize the black community, and, in fact, were rather negative toward the African Americans; however, through this revival many became Baptists and they ultimately gave rise to their own Baptist churches. The Spirit of God was moving, despite the fact that Finney, for example, was very skeptical about the possibility of revival occurring in the southern states, since that would appear to give some kind of divine approval upon the institution of slavery. Sometimes, however, God blesses in spite of the culture, and his blessing leads to the transformation of a culture that is contrary to his will. Slavery in the Roman Empire underwent the same process. The apostle Paul did not attack slavery, or speak against it, but Christianity was inevitably going to undermine it and bring about a great transformation.

What brought that revival to an end? For almost ten years it moved in great power and effectiveness, but toward the end of the 1830s, there came to the fore a New England Baptist preacher, William Miller (1782–1849), a self-educated farmer, former deputy sheriff, and justice of the peace.[17] After a fourteen year-long personal study of the Scriptures Miller came to the conclusion that Christ was going to return in October of 1843, and in the context of the great revival meetings preached this. People began to turn to the Lord seeking to be ready for the return of Christ. When Miller told them that the hour was at hand, many left their homes and farmlands, even climbed the hills in order to get an advantage over other Christians, and waited, and nothing happened. Miller explained that he had made a slight miscalculation, it was not October of 1843, but 1844. When it still did not happen, many people became totally disillusioned with Miller and his followers. Tragically, it also killed the revival. Because Miller was a powerful revival preacher, people did not just dismiss the foolishness of attempting to calculate the date of the Lord's return, they also dismissed the authenticity of the revival, one of the dominant notes of which was the teaching about the second coming of Christ.

One of the precipitous events that had prepared the church for the fresh outburst of revival was the 1826 translation of the book by the exiled Chilean Jesuit, Manuel Lacunza (1731–1801), *The Coming of the Messiah In Glory and Majesty* out of the original Spanish. Lacunza is credited with being the modern-day reviver of the pre-Augustinian teaching of Chiliasm or premillennialism. Most of the earlier revivalists and biblical scholars had been postmillennialists, but Lacunza was the first in almost a millennium and a half to put in writing the concept of a premillennial return of Christ, which teaching was further refined later in the revival in 1830 when the pretribulation rapture was prophesied by a Scottish girl who was also involved in the revival. Her prophecy was accepted as authentic and ultimately affected the doctrines of many evangelical groups even to the present.

Among the followers of Miller were some who were not prepared to take the same course of action that Miller himself did. Miller repented publicly of his date-setting techniques and returned to the quietness of private life, ceased his preaching activity, and was restored to the Lord and became a godly member once again of the local Baptist church, no longer in a position of leadership. Some, however, were not prepared to admit their error, among whom was the Baptist Ellen G. White (1827–1915), who together with her husband, James, claimed to have received a revelation that Christ had in fact returned, not to earth, as Miller had mistakenly expected, but from the inner sanctuary in heaven with the blood of the atonement heralding the beginning of a new era of grace. Out of the teachings of White, her husband, and those associated with her, arose the Seventh Day Adventist movement, initially called the Seventh Day Baptists, because of her insistence that the reason the church had missed what God was doing was because they had abandoned obedience to the Sabbath day as the correct day for worship and only those who worshiped on the seventh day were going to meet the Lord and be part of the rulership of the millennial kingdom.

A further movement that arose out of Miller's error was the Jehovah's Witnesses. When some years later Charles Taze Russell encountered the Miller's teachings and his method of approaching the Scriptures, he was fascinated and remolded them to form initially the Bible Students' Association and ultimately the Bible and Watchtower Association, later renamed as it is known today, the Jehovah's Witnesses. This revival was one of the most blessed and yet ultimately one of the most confusing of all the revivals.

Britain. The growth was phenomenal, not just in America, but also in other countries, in Great Britain. This was the time when William Booth came to Christ and began his great open-air ministry that ultimately led to the founding of the Salvation Army. In Wales, both in the north and the south, sporadic periods of revival occurred over the next twenty years, bringing the majority of the population into a saving relationship with Christ.[18] Similarly, in Scotland through the ministry of Thomas Chalmers, the leader of the evangelical party in the Church of Scotland, the brothers John (1806?–1870?), Horatius (1808–1889), and Andrew Bonar (1810–1892) of Edinburgh; Robert M. McCheyne (1813–1843) in Dundee; and William C. Burns (1815–1868), under whose ministry the phenomenal Kilsyth revival came in 1839, and then burst forth again in Dundee. Despite the disruption of the Church of Scotland over government interference, the revival continued in great power.

The revival in Ireland was so great that they called it a second reformation and more than 50 percent of the Irish population were converted to Christ. In the 1830s, the Roman Catholics in Ireland were the minority and the evangelical believers were by far the majority because the Spirit of God was moving in such power. Tragically, the potato famine of the late 1830s resulted in the emigration of large numbers to the United States of America, and the higher birth rate among Roman Catholic church members within a generation had largely restored the earlier Catholic majority. It was in Ireland among the evangelicals in Dublin that the Christian Brethren movement was formed led by John Nelson Darby (1800–1882) and others.

Scandinavia. In Sweden, the ministry of George Scott (1804–1874) was extremely effective, until he, being a British Methodist, was expelled in 1842. Carl Olof Rosenius (1816–1868), who was converted under Scott's ministry, took up the work and revival spread throughout much of Sweden, giving birth to the Swedish Evangelical Covenant church, out of which came the Evangelical Covenant movement in America among the many Swedish immigrants. In Norway, France, and Switzerland, *La Reveil* continued in great power, even reaching as far as the Netherlands.

Hawaii. Probably the most remarkable revival at this time was the revival in Hawaii, in which Titus Coan (1801–1881), an associate of Finney, and Lorenzo Lyons (1807–1886) were so powerfully used. In one day in Hilo, Coan received 1,705 members by profession of faith into his church.[19] In one church alone, in Honolulu, 7,557 people came to Christ during the course of the revival. Hawaii turned from being a predominantly cannibalistic and pagan country into being a predominantly Christian country. Throughout Polynesia, Tonga, and Fiji, the Spirit of God moved in great power. Even in predominantly Muslim Indonesia the great revival swept through. In Minahassa, in the northeastern peninsula of Celebes Island, a folk movement of such proportions swept through that every person living on that peninsula came to Christ and not one person was discovered who had not had a personal born again experience. In South Africa, also, Robert Moffat (1795–1883), the great missionary pioneer, experienced great revival.

Around the world this was a period of awakening, which generally came to an end about 1842, when God seemingly withdrew the moving of his Spirit. The birth of the Evangelical Alliance in 1846 came about as an attempt to stay the erosion that was fast taking place among evangelicalism. By 1850, almost all the gains of the 1830s in the Western world had been lost. The widespread backsliding and renunciation of evangelical Christianity that followed the Millerite debacle, opened the door to the inroads of German higher criticism that developed almost as a consequence of the failure of the revival. Philosophers took over from preachers; higher critics took over from consecrated revivalists. It would take a further revival to restore evangelicalism in the western world.

Endnotes

1 J. E. Orr: *The Eager Feet: Evangelical Awakenings 1790–1830* (Chicago, IL: Moody, 1975).

2 C. G. Finney: *Charles G. Finney, An Autobiography* (London, UK: Salvation Army, 1882 edn.), 4–6.

3 Ibid., 6.

4 Ibid., 17.

5 Ibid., 17, 18.

6 Ibid., 21, 22.

7 Ibid., 22.

8 Ibid., 22.

9 Ibid., 42ff.

10 Ibid., 51ff.

11 Ibid., 79ff.

12 Ibid., 91ff.

13 Ibid., 93.

14 Ibid., 144.

15 Ibid., 253.

16 Orr, op. cit., 136.

17 Earle E. Cairns: art. "Miller, William" in NIDCC, op. cit., 660.

18 Orr, op. cit., 147.

19 Ibid., 164.

Chapter 16

Mid-19th Century Awakening

1845-1870

The revival that came in the middle of the nineteenth century in North America began early in 1857 and lasted until about 1861 when the Civil War broke out. Among the Union and the Confederate troops, however, there were instances of limited outpourings of the Spirit, despite the intensity of the conflict.[1] In other parts of the world, the revival proper did not start until about 1859 and continued much longer than in the United States of America.

Preparation for the Awakening. The situation in North America prior to the awakening was one of substantial religious decline affected by four major factors. First of all, there was **division over slavery**. The churches of the old mainline denominations during the 1840s and early 1850s split into the Methodist Church North and the Methodist Church South; the Presbyterian Church in the North and the Presbyterian Church in the South; the Northern Baptist Church and the Southern Baptist Conference. The Southern churches generally permitted slave holders to be members of the churches, whereas those in the North usually excluded them from membership or from participation in church activities. In many communities along the dividing line between the Northern and Southern states churches divided with part of the church joining the Northern segment of the denomination and the remainder linking up with the Southern segment, bringing conflict and preaching against those in the other group, which exacerbated the division between former fellow-Christians.

Second, there also was **a rising tide of disillusionment,** especially resulting from the debacle of Millerite Adventism. Those who had been awakened in the earlier revival of the 1820s and 1830s and had been caught up in the fervor surrounding the prophetic movement represented particularly by William Miller in the later 1830s and early 1840s, became very deeply disillusioned by the failure of Miller and other prophetic interpreters. The turning away from God became so widespread that in 1846 the evangelical churches formed an alliance partly in an attempt to halt the forsaking of the churches, and partly to check the rising influence of sectarian groups, such as the Seventh Day Adventists, the Church of Jesus Christ of Latter-Day Saints, and the Spiritists. Although it gave the evangelicals a united voice, the Evangelical Alliance had little success in stemming the flood out of the churches and by 1856 church attendance in the United States had decreased by more than 50 percent from just twenty years previous, despite the population increase of over 30 percent in that same time period. The church was failing.

Third, there was **distraction over affluence.** People generally were being caught up in an orgy of indulgence, materialism, and affluence. The opening of the Midwestern fields to settlements, and the discovery of gold in California, prompting the great Californian gold rush, took people from the east, away from their settled homes and associations out to the west where there were no churches, and nothing established to care for them. Money became the god. Also, the developing of the railroads meant that the railroad owners sought investors. People could invest quite cheaply in railroad stock and, as the towns in the Midwest developed along the railroad routes, found that their stocks' value was growing at a phenomenal rate. In Britain, 150 years earlier, as the empire was expanding, people invested in stocks to develop the South Sea Islands and to import the products from there, but "the South Sea Bubble" burst, ruining many. Similarly, this great period of American affluence came to an ignominious collapse through the great bank panics. Within the space of about fifteen years there were three major runs on the banks, the last one shortly after the outbreak of the revival. Materialism inevitably distracted people from the things of God at this time.

The fourth factor in the religious decline was **a sense of desperation**. Many churches had come to rely on revival as the prime means of growth. It was very easy to grow a church in a period of revival. Simply open the doors and the Spirit of God would bring in the people. A popular revival such as began in 1825 packed the pews and escalated church membership. Twenty-five years later, however, most of those who were converted in the revival, were entering middle age or older and, as with normal demographics, were beginning to die off, leaving noticeable gaps in the pews. Also, the pulpit ministry had concentrated on the needs of the newly converted believers immediately following the revival and evangelistic preaching had virtually disappeared, leaving a rising generation that had not faced the challenge of the gospel. As the revival enthusiasm began to abate and the Spirit of God was apparently not bringing in the replacements as had happened at the height of the revival, the church entered a period of decline. A proliferation of committees and organizations devoted to finding a solution to the problem failed to change the situation. A sense of hopelessness began to pervade the churches.

A British Wesleyan Methodist, William Arthur (1819–1901), secretary of the Methodist Missionary Society (1850–1867), came up with a unique solution: "If the church needs a new beginning then let us return to the book of Acts and find out how things were when God began the church." In the year 1855 he was invited to deliver a series of lectures at the Methodist Training College in Sandusky, Ohio, which were subsequently published under the title of *The Tongue of Fire; or The True Power of Christianity*, in which Arthur turned to the opening chapters of Acts to ascertain how the ministry of the infant church began and by what means it would spread to the farthest parts of the earth.[2] His conclusion was that the church could only function as God intended—not on the basis of occasional outpourings of the Spirit, but a constant filling with the Spirit. Only as believers live in the Spirit can they truly experience God's power working through them. His book concluded with a prayer that became the prayer of the church of that day:

> And now, adorable Spirit, proceeding from the Father and the Son, descend upon all the Churches, renew the Pentecost in this our age and baptize Thy people generally – O, baptize them yet again with tongues of fire! Crown this nineteenth century with a revival of "pure and undefiled religion" greater than that of the last century, greater than that of the first, greater than any "demonstration of the Spirit' ever yet vouchsafed to men!"[3]

Within three years, between 1856 and 1859, Arthur's book had gone through eighteen reprints and sold over three million copies in the United States of America alone,[4] and a similar impact was observed in the UK. Among the people greatly influenced by William Arthur was an evangelistic couple, Dr. Walter (1804–1883) and Phoebe Palmer (1807–1874). Phoebe, and her sister, Sarah Lankford (1806–1896), were involved in the Tuesday Meetings for the Promotion of Holiness (1835 onward), a major tributary of the developing Holiness Movement in America. Palmer subsequently became a well-known camp meeting speaker, and a prolific contributor to various holiness journals, in addition to authoring and publishing several books herself. Having obtained the printing rights for printing and circulating Arthur's book from the original publisher, Harper Brothers (later named Harper and Rowe), the Palmers distributed it widely through their meetings.

The Beginning of the Awakening. In the fall of 1857, on their way back to New York from very successful camp meetings throughout Ontario and in Quebec, the Palmers visited a Thursday night prayer meeting at a Wesleyan Methodist Church in Hamilton, Ontario, and challenged the fifty present to a fresh dedication to the Lord. Promising to stay for an evangelistic meeting the following night, they were surprised when several hundred attended and twenty-one accepted Christ as Savior. As they continued the meetings over the weekend, fifty-five more professed salvation, and the meetings continued for almost three weeks, resulting in about 500 coming to Christ in that city.[5] A report in the Christian Advocate newspaper declared:

> The work is taking within its range . . . persons of all classes. Men of low degree, and men of high estate for wealth and position; old men and maidens and even little children are seen humbly kneeling together pleading for grace. The mayor of the city, with other persons of like position, are (sic) not ashamed to be seen bowed at the altar of prayer beside the humble servant.[6]

From the "gust of divine power," as the Hamilton revival was called, the Palmers went on from city to city across Canada, spreading the good news of the revival that had now begun.

As the revival in Canada was beginning, a young businessman, Jeremiah Lanphier (1809–1898), who had been appointed by the North Dutch Reformed Church in July 1857 to be the city missionary for lower Manhattan, in New York, felt strongly impressed to call a Wednesday noontime prayer meeting beginning on September 23, 1857. Lanphier had been converted in 1842 at the very end of the earlier revival, through the ministry of Charles Finney, on one of his last visits to the Broadway Tabernacle, the church that he had founded in New York. As one of the last fruit of the old awakening, despite having prospered in business, he longed for a return to the days of divine visitation. In preparation for the businessmen's prayer meeting, he distributed a flyer to the business houses in Manhattan inviting all interested to an hour-long prayer meeting in the Consistory building behind the church on the corner of Fulton and William Streets. Its message was:

How Often Shall I Pray?
As often as the language of prayer is in my heart; as often as I see my need of help; as often as I feel the power of temptation; as often as I am made sensible of any spiritual declension or feel the aggression of a worldly spirit. In prayer we leave the business of time for that of eternity, and intercourse with men for intercourse with God.[7]

For the first thirty minutes, nobody came and Lanphier was greatly discouraged. Finally, he heard a step on the stairs and six men joined him for the last thrity minutes of the meeting. The next Wednesday there was a considerably higher attendance; twenty-four men turned up for the prayer meeting. They were so touched by the Spirit of God that they asked that as of the following Monday the meeting should be held daily not just weekly. At the first Monday prayer meeting sixty were present; the next day, 200; and on the Wednesday, 500. The next week saw the collapse of the Bank of Pennsylvania and the subsequent bank panic, which in turn triggered the New York stock market crash, following which attendance accelerated even more rapidly and the Spirit of God began to move in an unprecedented fashion.

At the same time the news arrived of the revival in Hamilton and people began to seek God for such a revival in the United States of America, especially in the city of New York. New centers for prayer opened and within six months 10,000 businessmen gathered daily for prayer in New York City. In the first two years, one million converts were added to the churches in the United States of America.[8] That number did not include those already attending the church who were in a low spiritual state and were renewed in their commitment to God. Undoubtedly many millions more were touched by the awakening.

In a partial survey of attendance at various prayer meeting locations in Manhattan in March 1858, the *New York Herald* reported that at Fulton Street Dutch Reformed Church where it all began there were 300 present; at John Street Methodist Episcopal Church, 600; at Burton's Theatre, 1,200; at Ninth Street Dutch Reformed Church, a very small church, 150; at the Pilgrim's Congregational Church, also a very small building that would normally accommodate about 100, 125; at Broome Street Dutch Reformed Church, 300; at Waverly Place YMCA, 200; at Mercer Street, in a former bar that was transformed into a prayer meeting room when the owner of the bar and the patrons were converted, 150 were packed in that day; at Madison Square Presbyterian Church, 200; and at Thirty-Fourth Street Methodist Episcopal Church, 250. These figures were collected by a dozen reporters who ran in horse-drawn cabs from place to place, tallied the numbers present, and then moved on to the next place allotted to them.[9] Every meeting place in Manhattan was not included in the report nor were those outside the city. Later Finney recalled:

Daily prayer-meetings were established throughout the Northern States. In one of our meetings in Boston, a gentleman said, "I am from Omaha, in Nebraska. On my journey East I have found a continuous prayer-meeting all the way. We call it about two thousand miles from Omaha to Boston and here was a prayer-meeting about two thousand miles in extent."[10]

It seemed as though every city and town closed for prayer between noon and 2:00 p.m. to allow people the opportunity of attending one of the prayer meetings being conducted there. In every state and territory and in every denomination of Christians, including the Unitarians of New England, God moved in a powerful way, reaping a harvest before the devastation of the looming Civil War that would plunge so many into eternity. Finney mistakenly assumed that slavery had excluded the Southern states from the outpouring of the Spirit;[11] however, the evidence was totally contrary to his conclusion. Even the Confederate Army was not passed over in this awakening.[12] Orr summarized the situation:

The influence of the Revival was felt everywhere in the nation. It first captured the great cities, but it also spread through every town and village and country hamlet. It swamped schools and colleges. It affected all classes regardless of condition. A Divine influence seemed to pervade the land, and men's hearts were strangely warmed by a Power that was poured out in unusual ways. There was no fanaticism. . . . Nowhere was the Awakening more effective and without fanaticism than in the colleges and universities, from New England to the western frontier, from Virginia to the heart of Texas. Few were the institutions untouched by it.[13]

The Spreading Revival. It spread, not just to the United States of America, but overseas to other lands. Throughout Canada, the eastern states, the Midwest, the west, the south, as far as the Caribbean, Europe, Britain, Scandinavia, Switzerland, France, the Low Countries, eastern Europe, Russia, Germany, across the southern hemisphere, Australia, New Zealand, the Pacific Islands, and South Africa, ultimately reaching the mission fields of east Asia and Latin America, the revival spread until there was hardly a place where Christianity was known that did not experience the stirring of the Holy Spirit. The dimensions of this particular revival were greater than any seen previously.

From Philadelphia, Pennsylvania, the awakening spread to **Ireland**, first by a cable news report, which was followed by the visit of an official deputation from the Irish Presbyterian Church, Professor William Gibson, and the former Moderator, William McClure, whose report quickened interest throughout the island.[14] In Kells, near Ballymena, Northern Ireland, a young man, James McQuilkin, was reading the testimony of George Mueller (1805–1898), renowned for his faith and for the orphanage he founded in Bristol, England, during the earlier revival. That account together with the reports from America inspired him to ask why such "a blessed work" might not recur in his day. Calling together three friends, he began prayer meetings for an outpouring of God's Spirit in the nearby Ahoghill First Presbyterian Church in March 1859, which attracted such crowds that the meetings had to be moved outside lest the building collapse from the weight of numbers. Within a week the *Ballymena Observer* newspaper was carrying reports of the spreading awakening, which quickly transformed life throughout County Antrim and two months later reached Belfast, where crowds reaching twenty thousand gathered for prayer in the open air.[15]

Throughout the predominantly Protestant counties of Ulster and even among the scattered Protestant communities remaining in the rest of Ireland following the major immigration of Protestants to America during the potato famine (1845–1852), the revival spread with such effectiveness that more than 100,000 new converts were added to the churches.[16] Whittaker noted: "The revival was strongest in Protestant areas, but many Roman Catholics were converted and many abandoned their Catholicism as they embraced the teachings of God's Word."[17]

From Ireland the awakening quickly crossed the Irish Sea to **Scotland**, bursting forth in Aberdeen in the fall of 1858, whence it spread throughout the southwest. A year later a fresh wave, prompted by the ministry of Edward Payson Hammond (1831–1910), an American theological student in Edinburgh, spread along the Solway, coinciding with a powerful wave that inundated the northern Highlands, the western Islands, and the Orkneys. In 1859 a further wave of blessing also spread from Aberdeen to Inverness and down the east coast of the country into northern England, affecting virtually every town and village.[18]

As the awakening spread southward into **England**, the ministries of Walter and Phoebe Palmer (summer 1859–1863), Charles and Elizabeth Finney (winter 1859–1860), and Payson Hammond provided focal points for the intensifying prayer movement. By 1861 the awakening was burning at full strength and spreading rapidly from its urban beginnings into the surrounding countryside, from Tyneside in the north to Cornwall and Devon in the south. The spreading movement brought forth fresh faces, such as the young Methodist minister William Booth (1829–1912) and his wife, Catherine (1829–1890), who having been expelled by the Wesleyan Methodist Church for "religious zeal" (1855) and by the Methodist New Connexion (1861), became itinerant revivalists. Subsequently "in 1865 (they) started *The Christian Revival Association* in Whitechapel,"[19] which later became The Christian Mission and finally The Salvation Army (1878), and which was to benefit enormously from the next awakening:

> The 1859 Revival in Wales can be traced to the influence of the American Revival of 1858, but, unlike its Scottish counterpart, it owed nothing to the Ulster movement. Indeed, there is evidence to suggest that the outbreak of revival in Wales actually preceded that experienced in Ulster.[20]

The Welsh Calvinistic Methodist preacher, David Morgan (1814–1883), after praying for an outpouring of the Spirit in **Wales** for ten years, in 1859 went to hear the Wesleyan Methodist preacher, Humphrey Rowland

Jones (1832–1895) on his return from the US and was deeply affected by his message on "Lukewarmness." A few days later, he recounted:

> I went to bed as David Morgan. I woke up the next morning with a conscious sense of the anointing of the Spirit of God upon my ministry. I felt like a lyre. Every time I opened my mouth to preach people fell to the ground under great conviction of sin.

For the next two years the Spirit of God worked through Morgan in a phenomenal way. After two years Morgan said: "I went to bed like a lion and I woke up the next morning and I was David Morgan again" and the revival through his ministry was over.[21] He spent the rest of his life with a moderate, pleasant ministry, never again used in the powerful way that he had been in the revival. Only the sovereign Lord knows why the change:

> The Rev. John Venn, M.A., the Prebendary of Hereford, before an Evangelical Alliance gathering in the autumn of 1860 . . . claimed that almost every county in the principality had been influenced by a more or less remarkable work of grace. . . . Prebendary Venn estimated that about 100,000 persons in all had been received into full communion in the course of two years.[22]

In the spring of 1862 the American evangelists, the Palmers, began a month of stirring meetings in Cardiff, in which so many were converted that the crime rate dropped substantially. Their ministry was followed by that of the converted collier Richard Weaver (1827–1896), when the largest building in the area, the Music Hall, was packed with over 4,000 each evening and many hundreds turned away.[23] The following spring William and Catherine Booth, after a powerful time of revival in Cornwall, crossed the Bristol Channel, bringing a fresh wave of blessing to Cardiff, which continued under a further visit by Weaver as the Booths moved on to follow the Palmers into the English Midlands.

As news of the American awakening spread across the Atlantic to **Scandinavia**, the earlier revival movements associated with the ministries of Hauge in Norway, Ruotsalainen in Finland, Scott and Rosenius in Sweden, received fresh impetus. Localized stirrings occurred through the work of the Swedish Evangelical Mission, the influence of which spread across the region, especially under the leadership of Paul Peter Waldenstroem (1838–1917), the successor to Rosenius.[24] In Denmark "many from 'the awakened circles' joined the Grundtvigian movement. Others founded the more pietistic *Indre Mission*. Smaller groups joined the Lutheran Mission (Bornholmians)."[25]

Continental Europe. "The Ulster Awakening created great interest in Geneva, and stirred up revival movements in the French-speaking Reformed Churches in Switzerland, France and Belgium."[26] *Le Reveil,* in particular, gained a renewed impetus, "permeated the French Reformed Church, and rejuvenated hundreds of Dutch congregations."[27] Although there was no general awakening in Germany due to the political turmoil gripping the nation in the post-Napoleonic period, especially between the March Revolutions of 1848 and the final unification of the nation in 1871, there were localized sporadic outbreaks of revival among the Pietists and Evangelicals scattered throughout the region. Greater impact was actually experienced among the scattered German-speaking settlements of eastern Europe. For example, Orr noted:

> In the Russian Ukraine, German settlers (both Mennonite and Pietist) had experienced great awakenings in the mid-century. Their zealous outreach resulted in their Russian compatriots engaging in prayer, the movement taking on the name Stundist, from its hour of prayer.[28]

The spread of the awakening eastward prepared the way for what would take place in later revivals through the ministries of Granville Waldegrave, Lord Radstock (1833–1913), and the German-British evangelist, Friedrick Wilhelm Baedeker (1823–1906).

Although **Australia** boasted few major population centers in the mid-century, as the news of the awakening in America and Britain reached the colonies, the scattered churches began prayer meetings that prompted several local awakenings and prepared the way for a more widespread movement through the ministry of a relatively unknown American Methodist evangelist, William "California" Taylor (1821–1902). His arrival in 1863 marked the beginning of a remarkable period of growth for the Methodists, which spilled over into every denomination. "Most of 1864 he gave to ministry in Victoria and Tasmania; 1864 to New South Wales and Queensland, with a side trip to New Zealand; and 1865 to South Australia. His evangelism was very fruitful, for more than six thousand converts were received by the circuits."[29]

Almost simultaneously, revival spread throughout **the South Sea Islands** of Hawaii, Micronesia, Melanesia, and Polynesia. Similarly, there was a period of rapid growth in the churches of the Dutch-controlled Indonesia that "resulted in large part from the religious revival in the Netherlands itself. In the 1860s, missionaries from newer societies founded in the Netherlands through evangelical renewal began to arrive in the East Indies."[30] Sumatra, then under Prussian control, also experienced a major folk movement beginning in 1862 through the ministry of the Danish missionary, Ludwig Nommenson (1834–1918) and the German Rhenish Missionary Society, that swept the majority of the Batak tribespeople into the Christian faith.

The news of the revival in America and in Britain prompted a widespread call to prayer in both the Dutch-speaking and the English-speaking churches of **South Africa**. Although there was a noted increase in church attendance before 1860 "it could not be said, however, that there had been any significant awakening among either English or Dutch-speaking churches there until later."[31] That summer the awakening came in full force, sweeping many into the kingdom of God and transforming the local congregations. Almost two years earlier, however, God had begun to move among the Bantu of Transkei and the Zulu congregations of Natal,[32] a prelude to what would become a major outpouring in the next generation.

The Characteristics of the Awakening. The most outstanding characteristic was the feature of **extraordinary prayer**. While every revival has been marked by prayer, this particular awakening was distinguished by the prayer meeting in its earliest days in America. "Its contemporaries rightly called it 'the prayer meeting revival,' for it was universally marked by fervent prayer."[33] It was extended powerfully by the prayer meetings stemming out of Fulton Street, New York, to encompass much of the Christian world.

A second feature of the awakening was **spontaneous praise**. Congregations would burst forth in praise. In Wales, in particular, "a feature of the revival was 'moliannu' or praising, a peculiar form of worship described as a chorus of rapturous praise from preacher and people in turn."[34] Although critics accused those affected by the revival of emotionalism, there were few instances of physical manifestations or emotional extravagance.[35] Even where physical prostrations were noted, as in Ulster and Scotland, they were relatively short-lived.[36] The fact that conviction of sin was often followed by an inordinate sense of joy, and even laughter, was offensive to some sober-minded (and somber-minded) clergy was not surprising, but among enthusiastic proponents of the revival, especially in the emerging holiness movements, such times of exultant joy were thought of as a characteristic of being filled with the Holy Spirit.

The third characteristic was **the absence of strong personalities**. Although in every country there were individuals who rose to the occasion, there did not emerge prominent personalities like the Wesley brothers or George Whitfield or Jonathan Edwards from the Great Awakening, or Charles Finney from the Adventist Awakening. Although Finney was still active in this revival, he was simply one of the many individuals who were used by God, people without any other claim for fame than the fact that God laid his hand upon their life, took them up and used them, some for a very brief time period, as in the example of David Morgan of Wales. He was quite inconspicuous before the revival period and equally inconspicuous after the revival period but for some two years was a powerful instrument of God. Emerging out of the revival came some who would be used powerfully in the next major phase of awakening, the Gospel Mission Awakening.

The fourth element was **a strong impetus to missions**. The birth of denominational missions came about through the revival around 1800 but this revival gave birth to a new concept in missions, usually associated with the name of Hudson Taylor (1832–1905), namely the faith mission. Taylor went to China first with the China Evangelization Society in 1854. When that failed, he returned home in 1859, and six years later founded the China Inland Mission with an interdenominational home base of sympathetic believers who contributed to the support of the individual missionaries. In each supporting church a missionary secretary was appointed to receive the funds on a regular basis and forward them to a national headquarters, whence they were disbursed in support of these faith missionaries. This approach to missionary support, unknown previously, arose as a result of this revival period and characterizes much of the modern evangelical missionary endeavor.

The Christian church is greatly indebted to this revival because of its results both in the area of foreign missions and in the fact that many of the major personalities, who were to play important roles in the next great awakening in the last quarter of the nineteenth Century, emerged from it.

Endnotes

1 K. J. Hardman: *Seasons of Refreshing* (Eugene, OR: Wipf & Stock, 2006), 186–191.

2 W. Arthur: *The Tongue of Fire, or The True Power of Christianity* (New York, NY: Harper, 1856).

3 Ibid., 354.

4 D. W. Dayton: *Theological Roots of Pentecostalism* (Grand Rapids, MI: Zondervan, 1987), 73–74; J. E. Orr: lecture on the 1857 Prayer Meeting Revival at Oxford Association for Research in Revival (Regent's College, Oxford, July 26, 1977).

5 C. E. White: *The Beauty of Holiness* (Grand Rapids, MI: Zondervan, 1986), 45–46.

6 *Christian Advocate* (New York, NY) November 5, 1857, quoted in J.E. Orr: *The Fervent Prayer* (Chicago, IL: Moody, 1974), 2.

7 Quoted in Orr, ibid., 4.

8 Ibid., 5.

9 *New York Herald*, March 26, 1858, quoted in Orr, ibid., 9.

10 Finney, *The Life of Charles G. Finney*, op. cit., 369–370.

11 Ibid., 371.

12 Orr, op. cit., 28–33.

13 Ibid., 11.

14 Ibid., 46.

15 Davies, *I Will Pour Out My Spirit*, op. cit., 156.

16 Orr, op. cit., 51.

17 C. C. Whittaker: *Great Revivals* (Springfield, MO: Gospel Publishing House, 1984), 93.

18 Orr, op. cit.,55.

19 R. E. D. Clark: art. "Booth, Catherine" in NIDCC, op. cit., 145.

20 Orr, op. cit., 59.

21 D. M. Lloyd-Jones: *Preaching & Preachers* (Grand Rapids, MI: Zondervan, 1971), 322–324.

22 Orr, op. cit., 62.

23 Ibid., 61.

24 Ibid., 83.

25 N.O. Rasmussen: art. "Denmark" in NIDCC, 293

26 Orr, op. cit., 84

27 R.D. Linder: art. "Reveil, Le" in NIDCC, 843

28 Orr, op. cit., 86

29 J.E. Orr: *The Light of the Nations* (Exeter, UK: Paternoster, 1965), 161

30 J.E. Orr: *Evangelical Awakenings in the South Seas* (Minneapolis, MN: Bethany, 1976), 71

31 J.E. Orr: *Evangelical Awakenings in Africa* (Minneapolis, MN: Bethany, 1975), 54

32 Ibid., 63–66

33 Orr, *The Fervent Prayer*, op. cit., 6

34 Ibid., 60

35 Ibid., 44

36 Ibid., 54

Chapter 17

The Gospel Mission Awakening

1870–1900

In many respects, the revival that marked much of the last quarter of the nineteenth century was a direct result of the mid-century awakening. Many of the leading figures were the product of the earlier awakening and much of the interest in a fresh movement of the Holy Spirit arose from the reports circulating of that powerful time. Although in the English-speaking world the influence of **the Gospel Mission Awakening**, from 1870 to the late 1880s, would continue to affect future generations, in the rest of the Christian world, the successive outpourings of the Spirit from the late 1860s until the great surge of the twentieth Century from 1900 to 1910 would radically change the face of global Christianity.

Throughout **Scandinavia** came a fresh wave of revival beginning in Sweden following the death of Carl Rosenius in 1868 that gave birth to the Evangelical Mission Covenant (1878), which later impacted the Lutheran Churches in the US. Norway was also gripped by a powerful awakening in the 1880s, as was Denmark, especially through the ministry of a student of D. L. Moody, Frederick Franson (1852–1908),[1] founder of the Scandinavian Alliance Mission (1890), later renamed The Evangelical Alliance Mission (TEAM).

During this awakening, a significant impact on much of the English-speaking world was made by two remarkable characters, the international evangelist

D. L. Moody (1837–1899), renowned for his great evangelistic ministry on both sides of the Atlantic, and the missionary evangelist William "California" Taylor (1821–1902), whose amazing ministry affected every continent where the church was represented. To them may be added a multitude of pastors, missionaries, and evangelists, whose ministries either prepared the way for the revival, or helped extend its impact worldwide. Many became models for future generations of Christian leaders, and left an enduring legacy, such as Charles H. Spurgeon of London (1834–1892), Henry Grattan Guinness (1835–1910), the world missionary; Edward Payson Hammond (1831–1910), the international children's evangelist;[2] and Andrew Murray of South Africa (1828–1917). The spread of the awakening eastward across Europe prepared the way for what would take place in the next revival through the ministries of Granville Waldegrave, Lord Radstock, and the German-British evangelist Friedrick Wilhelm Baedeker.

In 1876 a poor, young Scottish woman, Mary Mitchell Slessor (1848–1915), who had been converted in the mid-century awakening, set sail for Nigeria to "the White Man's Graveyard of the Calabar" as a pioneering missionary with the United Presbyterian Church's Calabar Mission. Her effective ministry at the height of the revival not only won her the respect of the most savage and powerful chiefs but eventually led the British Imperial government to appoint her the first honorary female vice-consul. The lasting tribute to her revival ministry, however, was the conversion of the majority of the Ibo people to Christianity.[3]

The revival in the winter of 1880–81 in Williston Congregational Church in Portland, Maine, under the leadership of Pastor Francis E. Clark (1851–1927) resulted in the formation of a Young People's Society of Christian Endeavour (1882) to conserve the fruit of the awakening and promote further revivals among the youth. Four years later (1886), a thousand young people from many parts of the US attended the first national convention in Saratoga Springs, Florida, and the growth spread internationally following Clark's visit to England in 1888.[4]

Dwight L. Moody had been converted and brought into a position of usefulness by God during the earlier awakening; first, by beginning a Sunday school in a vacant saloon (1858), which grew into the largest in

Chicago and by 1860 had developed into a church, and second, by his involvement with the YMCA, becoming its president in 1865. Two years later, on his first visit to Britain, Moody met many prominent evangelical leaders, such as A. A. Cooper, Earl of Shaftesbury (1801–1885); George Mueller (1805–1898); George Williams (1821–1905), founder of the YMCA; R. C. Morgan (1827–1908), the editor of *The Revival* newspaper; C. H. Spurgeon; and the renowned international evangelist, Henry Varley (1835–1912), who was to play a significant role in Moody's life.

The following year (1868), a young British evangelist, Henry Moorehouse (1840–1880), whom Moody had briefly met on his visit to England, visited Chicago and preached for a whole week on John 3:16 at Moody's church in Farwell Hall, the headquarters of the YMCA and of Moody's Sunday school movement in Chicago. He extended an invitation to Moody to return to England and to visit the influential evangelical Mildmay Circle at St. Jude's, Islington, hosted by William Pennefather (1816–1873). The loss of Farwell Hall to fire shortly afterward delayed his plans but fortuitously in 1870 at the annual convention of the YMCA in Indianapolis he became acquainted with Ira D. Sankey, who was to become his crusade soloist for the next quarter century.[5] The following year, while visiting New York, he had a supernatural encounter with the Holy Spirit, a baptism with the Holy Spirit, which equipped him for ministry as an international evangelist. His second visit to Britain in 1872, brought him face-to-face with a challenge from his friend, Henry Varley: "Moody, the world has yet to see what God will do with a man fully consecrated to Him."[6]

The evident blessing of God upon his ministry prompted Pennefather, the host of Mildmay, to invite the evangelist to return, along with his team for a series of crusades. When Moody arrived in Britain in June 1873 for the crusades, none of the churches were aware of his coming due to his failure to maintain effective communication and the unexpected death of Pennefather, who had invited him. Despite the cancellation of his scheduled meetings, God still used him in a powerful way. Traveling at short notice to the city of York, the team began their first meetings rather inauspiciously. From there he moved on to Sunderland, Newcastle, Edinburgh, Dundee, Glasgow, Belfast, Dublin, Manchester, Sheffield, Birmingham, and Liverpool, steadily increasing in effectiveness and impact until the climactic finale in London in 1875, where in the space of twenty weeks more than two and a half million people thronged Moody's meetings. His ministry proved to be a phenomenal success. It was God's time for Moody and Moody was God's man for that time.

In 1875, he carried the revival back to the United States of America and began a remarkable series of revival meetings along the eastern seaboard of the United States and as far inland as Chicago. This period of revival with Moody came not in the setting of a period of decline, as far as the evangelical world was concerned, but during a period of assault and conflict between evangelical faithfulness and German rationalistic higher criticism that was attempting to make inroads into the colleges and universities of the major denominations in the United States of America. In the midst of that conflict God raised up this powerful evangelist to be a witness to his faithfulness to his Word.

Although Moody's later period of ministry in Britain (1881–83) was not attended by signs of awakening on par with his earlier visit, God's blessing was evident in several significant aspects. His Cambridge mission (1882) "was the beginning of a worldwide interdenominational student ministry movement."[7] As a result the renowned Cambridge Seven committed themselves to evangelism in China, departing in 1885. Through a later tent mission in East London in 1885 Wilfred Grenfell (1865–1940) was converted to Christ and later went as a missionary to Labrador (1892). The following year the Student Volunteer Movement for Foreign Missions was formed with the watchword: "We can evangelize the world in this generation" with the young John R. Mott (1865–1955) as chairman.[8]

Some have dismissed Moody as being nothing more than another evangelist. In reality, many of the things that happened under Moody's ministry and the responses to his ministry cannot be explained in terms of simply planning an evangelistic campaign. Just as in more recent days the beginning of the ministry of people like Billy Graham cannot be understood apart from the fact that in the post-World War II years, there was a rising tide of spiritual expectancy that finally, in 1947, burst forth in revival, affecting not only the ministry of the evangelical Billy Graham but also Pentecostal healing evangelists like Oral Roberts, William Branham, A. A. Allen, Jack Coe, T. L. Osborn, and a whole host of lesser-known preachers. Even where there were no prominent individuals, other signs of awakening were apparent. The rise of such evangelists cannot be explained except in the context of a general move of God's Spirit preparing the hearts of people for the appeal of the gospel. This is why Moody's ministry coming at the time that it did, was so spectacularly effective, even though Moody himself from his published sermons was not a great preacher, nor was he even a great organizer of meetings.[9]

William Taylor of California was actually born in Virginia in 1821, converted in the last year of the Finney revival in 1841, and began an itinerant ministry in the Baltimore Conference of the Methodist Episcopal Church in 1842, just one year after his conversion. His ministry was not attended by major success until in 1849 he decided to head west to the California gold fields and there to begin a ministry amongs the gold miners. He went from place to place simply carrying his belongings in a wooden box on which he stood on to preach while conducting open-air meetings, which resulted in several Methodist Episcopal churches being established throughout the gold fields. Despite the moderate success of his ministry, on hearing of the revival that was taking place in the east, in 1858 he returned to travel the eastern seaboard of the US and Canada, preaching and taking part in the revival occurring there.[10]

In 1863, however, he felt very concerned as he saw the revival fires in America ebbing and became convinced that he should carry the message of the awakening beyond the shores of North America out to the uttermost parts of the earth. Speaking only English he needed to go where English was spoken and so he chose **Australia**. On June 16, 1863, he landed in Melbourne, Australia, and began his ministry in the Wesley Church there. The Australians did not respond to his ministry as well as he had hoped because most of the preachers that they had had were English preachers. Taylor being an American was not as emotional as the typical English preacher of that day[11] and so the Australians decided that Taylor did not believe his message as fervently as British or English preachers did. His first meetings were not particularly successful until the Spirit of God began to move in a most remarkable way – first in Victoria, then in Tasmania, across New South Wales, and Queensland, then over into New Zealand, returning to South Australia in 1865. Through two years of ministry, more than six thousand converts were added to the Methodist church alone and considerable numbers joined other denominations out of a population of one million people. Undoubtedly, God was doing something through this man's ministry. In the State of Victoria alone two thousand converts were won to Christ and joined the church as a result of his ministry.[12]

From Australia, Taylor moved on to **South Africa**, arriving in Capetown in 1866. His arrival in South Africa was unusual in that when he arrived at Capetown he had no idea where he was going to minister or with whom. All he knew was that God had called him to South Africa to minister to the English-speaking people. His first meetings at the Wesleyan Chapel in Capetown, in Wynberg, Port Elizabeth, Uitenhage, and in Grahamstown, while blessed with many conversions, were not extraordinary in attendance or impact.[13] However, in Queenstown, he met a young Zulu lay-evangelist, Charles Pamla (1834–1917), who invited him to come and speak, not to the English or Dutch inhabitants, but to the Bantu tribespeople with Pamla as his interpreter.

Accompanying Pamla to the town of Annshaw, about twenty-five miles from King William's town, Taylor was amazed to find over 600 people had gathered there, dressed in the characteristic red blankets of the Xhosa tribe. Not realizing that his hearers were completely heathen, Taylor preached on the text that had been so effective for his sermons in Australia: "You shall receive power after the Holy Spirit comes upon you."[14] As he began to preach, the Spirit of God came upon the congregation and under intense conviction of sin, every person present repented before God and accepted Christ as Savior. Pamla later recounted: "There the Holy Spirit came mightily on us and many wonderful things were seen and done."[15] Even after Taylor's departure, 165 others came to Christ who had not been present at that gathering but had simply heard reports of the meeting from the attendees. God was moving. In Healdtown over a thousand natives crowded the 800-seat Wesley Chapel to hear the gospel of Christ.

Taylor found that his ministry, not among the Europeans but among the Africans, the Bantu tribespeople, was a phenomenal success under the Holy Spirit. He later recorded: "The awful presence and melting power of the Holy Spirit on these occasions surpassed anything I had ever witnessed before." Charles Pamla, his interpreter, traveled with him throughout Southern Africa translating for him. The Xhosa people gave Taylor the name of *Essiecunde* (the Blazing Firebrand) because wherever he went, he kindled the fire of the Holy Spirit. Even beyond the Xhosa people among the Zulus, he found a similar outpouring of God's Spirit beginning to take place. In three weeks of meetings among the Zulus, some 7,900 people made a profession of faith in Christ. From there, Taylor returned to America via the West Indies and Pamla continued a powerful revival ministry throughout Southern Africa. Within a short time, Taylor had departed once again for Australia but now a further call was on his life to head northwards to Ceylon and ultimately India.

On November 25, 1870, he arrived in **India** in the town of Lucknow.[16] On his arrival, he discovered that the letter that he had written to the Methodist Episcopal missionaries in Lucknow had not yet arrived. There was no one to meet him at the dockside and so he stopped an Indian man and asked him if he could direct him to the Methodist Episcopal mission. The man spoke some English and responded: "Certainly, I will take you there." Walking up the hill from the dock to the mission, Taylor noticed people sitting around, just idling the time away with nothing to do and decided that this was a good opportunity to do a little preaching. He told his guide to stop as he wished to say something to the people who were sitting on one of the street corners. Taylor began to preach and when he gave an invitation, many of those who were listening accepted Christ as Savior. He told them to follow him to the mission. At the next street corner, he decided to do it again and others were converted and followed him on his way up the hill to the mission. By the time he arrived at the mission, more than 340 people had accepted Christ as Savior within the three hours of his arriving in Lucknow.

He knocked at the door of the mission and the missionary, James M. Thoburn (1836–1922), answered, amazed to see William Taylor. When

Taylor explained the situation, Thoburn said: "But I am sorry, I did not know you were coming and in any case, we only have twelve converts here in Lucknow. It is not worth your being here to conduct meetings. There will be just a handful to listen to you. You would be better going on to another town." Taylor responded: "You may have had twelve converts, but you now have another three hundred and forty and here they are." The large crowd of Indians had filled the mission compound and was spilling over into the streets, ready to be instructed and received into the Methodist church. Thoburn was totally overawed by the work with which Taylor presented him. That was characteristic of Taylor's ministry.

Although a minister of the Methodist Episcopal Church, he made a practice of first going into a community, establishing a mission work and then contacting the Methodist Episcopal Church in America and inviting them to send a missionary or to establish the church on a regular footing while he went on somewhere else. By the time his letters arrived in America he had usually already left that community in the charge of elders that he had appointed to look over the work. His superiors would of course write back to him but they never knew where he was going next and so the letters to him would sometimes arrive months after he had moved on. From Lucknow to Bombay to Poona to Calcutta to Madras to Bangalore, Taylor went from place to place establishing Methodist Episcopal missions without any permission but simply presenting the Methodist church leadership with the information. "Here is a Methodist Episcopal Church, send a missionary." Of course, this created logistical problems for the denominational authorities because they did not know until the work was already established that they would need to send a missionary. Several months would elapse while they were getting a missionary equipped and sent out. By the time he arrived the work had been going on without the missionary for some time and Taylor already had gone on to two or three other cities and established further works.[17]

While in India, he received word from Moody inviting him to come back to an English-speaking area, in fact, to the meetings in Islington, London in England, and there to participate in the revival that was taking place. Consequently, he left his beloved Asia and became effectively involved in the revival in **Britain**. From there, he was summoned back to the United States of America but this restless traveler could not be content with having evangelized in North America, in Australia, in Asia, in Africa, and in Europe. There was a continent yet to be evangelized; he had not yet set foot in **South America**. That to his world vision was unthinkable and so in 1877 he set forth on yet another outreach down to the south first to Peru, then Bolivia, and Brazil, establishing self-supporting missions,[18] a new totally indigenous system of missionary enterprise.

This was something that William Carey, in the 1790s, had envisioned but had never effectively implemented. The early missions tended to revolve around the Western missionary who went in, established a center, built a compound, a home, even had the converts come and live in the compound or in its vicinity and attend the mission church. The church itself was controlled entirely from the mission perspective but was not indigenous in its leadership, nor in its approach. Taylor determined that the problems that he had faced and created in Asia, especially in the Indian subcontinent, would not continue in South America. In handing over these missions to the Methodist Episcopal Church and trying to get them to send missionaries, there was a colossal fallout rate. While the churches in Asia were waiting for the Methodist Episcopal Church to send missionaries to take charge of the work, there was a danger of leaders going astray and being deceived into false doctrine. Another danger was that when the missionary did come that he would quash the work because his attitudes and principles differed from those of Taylor. The inroads of German rationalism into the universities and colleges in America was affecting the potential missionary candidates and although most of the missionaries were godly, Spirit-anointed men, there were many going out in the 1870s who were greatly influenced by rationalistic concepts and were not thoroughly committed to Evangelicalism, such as happened in Ceylon in 1875 with the appointment of Reginald S. Copleston (1845–1925), "a brilliant young Oxford don,"[19] as Anglican Bishop of Colombo, who "withdrew the license to minister" from all the evangelical Anglican missionaries.

Taylor himself was a thoroughly committed Evangelical and therefore he felt very perturbed that he was in some instances handing over his new converts to the care of a "corpse." So, when he went to South America, he determined that he would establish not just an eldership to care for the church while awaiting a missionary, but also a functioning Methodist Episcopal Church in each of the South American countries, providing a network of elders to ensure that each church was established on a good footing with biblically oriented leadership. Across South America he established self-supporting missions entities; however, in 1879 he was summoned back to the USA to face discipline from the Methodist Episcopal authorities for "unacceptable" missionary activity. Although he had kept them informed, he had not sought their permission, nor was he operating in a fashion generally approved by the Methodist Episcopal Church.

His orders were to return to the US by the most direct possible route. Taylor interpreted that in terms of distance rather than speed of travel. So, he bought himself a donkey in Brazil, on which he traveled back to North America by way of Bolivia, Peru, Central America, and Mexico, establishing churches and self-supporting missions as he went. Finally, in 1884 after a five-year-long journey, he arrived in Texas in time for the Methodist Episcopal Church South's conference in San Antonio. What could they do with someone like this? They decided that there was only one thing to do with this kind of revivalist who traveled bringing spiritual awakening wherever he went and that was to make him a bishop. If they could not confine him to a diocese then they would confine him to a continent and so they appointed him the Methodist Episcopal bishop for the continent of Africa, with explicit instructions that he was not to leave the continent of Africa until such time as he was to retire.

As the appointed Bishop of Africa, he arrived in Angola in 1885 and traveling throughout sub-Saharan Africa, Angola, Southern Africa, the Free States, Portuguese East Africa, the Congo, and West Africa as far as Liberia, he conducted meetings, established churches, and self-supporting missions, spreading the gospel of Christ everywhere he went.

At the time of his appointment, he was sixty-three years of age. By the time he reached seventy in 1891, the compulsory retiring age for Methodist bishops, word reached him that he had to return home for retirement.

Aware of his earlier practices, his superiors said that on this occasion, he had to return home by the fastest means of travel at his disposal. He was at the time in Liberia. There was a freighter leaving Liberia for the US by way of Europe that would take some six months to get there; however, there was another freighter leaving Capetown, South Africa, that would make the journey direct to New York in only five months. So, he informed the Methodist authorities that he would be setting sail from Capetown for New York as soon as he could get to Capetown. The journey from Liberia to Capetown took him almost five years.

Finally, in 1896 he arrived in New York to face six years of "retirement," which, in reality, were spent traveling throughout the United States of America, promoting missions, and preparing the way for a revival yet to come. A major feature of D. L. Moody's crusades between 1896 and 1899, when Moody died, was the missions service that "California" Taylor would conduct to promote missions. As one of the prime movers in the Student Volunteers for Missions that Moody was so vigorously promoting, his ministry resulted in sending many thousands of young people out to the mission fields.

Although his ministry was unique in many respects, the most remarkable feature was that wherever this man went revival accompanied him. It seemed as though he embodied in himself the principles of this Gospel Mission revival. He would arrive in a pagan town with no known Christians, no support, simply find someone who spoke English, begin preaching, and one after another would come to Christ. He would establish a work and stay there as long as it took to get the work established on a good footing and then on to the next town.

He said that God had revealed to him that he would have revival wherever he went if he would simply remain true to the God who had promised to empower him. He only ever preached on one text, Acts 1:8: "You will receive power when the Holy Spirit has come upon you." And with that text, he visited every inhabited continent of earth, the first evangelist known to do so. It has been conservatively estimated that over three million people came to Christ through his ministry. "California" Taylor was a man that God singularly used in revival.

Shortly before his death D. L. Moody in a sermon on revival in 1899 made the statement:

> A revival is the only hope for our republic. I think it is getting very dark but don't think for a moment that I am a pessimist. Pentecost isn't over yet. Why shouldn't we now at the close of this old century have a great shaking up and a mighty wave from heaven?

Moody did not live to see the great revival come that he was looking for and expecting, but less than two years after his death God had begun to pour out his Spirit anew. That period of revival at the beginning of the twentieth century is the topic of the next chapter.

Endnotes

1 Orr, *The Light of the Nations*, op. cit., 196–7.

2 Orr, ibid., 171–2.

3 J. W. Meiklejohn : art. "Slessor, Mary" in NIDCC, 908.

4 Orr, op. cit., 209–210.

5 B. L. Shelley: art. "Sankey, Ira D." in NIDCC, 878.

6 Orr, op. cit., 191.

7 Davies, *I Will Pour Out My Spirit*, op. cit., 165.

8 Ibid; Orr, op. cit., 272.

9 Orr, *The Fervent Prayer,* op. cit., 58.

11 Orr, *Evangelical Awakenings in the South Seas*, op. cit., 56ff.

12 Orr, *The Fervent Prayer*, op. cit., 161.

13 Orr, Evangelical Awakenings in Africa, op. cit., 67 contra Orr, *The Light of the Nations*, op. cit. 163.

14 Acts 1:8.

15 Quoted in G. Meats: *Methodist Missionaries n. 2* (Cape Town, SA: Methodist Missionary Dept., 1958), 17.

16 Latourette, *History of the Expansion*, op. cit., VI, 170, 171.

17 Orr, *Evangelical Awakenings in Southern Asia*, op. cit., 70–71.

18 Latourette, *History of the Expansion*, op. cit., 118.

19 Orr, op. cit., 71.

Chapter 18

Early 20th Century

1900–1940

The twentieth century dawned with a spiritual awakening that is still underestimated by researchers more than a century later. Even the Pentecostal churches, while acknowledging the birth of the modern Pentecostal movement at the beginning of the twentieth century, seldom recognize that the Pentecostal movement was born in a general period of revival. The great Welsh revival has probably been written about more than any other awakening, except possibly the Pentecostal aspect of the revival, and although only one part of the awakening, has inspired others to seek a similar visitation.

A survey of the number of countries that were affected by the revival at the beginning of the twentieth century reveals that this awakening touched virtually every part of the world where Christianity was found. The US, Canada, Mexico, and the Caribbean all were convulsed by spiritual awakening at this time. In every part of the United Kingdom and Europe, from Scandinavia in the north down to the Mediterranean countries, and eastward to the borders of Asia and the Middle East, multitudes were affected by revival. Across Russia and throughout the Far East, God moved powerfully. The Korean (1907) and Manchurian (1908) revivals, in which the Canadian Presbyterian Jonathan Goforth (1859–1936) played a significant role, have been extensively written about. To a great extent, the revival in Korea transformed the Korean Christian church into one of the most powerful branches of evangelicalism. Japan (1900–1910) was visited by a decade of awakenings that deserves more attention than has been received. Southern Asia, from Punjab, Bengal, and Assam to Burma, Indonesia, and the Philippines, was stirred by a succession of spiritual awakenings that transformed long standing churches and gave renewed impetus to the missionary endeavor. The southern hemisphere, from Australasia and the Pacific Islands, to South Africa, and north through central Africa branching both west and east and reaching as far north as Egypt, was radically touched by the Holy Spirit. In South America, despite the uneven penetration of Christianity there, revival was noted in Chile, Brazil, and Argentina. Although there may have been few major stirrings in Central America, some areas were touched and renewed during this time period. Further investigation will probably reveal this to have been an even more extensive awakening than ever known before.

The origins of this awakening may be traced back to **a general prayer movement** in the Christian church, not always prayer for revival, but in many instances that was the prime topic. As Matthew Henry (1662–1714), the renowned Bible commentator, is reputed to have declared: "When God intends great mercy for his people, the first thing he does is to set them a-praying."

The second major factor in the origins of this awakening was **the "deeper life" meetings**. With the ministry of Moody and others associated with him, there came a great interest in a deeper life than had been apparent before. Much of this was associated with the town of Keswick in the Lake District of England. By the beginning of the twentieth century, the Keswick conventions had been duplicated in most parts of the Christian world. The initial Keswick began in 1883, but by 1900, there were several similar deeper life conventions throughout Britain, in the United States of America, and even in India, all of which made reference back to the English Keswick. At the Welsh Keswick in Llandrindod Wells as people turned to God and began to seek the Lord for revival, the young man Evan J. Roberts (1878–1951), who was to be so greatly used in the Welsh

Revival, found his heart being stirred to seek God for revival. Although the Indian Keswick typically was more of a preaching conference, with expositions addressed to Christians challenging them to a deeper spiritual life than they had previously known, John Hyde (1865–1912), the great missionary, had a powerful impact on the churches in India in 1904 by summoning them to prayer for revival.

The third area of interest is a strong emphasis on **evangelistic endeavors**. Moody promoted evangelism among the students of the universities of America and Britain with the theme "we can evangelize the world in this generation if we will," giving rise to the Student Volunteer Movement in the area of foreign missions. The closing decade of the nineteenth century was marked by forward movements in most of the denominations, which were evangelistic movements dedicated to fulfilling the Great Commission at home. It was also the era of the great evangelistic crusades of Reuben A. Torrey (1856–1928) and Charles M. Alexander (1867–1920), and then, after Torrey became the leader of Biola in California, J. W. Chapman (1859–1918) and Alexander, and then after Chapman took over the Philadelphia church, Billy Sunday (1862–1935); Seth Joshua (1858–1925), the Welsh evangelist; and Rodney "Gypsy" Smith (1860–1947), the British evangelist, who had a phenomenal impact on South Africa through the post-Boer War "Mission of Peace" (1904–1905).[1] One after another, these great evangelists came to prominence and exercised powerful evangelistic ministries as part of this strong evangelistic endeavor that was launched at the turn of the century. The goal was world evangelization, and certainly God was moving in power.

The general decline that usually precedes revival is not so apparent in relation to this particular revival. In fact, the crusading of Moody, Taylor, and others had lifted the church to a higher level of endeavor, and indeed the three factors identified above ensured that the spiritual fervor of the church was rising rather than declining. Nevertheless, alongside the promising aspects of evangelicalism there was **a continuing conflict with modernism and liberalism** that was robbing many of their faith and creating general discomfort in the churches, and especially in its institutions of higher learning. The seminaries and Bible institutes had been strongly impacted by modernism, producing great conflict both within their walls and with the denominations. A succession of heresy trials among the Presbyterians, the Methodists, and the Episcopalians over the inroads of modernism into the churches, saw the evangelical cause triumph in each instance but failed to halt the invasion. Instead it increased public sympathy for those who were being put out of office because of their failure to accept basic Christian doctrine. Sadly, ultimately, the evangelical cause was to lose the battle for the major denominations of the Western world. But on the mission fields, that was not so.

Modernism was not such a problem on the mission fields as it was in the West, and so the revival in many respects burned longer and more fervently there. In fact, that was where revival began. **The first signs of revival** was among the Boer prisoners of war from South Africa after the war with England, as far apart as Bermuda in the West and Ceylon in the East, resulting in many volunteers for missionary service.[2] Also in Northern China, the early 1900s witnessed localized outpourings of the Spirit.[3] These, however, were just stirrings—mercy drops preparing for the showers to come.

The revival proper began in the year 1900 in **Japan**. Japan, although subjected to missionary endeavor for some considerable time, had not seen any real growth of Christian witness throughout the missionary period. But in the year 1900, God began a powerful outpouring of his Spirit. First, there was an unusually effective **movement to prayer;** then, an intensive effort at **evangelism** matched by **an awakening** of the Japanese urban masses to the claims of Christ. In the cities, multitudes came to know the Savior. The total membership of the churches within a year had almost doubled in Japan. The church went from one-half of 1 percent of the urban population to 1 percent of the urban population. Even outside the cities in the countryside, people were being affected by the gospel of Christ. The war with Russia occurred just four years after the beginning of the awakening and effectively ended the revival in Japan. It also brought the Japanese church into a period of persecution and opposition and a loss of favor with the population at large. The Russians were ostensibly Christian and they were at war with Japan. Although Japan was victorious in the conflict, any Christian was suspected of being in some way allied with Russia.

News of the notable impact of the revival in Japan combined with the reports of the ministry of great evangelists to stir believers to a greater sense of expectancy. Torrey and Alexander found that the zeal for prayer during their crusades in New Zealand and Australia in 1900 gave their ministry unprecedented success. Although the revival did not break out in full force during their time in New Zealand and Australia, yet it was the surge in 1903 and 1904 that was to bring the full flood of revival to the Christian world. That was focused primarily in two areas: in the area of **Wales** on the borders of England in the British Isles; and in **the Midwest** of the United States of America.

The surge that affected **Wales** was associated first of all with the ministry of Seth Joshua, the renowned Methodist evangelist, and later with the young Calvinistic Methodist preacher, Evan Roberts. Evan Roberts is looked upon by many as simply a revivalist; however, he did not set out to be a revivalist, nor was he a revivalist of the classic style. He was simply a young man who had a great burden for seeing God move powerfully and through his ministry came a mighty stirring by the Spirit of God. It began with prayer meetings with a handful of intercessors who were fervently seeking God. Then a young Welsh girl, Florrie Evans, gave a very simple declaration that she loved the Lord Jesus with all her heart and that seemed to be the act that precipitated the major flow of the awakening.[4]

In two years, more than 100,000 thoroughly converted outsiders had been added to the church. Drunkenness was immediately cut in half and continued to decline. Many of the taverns and bars went bankrupt and were converted into chapels, churches, or houses of prayer. Even the pit ponies had to be retrained to respond to spoken English because they could not recognize the commands given without the usual oaths and curses that had accompanied them in the past. Crime was so diminished that judges often were presented with a pair of white gloves when they arrived to try cases because there were no cases to be tried—none in the community had fallen foul of the law. Many of the local police became unemployed because of the large-scale conversion rate in the valleys of

Wales where crime became virtually nonexistent. Some of those converted policemen formed singing groups that went around and ministered at the revival meetings. Others simply were left without income. Although the revival had a positive side, it also had a negative side, for example., if you lose your job because revival comes to your town, you are apt to take a very poor view of it.

In the initial stage, interestingly, there was a surge of cases that went through the courts. The first two months of the first phase of the revival saw an increase in the number of cases being tried and the number of criminals being sentenced. The reason for this was not that there was a sudden upsurge of crime, but rather, criminals, who for a long time had resisted the due process of law, seeking to avoid punishment, now openly and readily confessed to their crimes because the Spirit of God had convicted them, and in many instances, they were truly converted. Thus, cases were disposed of much faster than previously; instead of a case taking three or four days to argue before the court, it was over in just a matter of hours because the criminal pled guilty, and there was no need for the long presentation of evidence, crossexaminations, and legal arguments. The facts were presented, acknowledged, and judicial sentences handed down, leading to a very quick movement of cases through the courts, especially in some of the major Welsh cities like Cardiff and Swansea, because of the changed nature of the relationship between the criminal and the law. Truly a great transformation had taken place in Wales.

At the other side of the Atlantic was a similar movement of the God's Spirit in **the Midwest** of the United States of America. The ministry of people like Charles Fox Parham (1873–1929) and the phenomenal success of his ministry in places like El Dorado and Galena, Kansas, and later in Texas, is often attributed specifically to his Pentecostal persuasion, and undoubtedly the Spirit of God was able to move through his ministry because of his commitment to the full power of the Holy Spirit in Pentecost. However, the most successful period of Parham's ministry both in Western Missouri, Eastern Kansas, and in Texas came at the peak of the revival. The remarkable successes in the large numbers converted and physically healed at the birth of the modern Pentecostal movement may be accounted for by the fact that the revival was burning powerfully, and not solely because of the content of the teaching regarding the baptism in the Holy Spirit, and certainly not because of any special talents or abilities on the part of Parham and those associated with him. The Spirit of God was generally moving throughout the area convicting people of sin and bringing them to an awareness of Christ.

The reports of the meetings are typical of the revival meetings that were taking place throughout the United States of America. By 1905, most Christians in America were expecting a general outpouring of God's Spirit. God began to move in **Los Angeles** before William Seymour (1870–1922) ever arrived and the modern Pentecostal movement was born. This does not undermine the beginnings of the Pentecostal movement, because out of many revivals through the centuries a new denominational structure has arisen to accommodate the revival converts who could not be accommodated within the main body of the existent denominations. The Lord Jesus illustrated this by his examples of the repairing of an old garment and the reusing of old wineskins.[5]

F. B. Meyer, the great British preacher, visited Los Angeles and spoke at the First Baptist Church, as a result of which that church experienced a mighty awakening. Although there was a division in the church and some of the revived ones pulled out to form a New Testament Church, many remained and continued the revival in face of the resistance of many of their Baptist fellow worshipers. The same revival spirit that had moved there also moved in the First Baptist Church in Glendale and brought a similar division to that church. It was among those revived people that the Pentecostal work in Los Angeles had its roots.

In the Grand Opera House in Los Angeles, there were united meetings with attendances of up to 180,000 people, filling the Grand Opera House and every available building in the vicinity and overflowing into the streets. At that same time, as God was pouring out his Spirit, William Seymour came in and was used by God as one of the revival preachers. In fact, the very Wednesday evening, April 9, 1906, when God's Spirit was poured on the group that met in the home of Richard and Ruth Asbury and they began to speak in tongues. According to the *Los Angeles Times*, there were revival meetings taking place all over Los Angeles with 180,000 people in the churches seeking God for an outpouring of the Holy Spirit. The birth of the Pentecostal Movement was part of God's answer.

On **the East Coast**, in the year 1906, Atlantic City, New Jersey, with a 60,000 population, encountered such a move of God's Spirit that by April that year, the very time that the Spirit of God was being poured out so generally on the West Coast, there were only fifty adults who had not yet surrendered their lives to Christ.[6] So powerfully was the Spirit of God moving. The Methodist churches in Philadelphia that same month admitted 6,101 new converts into membership in their meetings.

In **the Southern States**, the First Baptist Church in Paducah, Kentucky, added 1,000 new converts within the first few months of 1905, and the old pastor, Dr. J. J. Cheek, who was in his eighties and preparing for retirement, died of overwork from counseling so many new converts. Believer's baptisms among the Southern Baptists rose by over 25 percent in 1905, a further 25 percent in 1906, finishing off with about a 15 percent increase in 1907. God was moving.

In **the Upper Midwest** in Burlington, Iowa, every store and factory closed for a whole week in order to allow the employees to attend services, prayer meetings, and rededication of their lives so they could get their lives straightened out. Denver, Colorado, declared a day of prayer and by 10 a.m. the churches were filled and by 11:30 a.m. every store in the city was closed. Over 12,000 people were attending prayer meetings. Every school was closed, and even the Colorado legislature, which was meeting in Denver at that time, was closed. For a year afterwards, walking through the streets of Denver, Colorado, was like walking through a new Jerusalem. There was such a sense of the presence of God there.[7]

The Pentecostals were not the only recipients of blessing at that time. Over the two year period, 1904–1906, the seven major Protestant churches in the United States of America increased in membership by more than 2,000,000 new converts.[8] Even in **South Africa**, the Methodist church grew by over 30 percent during the three major years of the revival.[9] During the main period of the revival from 1905 through 1906, there was a great move of God in India and throughout Southern Asia. In all the states of **India** where there was a Christian presence, the Christian population increased by over 70 percent.[10] In **Burma**, the American Baptist Missionary Union baptized over 2,000 Karen tribesmen into their church that year. In **Korea**, wave after wave of revival came through. First in 1903, which doubled the churches; then in 1905, which doubled the churches again; and in 1907 the churches doubled yet again and instituted a movement for prayer that has characterized the churches in Korea ever since.

Jonathan Goforth's meetings in **Manchuria** have been well recounted, as have the amazing things that occurred throughout his ministry from the Boxer Rebellion until the 1911 revolution.[11] The leader of the revolution, Sun Yat Sen, who became the first president of the Republic of China, was a born-again Christian. The number of evangelical believers in **China** doubled from a quarter of a million to a half a million. It was the first known evangelical awakening in China in the modern era. In **Indonesia**, 100,000 evangelicals in 1903 by 1910 had risen to 300,000 and subsequently continued to grow.

In **Latin America**, the revival in Brazil, Chile, and other countries was also marked by powerful growth. In fact, the revival in Chile brought into being one of the most powerful Pentecostal movements that was in existence until the middle sixties the Pentecostal Methodist Church. A Methodist Episcopal preacher, William C. Hoover, was baptized in the Holy Spirit after hearing about the revival that had taken place in Mukti, India, under Pandita Ramabai. He began to seek God for a similar outpouring of the Spirit in Valparaiso, Chile, and the Spirit of God came upon them as at Pentecost.[12] He heard of what was happening in North America in Azusa Street and so decided to travel there to see for himself and discovered that what they were experiencing in Chile was the same as was being experienced at Los Angeles. On his return, he testified to what God had done and as a result the Methodist Episcopal denomination expelled him and the churches that had accepted his message, and so the Pentecostal Methodist Church was born, which by the early 1960s had the largest church in the world as part of its fellowship, the 60,000-member Jotabeche Church in Santiago, Chile.

Sadly, the Methodist Church, which expelled them, numbered 75,000 believers at the time, and by 1960 still numbered 75,000 believers, even though the population of Chile had doubled since 1906. The Pentecostal Methodist Church, on the other hand, had grown to not 75,000, but 750,000, and since then has continued to grow. Today the Pentecostals number approximately one and a half million believers out of population of about 8,000,000 people.

God was moving, and has continued to move throughout the 1900s. Probably the most renowned evangelist of this time period was Billy Sunday, a converted professional baseball player. He had come into a saving experience through the ministry of the Pacific Garden Rescue Mission in Chicago while playing for the Chicago White Stockings, a professional baseball team that a few years later became the well-known Chicago Cubs. He began to work first in the YMCA and then became the crusade organizer for J. Wilbur Chapman. On Chapman's leaving the evangelistic field to take up the pastorate of John Wannamaker's Bethany Church in Philadelphia, Sunday was thrust into evangelistic ministry himself as an evangelist. Although his ministry in the Midwest, especially around Iowa, was moderately effective initially, it was not until the great move of the Spirit in the middle of this decade that Sunday's ministry leapt into national prominence. He began to take with him his own portable tabernacle, a wooden building, which would accommodate 25,000 people, for erection at each new site, and people would come from the supporting churches.

The impact of this very effective evangelistic ministry was not independent of the revival but a part of the revival. Homer Rodeheaver, the founder of Rodeheaver Hall Songwriting Company, was Billy Sunday's permanent staff member (he was to Billy Sunday what Bev Shea was to Billy Graham), and exercised a powerful singing ministry. He was associated with Sunday quite early in his ministry, and the impact of the Sunday and Rodeheaver meetings was often quite phenomenal.

Although Sunday's campaigning against alcohol consumption is well known, that was only part of his ministry. He was a strong evangelistic preacher, who used the language of the street to appeal to the man in the street, and who scattered sawdust down the center aisle of the tabernacle to deaden the sound of the marching of the feet coming forward to shake his hand and accept Christ as Savior. In his crusade in New York, 98,264 people surrendered their lives to Christ, approximately one-tenth of the city's population, during his crusade there. In Boston over 64,000 people came to Christ; in Chicago, nearly 50,000; in Philadelphia, over 41,000; in Buffalo, New York, out of a population of only about 100,000 at that time, 38,800 accepted Christ.[13] That is more than evangelism; it is revival. The impact of this decade of revival was truly phenomenal.

Endnotes

1 Orr, *The Flaming Tongue*, op. cit., 117ff.
2 Ibid., 188.
3 Ibid.,158.
4 Ibid., 3.
5 Matthew 9:16, 17.
6 Orr, op. cit., 71.
7 Ibid., 70ff.
8 Ibid., 81-90.
9 Ibid., 121.
10 Ibid., 191.
11 J. Goforth: *By My Spirit* (Minneapolis, MN: Bethany, 1964).
12 Acts 2:1–4.
13 Hardman, *Seasons of Refreshing*, op. cit, 225-37.

Chapter 19

Post World War II

1940–1960

Edwin Orr describes this as the sixth wave of revival in the modern era of evangelical awakenings. The revival stirrings between the wars had taken place in a time of economic and social depression but the coming of World War II and its end brought a period of almost unprecedented prosperity to the Western world. Yet in the midst of that prosperity people began to turn to God. In part, particularly in Western Europe and the Pacific Rim, this arose because of **the devastation** that the war had brought to so much of their world. Another factor was **the fear** that the communist control of Eastern Europe would spread westward unless a moral and spiritual awakening would undergird the fabric of society, strengthening it against the kind of Communist aggression that the Eastern Europeans were encountering. A further factor, especially in the United States of America, was **a nationalistic fervor**, in which the American people saw their nation as the bastion of freedom in the world and part of that was a nostalgic patriotism that included evangelical Christianity as an integral element. Thus, evangelicalism, in particular, showed signs of an upsurge during and following World War II, which continued well into the 1950s.

The first signs of revival, however, in the post–World War II days came not from the west but from the south. In 1946, in Madagascar the fourth major revival for that particular island nation broke out. God once again began to move in a powerful way. Prayer, confession of sins, the exorcism of evil spirits, and the restitution of goods and those things that had been spoiled by sinful actions in the past were all characteristics of that awakening. An interesting exercise in the study of revivals is to trace the frequency with which restitution as an aspect of real repentance is emphasized. Even where repentance is stressed outside of a revival situation, restitution is not as prominent a theme as in a time of revival.

Tragically, that revival was somewhat short-lived due to the unexpected death from tuberculosis of its most notable figure, Daniel Rakotozandry (1919–1948). Those who followed in his footsteps did not have the spiritual stature that he did and so within a few years the largely leaderless revival began to peter out and by 1950 the great work that had begun there was virtually over.[1]

The East. In 1947, the Korean Christians began to hold prayer meetings for revival, especially in northern Korea, which was newly liberated from Japanese occupation. The city of Pyongyang was marked by massive prayer meetings with more than 10,000 in attendance. This prayer meeting movement was called to commemorate the great revival of more than forty years before, in the opening years of the century. God began to pour out his Spirit yet again, and that revival continued even into the period of the Korean War. The final conquest of the north by the Chinese and their Communist associates resulted in the ending of the revival there, but not the ending of the revival in the south.[2]

The refugees who fled to the south continued the revival spirit, which burned brightly into the 1950s and, despite a brief lull at the end of that decade, resumed again in the 1960s and continues to burn very brightly to this day. God was answering the prayers of his people.

North America. From Madagascar, the revival fervor moved on to Korea, and then northward and eastward into North America. Mexico also experienced its first spiritual awakening at this time through the ministry of William Cameron Townsend (1896–1982), missionary to the Cakchiquel Indians of Guatemala, and the founder of the Wycliffe Bible Translators in 1942. Through his travels through northern parts of South America, Townsend helped spread the revival fervor.

By 1949, the Spirit of God was also being poured out in North America. That year heralded the first signs of a series of extraordinary revivals in several Christian colleges and universities, beginning at Bethel College in Minneapolis. Initially, this outpouring of God's Spirit in 1949 was not widely reported until the later outpouring at Wheaton College in Illinois brought it to public attention,[3] signaling that the move of God was definitely on.

At the same time as God was pouring out his Spirit on the colleges and universities across America, a young Youth for Christ evangelist, William Franklin "Billy" Graham (1918–2018), was invited to hold a major crusade in the city of Los Angeles. A personal renewal conference had been held in Forest Home, near Los Angeles, organized by Henrietta Mears (1889–1963) and J. Edwin Orr (1912–1987), out of which came the Hollywood Christian group which was very effective in evangelizing the stars and starlets of the Hollywood movie scene, many of whom came to faith in Christ. One of the young people present at the Forest Home meetings was Billy Graham, who as a result was invited to conduct a mass evangelism crusade in California later that year. Graham's crusade in Los Angeles continued for sixteen weeks; every time they were about to close, first after three weeks, then after a month, and then the next month, God poured out his Spirit afresh and gave indication that the crusade should continue. Continue it did, until multiplied thousands had come to faith in Christ. Across the United States of America people began to turn to God in prayer, seeking a general outpouring of God's Spirit upon the continent.

That outpouring almost came. In Billy Graham's autobiography he tells how in January of 1950 he was invited by Harold Ockenga (1905–1985) to conduct a crusade in the city of Boston. Ockenga and the crusade committee rented the Mechanics Hall, then moved to Ockenga's Park Street Church, returned to the Mechanics Hall and the Opera House, culminating in the Boston Gardens, the great public arena. The latter was packed to the very doors, until it was impossible to hold more people in the 13,000-seat arena, and over 10,000 had to be turned away. Seldom had even the greatest orators of the past drawn together such numbers in the city of Boston, but God was moving by his Spirit. Billy Graham had doubled the original schedule of meetings in the Boston area but had a pressing engagement in Toronto, Canada. Even as he departed from Boston by train for Toronto, he felt a strong compulsion to get off the train, first at Worcester and then at Springfield, and to telephone Boston to say that he would stay in New England. Repeatedly the feeling came to him that now was the hour for revival.[4] New England was being swept by the Spirit of God. Invitations had poured in from across the region. Any city in the whole of New England would throng to hear him. The press, even the *Boston Post*, whose editor was a devout Roman Catholic, suggested that Billy Graham should stay in New England and not go to Canada because this was, as he put it, the hour of God's visitation. But Billy had an engagement and he was desperately tired and frightened of the press. He said:

> Whatever I said was being quoted. I knew I wasn't qualified; I didn't have the experience to say the right things. I was afraid that I was going to say something that would bring disrepute to the name of Christ and so I decided to stay with the train and go on to Canada.[5]

Even at Niagara, as they crossed the border, Billy said: "Again I felt tremendously impelled to call back to Boston and say we should continue." But he resisted the impulse. Later he acknowledged: "I unwittingly disobeyed the voice of God."[6]

The revival that could have come to Boston and to New England never was, because the hour of God's visitation passed and it just never happened. How many other times has a great revival that could have had national dimensions been missed because the people that God had chosen to lead that revival refused to obey God, wittingly or unwittingly? When God says "Do it!"—do it. You do not know when the opportunity will come again—and certainly that opportunity did not come again to New England in that generation.

The Hebrides. Nevertheless, even though the general awakening in New England that could have happened did not happen, God continued to move in a very powerful way through others and in other places. At the other side of the Atlantic in the Gaelic-speaking Hebrides Islands of Scotland, especially on the island of Lewis, God began to pour out his Spirit again, largely through the ministry of the little-known Scottish preacher Duncan Campbell (1898–1972). Campbell's ministry in Lewis was marked by some phenomenal manifestations of the Spirit of God.

The revival there began simply through a cottage prayer meeting called by two elderly sisters, one Peggy Smith (1865– ?), blind, and her sister Christine (1867– ?), crippled with arthritis, and yet it was their prayer time that brought about a great move of God in that area. At the same time as they were praying, some young men were also praying and seeking God. One of the youngest, himself a deacon, read Psalm 24:34: "Who shall ascend into the hill of the Lord, or who shall stand in his holy place? He that hath clean hands and a pure heart, who has not lifted up his soul into vanity or sworn deceitfully . . ." Then he stopped, declaring: "Brothers, we have been praying for weeks, waiting on God. And what I want to know is this, are our hands clean? Is our heart pure?"[7] That was what it needed. The Spirit of God swept in and brought to each one a real sense of the power of God.

In prayer, the Smith sisters' pastor, Rev. James Murray MacKay, felt impressed to invite Duncan Campbell to come to Lewis for meetings in the parish church in Barvas. Campbell was in Ireland speaking at a convention when he received the invitation and he knew that God had called him to come. The sisters said: "He'll be here within two weeks"—and he was.

There was a great sense of expectancy, but in that first night's meeting nothing unusual happened. Campbell went home to his bed and during the night, at about 3:00 a.m., was awakened to the sound of feet in the road outside the house where he was staying. He opened the curtains of the bedroom and looked out. There, heading down the road from all parts of the island, was the light of lanterns and lamps as people were making their way to Barvas church. There was no meeting scheduled for that hour of the morning but the Spirit of God had begun to draw the people together. Even the man who owned the coach company in Stornoway, felt strongly impressed that he should get out his bus, drive into the center of the town, pick up the people who were waiting there and drive them across to Barvas about twenty-six miles away. Who would be there at 1:00 a.m.? But he went with his coach and found that the center square was filled with people. Not only he, but other coach operators had also come. They loaded up the people onto the coaches, and amazingly there were exactly enough coaches to accommodate all the people. Nobody knew where they were going, and so they just followed the direction that the Holy Spirit gave them—coach after coach, going along the narrow country lanes thronged with people heading to Barvas.

The unique thing about this particular awakening was the sensible presence of the Spirit of God that drew people together, without advertising, not even by word of mouth, but simply by an overwhelming impression that they should go to the epicenter of the revival. The Spirit of God moved in amazing power; the unconverted came to Christ; the converted were revived, set on fire for God, and went back to their homes and communities to spread the revival blaze over the whole island.

An airplane on its way out to the Orkney Islands loaded with passengers had to put in at Stornoway airport because as it flew over the Hebrides, the Spirit of God swept across the passengers and crew of that plane. Feeling that they could not continue their scheduled flight to the Orkneys, the pilot landed at Stornoway to seek someone who could lead them to a saving knowledge of Christ. Fishing boats passing along the Sound, the water between the Hebrides and the Scottish mainland, also made unscheduled stops in the harbors on the islands, especially on Lewis, because the fishermen, though some ten to fifteen miles out to sea, were falling under great conviction of sin and needed someone to lead them to faith in Christ. Their home ports were in other parts of Scotland, but the sense of the Spirit of God was so powerful in that whole area that they could not continue.

Duncan Campbell said that the greatest of all the miracles was in one particular village called Arnal, where there was a lot of opposition. One lone believer began to pray publicly for revival in that village. People in the village later said that as he prayed the Spirit of God swept in with such power that the very house where he lived was shaken. They thought an earthquake had come, and across the village people began to fall to the ground and call on the Lord to save them, as the Lord began to minister to them by the power of the Spirit.

Despite all the extremes of these unusual manifestations, however, there is no evidence of peculiar emotional responses on the part of the people. There were no signs and miracles such as had been evidenced in Pentecostal type of revivals, no extraordinary physical manifestations such as were apparent in Kentucky in the revival of 1800, but a deep sense of conviction, a breaking down before God, as people all over this island community were smitten by the sense that God was there on their island. The revival continued less obviously from about 1949 to 1956, when a further visitation on another of these Scottish islands, South Uist, was also marked by similar manifestations.

It was my privilege to meet Duncan Campbell in September 1959, just three years after the South Uist revival. We stayed in the same home in Sheffield, England, and sat up until the early hours of the morning talking about these two revivals and the way that God's Spirit had moved in such power. That gave me a great hunger for revival, to study it, but more than that, to experience it and to live in that kind of awareness of the presence of the Spirit of God. One cannot come into contact with a man like Duncan Campbell without learning something, because he certainly was a man who seemed to carry with him the very sense of God's presence.

Britain. In 1950, the British Methodist movement, hearing of the revival that was taking place in the Scottish Hebrides islands, launched their mid-century crusade of evangelism in an attempt to turn the British public back to God. That was a human effort which, although it had moderate success, was unsuccessful in the long run at stopping the slide of the British churches into the night that was to come upon them by the end of the 1950s and it was simply not a revival. Crusade, yes. Evangelism, yes. The best effort that they could put forward, yes. Perhaps things would have been different in 1954 following the great crusade of Billy Graham at Harringay Arena in England. When Graham was invited and encouraged to return in the fall of 1954 for another major crusade, to cover the whole of Scotland, England, and Ireland, he consulted with the then Archbishop of Canterbury, Geoffrey Fisher (1887–1972), who was by no means an evangelical by persuasion. He felt that for Graham to return within a few months of the ending of the Harringay crusade would not be within the capacity of the English churches to handle effectively. So, he and his fellow church leaders asked him to plan his return to England for 1955, following his All-Scotland crusade, when they would book the great stadium at Wembley, which would accommodate 120,000 people.

Graham accepted the advice of those English churchmen but sensed once again that he had unwittingly disobeyed God, because when he returned for the All-Scotland crusade, as successful as it was, it was not revival; nor was the subsequent crusade in Wembley in London, which was also well orchestrated and well planned. Many were convinced that if Billy had returned the year before, in the fall of 1954, the revival would have gone forward in great power.[8] That was the last major opportunity that the British were to have for experiencing the moving of the Spirit of God for some considerable time. The decline of the churches following the 1955 Wembley crusade quickened to a landslide and by the 1960s, the churches were expending herculean but vain efforts in trying to stop the downhill slide. It is tragic to consider what might have been. That whole period of revival is fraught with similar problems.

The Pentecostal Phase. Alongside of the evangelical revivals were the revivals among the Pentecostals. In 1947, the World Pentecostal Conference was convened in Zurich, Switzerland. That first attempt by the Pentecostal movement to get together with fellow experientialists, despite differences in church government and some minor points of doctrine, was to precipitate an atmosphere in which revival could occur. The following year the Pentecostal Fellowship of North America was formed. Although these were organizational, about the same time in 1947 at Sharon Bible Institute in North Battleford in Canada, God began to pour out his Spirit. George P. Hawtin (1909–1994), his brother Ernest (1911–2006), and Percy G. Hunt (1910–1997), the leaders of that school, experienced a significant outpouring of God's Spirit that regrettably gave rise to a peculiar doctrinal aberration called The Latter Rain movement or The New Order of the Latter Rain. While the New Order of the Latter Rain may have begun in a genuine spiritual awakening, because of the leadership's resistance to the genuine leading of the Holy Spirit, and their unwillingness to correct, or even check public prophecies, the work soon foundered.[9]

The Healing Revival. But God was moving. Aimee Semple MacPherson (1890–1944), the great female evangelist of the preceding period, died in 1944 and during the next three years so did most of the older pre–World War II revivalists, including Dr. Charles S. Price (1887–1947), the great Canadian healing evangelist, and Smith Wigglesworth (1859–1947), the British healing evangelist. By 1948, many young men began to seek God for a fresh outpouring of God's Spirit and the raising up of a new generation of healing evangelists and God answered that prayer. The book by David Edwin Harrell, *All Things Are Possible*, tells the story of some of the more prominent evangelists, such as William M. Branham (1909–1965), G. Oral Roberts (1918–2009), Gordon Lindsay (1906–1973) and those associated with The Voice of Healing, Jack Coe (1918–1957) of the Assemblies of God, T. L. Osborn (1923–2013) from the Pentecostal Church of God, and A. A. Allen (1911–1970), also from the Assemblies of God. One after another came to the forefront in those early days. By 1950, revival was burning through the ministry of these men. It was estimated that any particular Tuesday evening over ten million Americans could be found sitting under canvas in the tent crusade meetings throughout the United States of America, listening to some of the two hundred or so evangelists associated with this great healing revival. God was moving in power in an unprecedented way.

The halcyon days of awakening at the beginning of the 1950s quickly faded as problems began to emerge within the ranks of the healing revivalists. One problem was that those who had been involved in the healing revivals at the very beginning had ministries that were powerfully owned by God with miracles and great manifestations of the Holy Spirit. People were being converted; their tents were thronged with people intent on seeking the Lord. As others began to embark on this evangelistic ministry, they sought to imitate the forerunners of the movement, especially prominent early leaders like Oral Roberts, William Branham, and Jack Coe. The younger evangelists could not match the claims that these men could genuinely make regarding their ministries. The temptation was for them to exaggerate the results occurring under their ministries to put themselves on a par with those so obviously used by God at the beginning of the awakening. They saw that unless they could claim as many or more conversions or miracles, then people would not come to hear them. This desire for position and prominence led so many to make outrageous claims that brought disrepute to the work. In their attempts to outdo the older evangelists the results claimed by the newer evangelists became increasingly incredible. This brought the work into disrepute, which proved tragic for the continuance of the awakening.

In 1951 and 1952, for instance, in the published accounts of the more than 200 healing evangelists regarding ministry in Jamaica, one of the favorite cross-cultural places for ministry, the number of converts claimed was double the entire population of the island.[10] Also, the number of blind people reported as healed in Jamaica was almost equal to the island's population. Either almost everybody in Jamaica was blind or some received and lost their sight repeatedly. The movement was foundering on a rock of human imitations, exaggerations, and falsehoods. God will not bless a work built on falsehood. Thank God for what he is doing, but do not exaggerate the results.

This was one of the few awakenings that was aborted because, although there was initially both among the evangelicals and among the Pentecostals a genuine move of God's Spirit, first one then another proved to be unresponsive to the leading of the Holy Spirit and either ran off into fanaticism as did the New Order of the Latter Rain, or drew back from following the Lord as closely as they should like Billy Graham and others of the evangelical wing did, or began to substitute human imitations for the genuine move of the Spirit as in so many of the healing evangelists' ministries.

From the debacle at the end of this revival period that effectively brought the whole thing to a conclusion, it looked as though God was withdrawing, but God does not. When a revival does not flow in God's direction, then God will temporarily withdraw the moving of the Spirit, but return in even greater power, which is exactly what happened in the late 1950s to the 1960s. Many of the preparatory events for the next major revival period arose out of those turbulent days. The union meetings of the healing evangelists; the emergence of the Full Gospel Businessmen's Fellowship as a viable means of communicating the Pentecostal message to the business community; and the great area-wide crusades of Billy Graham and others served as orchestrated and organized events bringing Pentecostals and non-Pentecostals into an effective working relationship. These factors would contribute toward the great revival that would dawn in the 1960s and early 1970s.

Endnotes

1 Orr, *Evangelical Awakenings in the South Seas*, op. cit., 201.

2 J. E. Orr: *Evangelical Awakenings in Eastern Asia* (Minneapolis, MN: Bethany, 1975), 111–19.

3 M. Dorsett: *Revival at Wheaton* (Wheaton, IL: International Awakening Press, 1994), 12ff.

4 W. F. Graham: *Just As I Am* (New York, NY: HarperCollins, 1997), 160–61.

5 J. Pollock: *Billy Graham* (London, UK: Hodder & Stoughton, 1966), 99.

6 Ibid.

7 D. Campbell: *The Price and Power of Revival* (Edinburgh, UK: Faith Mission, 1956), 60.

8 Pollock, op. cit., 180–81.

9 R. M. Riss: art "Latter Rain Movement" in *The New International Dictionary of Pentecostal and Charismatic Movements* (Gand Rapids, MI: Zondervan, 2002), 830–833.

10 D. E. Harrell, Jr.: *All Things Are Possible* (Bloomington, IN: Indiana University Press, 1975), 142.

Chapter 20

The Charismatic Renewal

1960–1975

The Charismatic Renewal is usually dated from about 1960 and was marked by a reviving of the church members and the entry of many into the fullness of the Spirit that was to herald an epochal change to the structure of Christianity. A further remarkable surge of spiritual life came from 1969 to 1975 in many established denominations arising partly out of the initial stages of the outpouring at the beginning of the '60s, and providing a counterbalance to much of the radical conflict that was currently taking place, but also developing in some surprising ways. There were three distinct aspects to the Charismatic Renewal.

The Protestant Renewal. Although the move of God's Spirit within the mainline Protestant churches had begun earlier, attention was drawn to it in April 1959 through the public testimony of Dennis Bennett (1917–1991), the priest of St. Mark's Episcopal Church in Van Nuys, California, regarding his personal reception of the fullness of the Holy Spirit.[1] Two years later, in August 1961, the renewal spread into the Lutheran Church in America when Larry Christenson (1928–2017), pastor of North Heights Lutheran Church, in Minnesota, was baptized in the Holy Spirit through the ministry of a female evangelist, Mary Westberg.[2]

The Youth Renewal. Alongside the Protestant renewal that ultimately was to penetrate all the main line Protestant denominations, there was also a youth aspect which is sometimes called the Jesus People movement or the Jesus Revolution, which began almost simultaneously in different parts of the USA and other countries about 1967, but particularly came to public prominence in 1969 with the spectacular baptismal services of a thousand-plus people in the Pacific Ocean by leaders like Charles W. (Chuck) Smith (1927–2013), Arthur O. Blessitt (b. 1940), and others of fame or notoriety. Emerging out of this youth movement were some heretical groups that creamed off a lot of the impetus of the movement, groups like The Children of God (now known as The Family International) or The Way International or other similar groups.

The Catholic Renewal. This third area has an interesting background in some of the deliberations that had been going on within the Roman Catholic Church. It ultimately came to the fore with the Vatican II Council, at which seemingly an open door was given for charismatic renewal within Catholicism, as the goal of that conference was, according to the Roman pontiff John XXIII (1881–1963), a new Pentecost in our day. Many Catholics wholeheartedly embraced the concept of having a new Pentecost, in which God's Spirit would be poured out upon all nations, Catholic, Protestant, from all branches of the Christian faith and, strangely, even outside of the Christian faith. They expected that this would be an age of a turning back to God and of some remarkable things taking place. Although the opinions about the Catholic renewal may differ, in reality, through that movement many did come to a vital and living faith in God; their lives were transformed; and many of the changes that are taken for granted in the modern Roman Catholic Church originated from the Catholic Vatican II Council in the mid-60s and the renewal that began shortly thereafter.

While the initial development may have been Protestant, it was the outpouring on Catholics, especially the surprising move of the Holy Spirit in 1966 at Duquesne University in Pittsburgh, Pennsylvania, that spurred a full-scale renewal throughout the Catholic world. Leon-Joseph Cardinal Suenens (1904–1996), Archbishop of Malines-Brussels in Belgium, was appointed the leader of the Catholic renewal forces within worldwide Catholicism and things began happening that would have been unimaginable just a few years earlier.

This not only brought changes to Catholicism, but also on the other side opened the door for a greater Pentecostal penetration into countries that had traditionally been reserved to the Catholic faith, but had practically lost sight of any real religious fervor. In **Italy**, for instance, where 98 percent of the population was nominally Catholic but, in practice, only one million out of sixty million people had any active religious faith, and possibly one and one half percent were practicing Catholics, the Pentecostal movement, after the Vatican Council and especially after the charismatic renewal in the Catholic Church began, was able to grow phenomenally. By the end of the twentieth century the Pentecostal movement alone in Italy embraced almost a million believers as its total constituency. There was only slightly more than a million practicing Roman Catholics in Italy and it is expected that within the second decade of the present century the Pentecostals will have far surpassed the Catholic Church in active participants. The situation within Pentecostalism is different from that within Catholicism in that there are few nominal Pentecostals but many active participants, whereas within the Catholic framework because of its long traditional role there are fewer active but more nominal participants. Therefore, although there may continue to be a majority of nominal Catholics in the foreseeable future, the active participants are considerably fewer. Nevertheless, God has certainly been doing remarkable things within Catholicism and notable changes have taken place.

The Third-World Revival. During the same time period as these various components of the charismatic renewal occurred, there were some remarkable outpourings of the Holy Spirit throughout the third-world. These were not two independent movements but part of a widespread movement of God's Spirit. As these dramatic changes were taking place within church life in the Western world God was pouring out his Spirit in countries like **Indonesia, Brazil, Korea,** and **Southern Africa**. Great revival continued in the war-torn countries of **Indochina, Cambodia, Southern Vietnam,** and **Laos**, countries that were to be devastated by the communist conquest of southeast Asia. The final fall of those countries in 1975 serves as a cutoff date for the awakening, because with the Western nations' final withdrawal from Indochina came a toppling of the free governments of those countries and a closing of the door to the opportunity for missionary work and evangelism there.

Furthermore, the predicted domino effect spread across the rest of the world as in nation after nation the revival fires extinguished, as though God himself were expressing his opinion of the Western nations's abrogating their agreements with that tiny enclave of freedom, abandoning it to whatever fate should overtake it. What may have been a sound political decision, produced multitudes of martyrs and created many problems for the work of God in those countries. God, however, is not limited by political decision-making and the work, although submerged and no longer in a revival phase, still continued.

The same thing could be said regarding **China**. The Western withdrawal from China after World War II, leaving the country to fall to the Communist forces, resulted in massive destruction for the work of God and the driving of the church underground. But what man may have meant for evil, God brought good out of. The submerging of the church spread it even further and after some thrity years of being submerged the church emerged even stronger out of that. The same will happen in Indochina, by the mercy of God.

The Indonesian Revival. Many things have been written about the revival in Indonesia and many exaggerations have filled the minds of miracle-hungry Westerners with unsubstantiated stories. Sadly, when we look at what has happened in Indonesia, we find that the stories of miracles being performed in great profusion originate primarily out of the writings of Mel(chior) Tari, an Indonesian young man[3] who was personally associated only with the fringe of the revival. His sister, however, was very closely involved in the original evangelistic teams that helped precipitate the revival in Indonesia. This young man's writings were full of the kind of exaggerations to be expected from someone thinking back into his early adolescence, and who is now influenced by publicity-hungry people. It is not surprising that his tales of multiple people being raised from the dead are a considerable development from his original testimony of one or two people that he knew had been raised from the dead.

Regrettably, other writers expand the accounts even further. The twenty instances of water turning into wine between October 1967 and the end of 1971 that could be and have been authenticated,[4] became such a common occurrence that in almost every communion service water turned into wine. When an evangelistic team needed to cross a stream that was running at full spate and all the signs of the footpath that crossed the shallow point of the stream had disappeared, a supernatural light appeared and guided that evangelistic team across the stream at the right point even though they could not see where the stepping stones were. In Tari's later accounts, this became not one but several instances of actually walking on water, despite the fact that in his initial testimony, as in all the testimonies coming out of the country, it was not mentioned. It sounds better to walk on water than it does to be supernaturally guided to the place where it is possible to cross the stream because of the minimal depth of water.

Such exaggeration led some to dismiss the Indonesian revival as being largely the creation of that young man and his two books on the Indonesian revival. But careful investigators have established beyond any shadow of a doubt that there was indeed a revival. Following the successful evangelistic ministry of Johannes Ratuwalu in 1964, the revival began in earnest in 1965 in the Bible college of the Christian Evangelical (Dutch Reformed) Church. From that beginning in Batu, **East Java**, and the sending out of sixteen evangelistic teams of ten students in each, God began to move in a remarkable way, especially on the island of **West Timor** and through the Soe Dutch Reformed Church on that island. Christians confessed their sins to God and to each other; experienced personal renewal; nominal Christians were soundly converted; miracles did occur, confirming the message that was being preached; healings were not commonplace but were there nevertheless; demon-possessed people were totally delivered; amulets, charms, and taboos that had featured so strongly in the people's lives in that largely pagan society were forsaken; and people were wholeheartedly committed to the Lord. In West Timor itself, the single visiting team from East Java gave rise to about ninety further teams that went all over the island evangelizing and witnessing. The result of that revival movement in West Timor was quite remarkable; there were many thousands brought to faith in Christ. The numbers in Java were even more impressive, between 1965 and 1971 more than two million Muslims converted to Christianity, the largest such conversion in modern history.

In 1953, when the Indonesian Islands became independent of Holland, there were slightly more than 250,000 Christians on West Timor and at the next official count in 1972 at the end of the revival there were over 500,000 believers. These are the only official figures available as no count of the numbers of Christians was permitted during the whole reign of Sukarno and his radical regime that came into power in Indonesia. The total increase of those added to the church in that nineteen-year period in fact would be closer to 264,000, allowing for normal demographic change and emigration. Normal population increase for that period would have produced an expected growth in membership of about 100,000 if the population increased at just over 2 percent per year during the nineteen-year time period; therefore, it is necessary to account for at least another 164,000 added to the church beyond the normal expected growth. The growth of the Christian population far exceeded the general growth because of the large numbers who had come to Christ.

The largest Protestant church, the Batak Protestant Christian Church, had an estimated membership in 1972 of about 1,000,000 members. The second largest was the Minhasa Evangelical Christian Church with 500,000[5] and then the Pentecostals with about 300,000 members and other smaller groups. What could account for that kind of growth? The only thing that can account for that kind of growth in a predominantly pagan or Muslim society is a moving of the Spirit of God. Undoubtedly, revival does not need exaggeration in order to make it a phenomenal move of God. It was truly a remarkable move of the Spirit of God and many thousands had come to faith in Christ. Some of the more responsible books tell of the occurrence of remarkable miracles, especially in the area of the healing of the sick and the deliverance of the demonized. The unusual miracle, however, of changing water into wine was the one that was finally to prove the undoing of the whole revival.

The wide circulation of Tari's stories of the multiplicity of miracles and especially of the changing of water into wine prompted some to resort to artificial means of duplicating the miracle. The leader of an evangelistic team from Soe working in Kupang believed that the Lord would repeat the miracle under his ministry and, to ensure its occurrence, secreted red dye *kesumba* in the bottom of his vessel. When his deception was exposed, he was forbidden to be involved further in ministry.[6] What he thought would enhance his reputation and that of the revival did two things: first, when it and other similar instances of deception became known, they cast doubt upon the authenticity of the revival movement in Indonesia where God had been moving so strongly by the power of the Holy Spirit. Secondly, such deceptions hinder the moving of the Spirit of God, who does not need the help of our human imitations.

The year 1972 marked the end of the revival in Indonesia. It did not resume for more than ten years, until 1984, and then it did not resume among the Dutch Reformed churches but among the Methodist churches that had not been directly affected by the earlier revival on West Timor. It was, however, not on West Timor but in **Sulawesi** that the revival began to pick up and to move and is still moving strongly throughout Indonesia. Timor has been largely untouched by the latest phase of revival because of the foolish intervention of a well-meaning man who felt that God needed a helping hand in order to perform a miracle.

God moved in a phenomenal way and in the new phase of the revival is still moving in a phenomenal way. He is doing incredible things that are not so incredible as to be unbelievable but incredible enough to challenge our faith for a like move of God in our day and in our lands. God is again moving in power in Indonesia and certainly the latest phase of the revival has been marked with similar signs and wonders and miracles but even more so marked with deep conviction and sound conversion on the part of the people who are being affected by it.

Revival is the desire of many in our day, and even if we may not be privileged to see a widespread revival in our communities, yet we know that whenever God's people are willing to turn from sin and seek the face of God with all their hearts, God has promised to pour out his Spirit even in the Western world. Even here, there have been those bright moments when the Holy Spirit has swept in and done a remarkable work in a community that was eager for such a thing to happen.

A personal note. At the latter end of this revival move between 1969 and 1975, I was pastoring a church on the Isle of Wight in the English Channel. On the first Sunday of August 1974, the Spirit of God swept in upon us in a most unusual and unexpected fashion. We had had special prayer for revival about a year before but were not currently engaging in prayer for revival. There had been some unifying influences among the churches in the months before the revival actually began, one of which was the presentation in various centers throughout the island of a very interesting musical called *Come Together*, written by Jimmie and Carol Owens from the USA, which in a musical way expressed Pentecostal type of worship and gave an openness to many evangelical churches that had not been particularly inclined toward the Pentecostals or Charismatics. Also, there had been a united evangelistic crusade with Eric Hutchings (d. 1982), a British evangelist, which had had some impact upon the island as a whole, although there were not many conversions. In my own local church, we had begun a Sunday night after-church fellowship for visitors and vacationers so they could get to know the people in the church and have some fellowship before returning to their lodgings.

The first Sunday morning in August began like any other Sunday morning service did, with hymns, prayers, Bible reading, and a brief message, followed by Holy Communion. As we gathered around the Lord's table, a lady of mature years, sitting at the front of the church, began to sing softly in the Spirit. The two people sitting behind her and the person alongside her also began to sing in the Spirit. Like an ever-widening ripple going across the congregation one after another of the approximately 150 people present began to sing in the Spirit, including some people who were not yet baptized in the Spirit but were at that instant so baptized and did not speak in tongues but sang in tongues. Some people present were visiting from an Anglican retirement center where a lady from the Hastings Elim Pentecostal church worked. They had come on vacation to the Isle of Wight and although most of them were not committed Christians, they had come for the first time to a Pentecostal church. Several of them were soundly converted and filled with the Holy Spirit within moments and sang in the Spirit. The rest of the group, who were not converted in the service, did accept Christ in the bus on their way back to the place where they were staying on the island.

The remarkable moving of God's Spirit that Sunday morning service just seemed to lift us onto a new plane of relationship with God. It was a blessed time but it was a preparation time for what was to come Sunday night. After I had opened church about 6:00 p.m. for early comers to gather for the 6:30 p.m. service, I was busy on the platform preparing everything for the service. When people began to arrive, they came in through the foyer and as they began to enter the sanctuary, suddenly the Spirit of God fell upon them. Those who were not right with God found that they could not come into the sanctuary without coming under such great conviction that some fell prostrate to the ground and began to weep, calling upon the Lord for forgiveness for sins long hidden in their lives. Those who were able to move helped them into the pews at the back of the church but soon those pews were crowded and others were arriving and were trying to get into the church. Some were falling, others were sitting, and yet others were just struck immobile by the sense of God's presence in the sanctuary.

Inside the foyer, we had offices, one mine, the other the deacons's office. We opened those up and the people went in there to seek God for personal renewal before coming into the sanctuary. The service was somewhat chaotic in its commencement because we simply began to worship the Lord as those who were renewed came on in. As others were renewed, they too came in and shared testimonies, joyfully exhilarating in what God had done in their lives. The service continued until late in the evening. We realized that God had indeed visited us. After church when the last person had finally departed, I was closing the outer gate to the church, part of the iron fence surrounding the church property. I noticed the bar at the end of the street had closed and the people were leaving. One old drunk came staggering along the street until he came to the edge of our property and suddenly stopping, caught hold of the iron railing. Thinking he had taken ill, I went back down the steps and asked him, "Are you ill? Do you want me to call for an ambulance?" Weeping, he declared: "I am a wicked, wicked man. I have wasted my life. I am such a wicked man." He began to weep before the Lord and confess his sins there in the street. The presence of God in the church was so powerful that he could not even walk past the church without falling under conviction of sin, although he knew nothing of what had occurred inside.

Our next service was the Tuesday night prayer meeting. Our custom was to begin with just a couple of songs followed by a brief time of worshiping the Lord, after which I would lead in prayer and then read the Scriptures with a brief exposition. Then we would take requests and devote the remainder of the service to intercessory prayer. Following this normal pattern, we sang and began to worship the Lord. As we worshiped the Lord, none of us were particularly conscious of the passing of time. I then began to read the Scriptures and the congregation paid good attention. When I was about to expound the Scriptures, one of the deacons pointed out to me that in fact the time was ten minutes after 9:00 and we had started at 7:30. No one had realized that more than an hour had passed while we were simply lost in the presence of God. I cannot tell what was revealed during that time to me or to other people who were present, for some things are not to be spoken of to those who were not present at the time. But God did some remarkable things in many people's lives during that worship time. It seemed as though as Paul said: "Whether in the body, or out of the body (we) could not tell," but we were caught up to the heavenly realms and we met God and he met with us.[7]

From that church the work spread out. Over the next several months, church after church throughout that island was revived. Every Anglican parish on the island was visited by the Holy Spirit. Almost a year later, there were seventeen charismatic prayer groups functioning in the Anglican parishes of the island; almost every parish had its own. More than 25,000 new believers were added to the various churches during the same period.[8]

Endnotes

1 Dennis J. Bennett: *Nine O'clock in the Morning* (London & Eastbourne, UK: Coverdale House, 1971), 1ff.

2 M. Harper: *As at the Beginning* (London, UK: Hodder & Stoughton, 1965), 86, 87.

3 D. J. I. M. Tari: *Like a Mighty Wind* (London, UK: Coverdale House, 1973).

4 K. E. Koch: *Wine of God: Revival in Indonesia, Formosa, Solomon Islands and South India* (Montreal, Canada: Christian Evangelism Publications, 1974), 39.

5 D. Coomes: *The Flame Still Spreads* (Guildford, UK: Lutterworth Press, 1974), 94, 95.

6 Koch, op. cit., 163,164.

7 2 Corinthians 12:2–4.

8 Minutes of the IEC (Island Evangelical Fellowship) August 1975, 1, 2.

Chapter 21

Late-20th & Early-21st Century Stirrings

1975-Present

By the mid-1970s, the Charismatic Renewal in western Christendom began to stratify into the Protestant, Catholic, and House Church streams. The latter was especially affected by the growing chaos that ensued from the rise of the Shepherding movement, which may be traced back to the New Order of the Latter Rain (1948),[1] and to the Positive Confession (Word of Faith) movement, which had its roots in the teachings of Essek W. Kenyon (1867–1948), which in turn were strongly influenced by the New Thought philosophy of Phineas P. Quimby (1802–1866).[2] The demise of the Shepherding movement in the early 1980s coincided with a fresh wave of the Holy Spirit's activity, mainly among evangelical Protestants, who were disenchanted with the obvious problems that had emerged in the Charismatic Renewal, but who, nevertheless, were hungry for a fuller experience of the Spirit's presence.

The Third Wave. The term was coined by C. Peter Wagner (1930–2016), formerly professor of Church Growth at Fuller Theological Seminary, in California, "to describe noncharismatic evangelicals who believe that signs and wonders of the Holy Spirit will accompany the proclamation of the gospel."[3] Because of some similarities with the First Wave (the modern Pentecostal movement) and the Second Wave (the Charismatic Renewal) some of those affected by the Third Wave began to identify themselves as "neo-charismatics" or "neo-pentecostals."

The movement was largely inspired by the Argentinian Revival, which began in the early 1980s, associated with the ministries of Omar Cabrera (Fondacion Vision de Futuro), Hector Anobal Gimenez (Ondas de Amor y Paz), and Carlos Annacondia (Asociacion Evangelista Mensaje de Salvacion).[4] The latter had a considerable impact upon Wagner and his former associate at Fuller, John Wimber (1934–1998), who, following his leaving Fuller to plant Calvary Chapel of Yorba Linda, later renamed the Anaheim Vineyard Christian Fellowship, had experienced a dramatic transformation in his ministry. On Wimber's return to Fuller as a guest professor in 1981, his class on "The Miraculous and Church Growth" had a profound effect on the students and helped popularize the Third Wave in America.

The parent organization of Wimber's church plant "Calvary Chapel" had resulted from the ministry of Charles W. "Chuck" Smith (1927–2013), a prominent leader of the "Jesus People" stream of the Charismatic Renewal, and former campaign manager for Paul Cain (1929–2019) in the late 1950s prior to the latter's extended "period of silence" resulting from a nervous breakdown. Disagreement over the emphasis on the "Power Gifts" of the Spirit between Smith and Wimber and the failure of Smith's prediction of the visible return of Christ and the end of the world on New Year's Eve, 1981, prompted Wimber and a small group of churches to withdraw from the Calvary Chapel movement in 1983 and join up with Kenn Gulliksen's small Association of Vineyard Churches, of which Wimber was subsequently designated leader. The growth of the Association of Vineyard Churches under Wimber's leadership may be attributed substantially to the popularity of his book Power Evangelism, which made the contents of his course at Fuller more widely available.[5]

The Kansas City Prophets. In 1982 Mike Bickle (b. 1955) moved his ministry from St. Louis, Missouri, across the state to Kansas City, to plant the Kansas City Fellowship (KCF), in response to a prophecy that he would "raise up a work that will touch the ends of the earth."[6] The following year the controversial "prophet" Bob Jones (1931–2014) became the "resident seer" at KCF and helped Bickle with the development of the umbrella

Grace Ministries, which in turn attracted other "prophets," including Paul Cain, Lou Engle, James Goll (b. 1952), Bill Hamon (b. 1934), John Paul Jackson (1950–2015), Rick Joyner (b. 1949), and Larry Randolph (1940–2020). Cain's association with Bickle in 1987, following his "period of silence," solidified the commitment of KCF and Grace Ministries to the Latter Rain teaching, particularly the Manifested Sons of God, and the Restoration of Apostles and Prophets as a preparation for an end-time revival immediately preceding the return of Christ.[7] Within a short time KCF and the "Kansas City Prophets," as the leaders had become known, had aroused such controversy that Wimber and his Vineyard Association agreed to provide covering for them. The temporary departure of Jones for immorality, and of Cain for homosexuality and alcoholism did little to staunch the influence of the growing Apostolic-Prophetic Movement, as many earnest believers within and on the fringes of the Pentecostal, Charismatic, and Evangelical streams of Western Christendom eagerly anticipated the prophesied revival.

The "Laughing" Revival. In late 1987, a young South African "Word of Faith" evangelist, Rodney M. Howard-Browne (b.1961), and his family began ministry in the US His meetings became increasingly marked by unusual phenomena, such as uncontrollable laughter which he attributed to the Holy Spirit. In the spring of 1993, he was invited to conduct a week-long evangelistic crusade at the Carpenter's Home Church (Assemblies of God) in Lakeland, Florida, pastored by Karl D. Strader (1929–2020). As wave after wave of "holy laughter" gripped the congregation the meetings were extended to three weeks, then to sixteen weeks, broadcast throughout America and into many other countries, and welcomed visitors from around the world. The stirring created by the initial meetings and those that followed came to an embarrassing conclusion, when Strader's son Daniel was arrested and the next year, convicted for fraud. The exodus of support for Strader's ministry in Lakeland resulted in the closing of Carpenter's Home Church in 2002 and its sale to Randy and Paula White's now-defunct Church without Walls three years later. The remnant of Strader's congregation was divided between two churches, one in Auburndale, Auburndale Life

Church, and the other, Ignited Church in Lakeland, pastored by Stephen R. Strader (b. 1955), another of Strader's sons.

The Toronto Blessing. In August, 1993, a young Vineyard Pastor, Randy Clark (b. 1952) of St. Louis, Missouri, experienced a revolutionizing "touch from God" at a Rhema (Word of Faith) Conference in Tulsa, Oklahoma, at which Howard-Browne was the main speaker. The following January, he was invited to conduct four days of Revival meetings at Toronto Airport Vineyard Church, Toronto, Canada, pastored by John Arnott (b. 1940). He later recounted:

> What began as a simple series of revival meetings developed into a mighty outpouring of God's Spirit, complete with such biblical manifestations aspeace, healing, shaking, falling under the power of God, laughter and diversities of tongues.[8]

As the meetings continued other highly controversial manifestations became apparent, such as animal noises, spiritual drunkenness, and physical distortions. Nevertheless, as the news spread multiplied thousands flocked to the meetings from around the world, seeking an "impartation" of the Spirit. Returning home, many took the "Father's blessing" with them and similar manifestations were reported in centers around the world. Of particular note was the impact made by Eleanor Mumford, a London (UK) Vineyard pastor, who on her return from a visit to Toronto in May 1994, was invited to share her experience with the Holy Trinity Brompton Anglican Church (HTB), led by J. A. K. (Sandy) Millar (b. 1939), who would become one of the leaders of the Charismatic Evangelical Anglicans and later (2005) be consecrated Anglican Bishop of Kampala, Uganda.

The church was revolutionized and became a center of pilgrimage, not only for Britons seeking renewal, but also throughout the British-influenced world. So many were brought into the faith that a course for new converts, *Alpha*, was developed that gained wide acceptance and was translated into multiple languages. In the twenty years that followed HTB also served as the mother church for some twenty-eight "church plants," many of which were reborn, formerly defunct parishes.

The initial enthusiastic support from Wimber for Toronto Airport Vineyard Church quickly changed as the meetings continued. Finally, in December 1995, despite Wimber's own early experience,[9] disillusioned by the seemingly unbridled and increasingly bizarre manifestations and exaggerated claims emanating from Toronto, the Vineyard churches severed their relationship with the church, which then adopted its current name, Toronto Airport Christian Fellowship, and began to identify more closely with the "Apostolic-Prophetic Movement" led by Wagner. The meetings continued for some time, but interest was lessening as attention was being drawn elsewhere.

The Brownsville Outpouring. In January 1995, Assemblies of God evangelist Stephen (Steve) Hill (1954–2014), who had spent eight years as a missionary evangelist in Argentina, working in the revival alongside Annacondia and Claudio Freidzon (b. 1955), after reading a *Time* magazine article about the events at HTB, arranged to visit, and Millar, laying hands upon him, prayed for an impartation of the same spiritual power. Shortly afterward, while conducting evangelistic services in Wisconsin, Hill made a side-trip to Toronto, where he was also prayed for by Carol Arnott, the pastor's wife.

On Father's Day (June 18), 1995, Hill was invited to preach at Brownsville Assembly of God, Pensacola, Florida, by the pastor, John Kilpatrick (b. 1950), whose wife, Brenda, had personally made two trips to Toronto, along with other leaders from the congregation. Although the official videotape of the service The Father's Day Outpouring shows a considerably lower key conclusion to the service, than that described by Kilpatrick in his book *Feast of Fire,*[10] this marked the beginning of a remarkable series of meetings which continued unabated for the next five years, until Hill finally moved his ministry to Dallas, Texas. Eager crowds, often into the thousands, began to attend the nightly meetings encouraged by the highly publicized approval of the Assemblies of God denominational leadership, which had been more reticent about Toronto, the renowned Korean megachurch pastor, David Yonggi Cho (b. 1936), and affirmations by noted Pentecostal scholars, such as Cecil M. Robeck Jr. (b. 1945) and H. Vinson Synan (1934–2020), who declared: "This is probably the most important

315

revival to come out of a local church since Azusa Street."[11] Although Kilpatrick and Hill initially sought to distance the occurrences at Brownsville from those at Toronto, Hill did acknowledge: "We've received a lot from the Toronto church on how to pray with people and care for folks. We model a lot of what is going on here from them."[12]

As the news and influence of Brownsville spread, accounts of further stirrings from across America and beyond fed the flames, despite the public criticism by prominent figures like Hendrik "Hank" Hanegraaf (b.1950), "the Bible Answer Man" and president of the Creation Research Institute, and Albert J. Dager, editor of *Media Spotlight*.[13] From November 1997 to June 1998, the local newspaper, *The Pensacola News Journal*, which had initially published favorable reports about the meetings, published an extended series of highly embarrassing investigative articles, exploring the financial affairs and contradicting many of the leadership's claims of impact upon the community, the large numbers of conversions and spectacular miracles.

By the dawn of the new millennium, it was obvious that the movement was losing its impetus, as Hill departed for Texas; and Dr. Michael L. Brown (b.1955), the leader of the Brownsville Revival School of Ministry (1996–2000), which at one point had boasted an enrollment of 1,200, was ousted along with several faculty members. The following year Brown set up a rival Fire School of Ministry, which has since relocated to Charlotte, North Carolina. In 2003 Kilpatrick also resigned from the church, which was left with a dwindling congregation, massive indebtedness, and memories of a revival that had been expected to transform the world before the return of Christ.[14] After several years of itinerant ministry, in 2006 Kilpatrick established a new base, The Church of His Presence in Daphne, Alabama, some forty miles from Pensacola, which was to be the epicenter of a fresh stirring four years later.

The Lakeland Healing Revival. In April 2008, Pastor Stephen Strader, son of Karl Strader, who had pastored the former Carpenter's Home Church, the scene of the earlier "Laughing Revival" (1993), invited the Canadian evangelist Todd Bentley (b. 1976) of Fresh Fire Ministries to conduct five days of special meetings at the Ignited Church, in Lakeland, Florida. The overwhelming enthusiasm for and response to Bentley's ministry attracted such crowds that by the end of June an estimated 400,000 from over 100 nations had attended the meetings,[15] necessitating regular changes in venue to accommodate the burgeoning congregation. An earlier report on MSNBC[16] estimated that a further 1.2 million TV viewers had also tuned in to the meetings.

In addition to the controversial manifestations that had marked the earlier stirrings in Lakeland, Toronto, and Brownsville, the new movement was marked by visions, prophecies, numerous miraculous healings, and multiple claims of the resurrection of the dead.[17] Unfortunately, the investigative report broadcast on ABC's *Nightline* was unable to verify any miraculous healing or resurrection of the dead.[18] On June 23, 2008, Wagner, together with leading fellow-apostles of the International Coalition of Apostles, a core group of the Apostolic-Prophetic movement, Che Ahn (b. 1956) of Pasadena, California; Pastor Bill Johnson (b. 1951) of Redding, California; and Arnott of Toronto, formally commissioned Bentley as a recognized healing evangelist to bring revival to the whole world. After a brief absence in July, on August 11, 2008, Bentley finally severed his relationship with the revival, resigned from Fresh Fire Ministries, and announced his separation from his wife because of his "inappropriate" relationship with the female worship leader of the Lakeland meetings. Although the meetings continued at the Ignited Church until mid-October, the growing scandal swirling around Bentley's private life; his proclaimed repeated visitations and dependence on the angel Emma, the Japanese goddess of the dead; his physical violence toward some of those seeking prayer; and the highly exaggerated and unsubstantiated claims of miracles, healings, and conversions quickly overwhelmed whatever good had been achieved in the revival. Subsequently Ignited Church closed completely.

The Bay of the Holy Spirit Revival. On the last night of the annual church conference (July 23, 2010) at the Church of His Presence, Daphne, Alabama, according to the pastor John Kilpatrick of Brownsville fame, while visiting British evangelist Nathan Morris (b. 1979) was preaching the scheduled sermon, there came a fresh spiritual outpouring, comparable to the "Father's Day" outpouring in Pensacola five years earlier.[19] In mid-August the meetings were moved to the larger facilities in the convention center in nearby Mobile, Alabama. Shortly afterward, the well-known Gospel singer, Delia Knox, wife of Bishop Levy H. Knox of Living Word Christian Center in Mobile, was able to walk following prayer by Morris, after being wheelchair-bound for more than twenty-two years as a result of an automobile accident on Christmas Day, 1987. The resulting enthusiasm from this confirmed and videotaped miracle spread rapidly and in April 2011 Kilpatrick and his team decided to begin a nationwide tour to encourage similar stirrings throughout the USA. Apart from occasional reports of miraculous healings, there has been little publicity regarding the results of subsequent meetings, despite considerable excitement in the various centers visited.

Eastern Europe Awakenings. In the latter years of Communist control there were periodic stirrings throughout Eastern Europe, such as the Romanian evangelical renewal in 1979–80 centered on the Second Baptist Church in Oradea, pastored by Iosif Tson (b. 1934) and resulting in 850 new converts being baptized.[20] With the collapse of most of the Communist regimes in 1989 came a new period of openness and opportunity for the churches, accompanied by an intense eagerness to hear the gospel on the part of the general population. Churches grew rapidly and multiplied as whole communities embraced the Christian faith, so long denied them. As one of the first Western missionaries in Romania after the 1989 revolution, I personally saw the results of the Spirit of God's activity in that country, which were not orchestrated by Western missionary organizations, nor promoted by slick advertising, nor padded by inflated statistics. Because initially the duration of visas was limited to thirty days, it was necessary temporarily to exit Romania for the same time period, which gave opportunities of ministry in neighboring countries such as the former Yugoslavia, and Bulgaria, where I observed the same characteristics as noted in Romania.

The renewal was marked by an expressed intense hunger for God and his Word, the preaching of the gospel, fervent prayer, and a strong anticipation of lasting results. In the closing decade of the millennium:

…the Pentecostal Union in Romania, for example, grew from 795 to 2,153 sovereign churches and about 1,000 other preaching points, with more than 500,000 baptized adult members, and a further 126 churches with some 5,000 members outside the union in the AG Association of Romania, the Nehemia (German-supported) fellowship, Pentecostal Holiness Churches and independent charismatic churches.[21]

Similar growth was noted in other Christian denominations and in much of the former Communist world, especially the former Soviet Union. Unfortunately, the impact of the awakening in the former Communist world was diminished by the importation of Western practices and doctrinal divisions. The highly publicized decline of Christianity in parts of Western Europe in the last decades of the twentieth century and in the first decade of the new was more than off-set by the rejuvenation of the faith in the east.

Latin America. Although the area is traditionally considered predominantly Roman Catholic, and the evangelical Protestants were "once considered essentially a foreign faith introduced by northern European immigrants and numbers of evangelical missions to culturally unassimilated Indians, it is now seen as a mass movement."[22] It is asserted that the 50,000 Protestants in Latin America in 1900 (about 1 percent of the population) grew to some 64 million by 2000 (almost 15 persent), three-quarters of whom identify with the Pentecostal and charismatic churches.[23] The conversion rate, which kept pace with the population growth during the first third of the last century, showed steady increase during the next third, exploded in the final third, and has continued to accelerate in the new century, showing all the signs of a major folk or mass movement into the evangelical Pentecostal-charismatic faith. The five most populous countries, Brazil, Mexico, Colombia, Argentina, and Peru, are steadily moving toward evangelical majorities by the end of this century.

Sub-Saharan Africa. Comparable with the growth in Latin America is the accelerating conversion of sub-Saharan Africa to evangelical Christianity, despite the resurgence of the Muslim faith in much of the northern fringe of the area in the new century. Throughout the nineteenth and most of the twentieth century, Africa was the focus of much of the European and American missionary activity; however, in the second half of the twentieth century the rising indigenous Christian movements in Southern, Central, and Western Africa increasingly overtook the role of the foreign missionary work, and accounted for most of the explosive growth. Periodic and limited outpourings of the Holy Spirit have brought in great local harvests, but reluctance on the part of the institutional church leadership has often resulted in efforts being diverted into prophetic fringe movements, some of which have combined Christian teaching with traditional pre-Christian practices. With the passing of the "prophetic" leaders, however, and the availability of native-language translations of the Scriptures, some of the fringe movements have shown signs of a return to a more biblically oriented faith. The intermittent revolutionary conflicts in East Africa, the violent expansion of Islam and the recurrent droughts, prompting major population movements, have limited the growth of Christianity there to the brief periods of peace and prosperity. According to the Pew Research Center, "The number of Christians on the continent rose from 7 million in 1900 to 470 million in 2010."[24] Much of the growth in Africa, as elsewhere, is demographic rather than evangelistic in areas with a substantial nominally Christian population.

China. The world's most populous nation has long been the focus of Christianity's missionary attention, despite becoming officially "atheistic" in the 1949 Communist Revolution, the expulsion of foreign missionaries, the official closing of almost all the existing churches, and the rigorous persecution of the remaining Christians. The 1966, Maoist Cultural Revolution sought to complete the work of obliterating all religions, including Christianity; however, following the death of Chairman Mao Tse-tung (1893–1976) ten years later, it became obvious that Christianity was still alive, if not publicly thriving. Since then the modernization programs of Deng Xiaoping (1904–1997) opened the door to increased foreign collaboration, tourism, and prepared for the tentative reemergence of the church into public life. The explosive growth of the church since the days of Chairman Mao is a powerful testimony to the direct work of the Holy Spirit, and as in Latin America has all the characteristics of a folk movement:

China's Protestant community, which had just one million members in 1949, has already overtaken those (sic) of countries more commonly associated with an evangelical boom. In 2010 there were more than 58 million Protestants in China compared to 40 million in Brazil and 36 million in South Africa. . . . Professor (Fenggang) Yang, a leading expert on religion in China, believes that number will swell to around 160 million by 2025.[25]

The vast majority of China's Protestants, at least 65 percent, and many of the Roman Catholics, about one million strong, would identify with the Pentecostal-Charismatic movement, as would almost all those involved in the unregistered house churches.[26]

South Asia. Formerly under British suzerainty, **India**, the world's second most populous nation, and its neighbors were also a major attraction for Christian world missions in the last two centuries. The post-independence resurgence of the indigenous religions of the region brought periods of severe persecution for those who had adopted the faith of the former conquerors, despite the almost two thousand years of Christian history in the region. Occasional awakenings, often precipitated by instances of miraculous healings, usually resulted in a fresh outbreak of persecution especially in the North where Islam also held sway and threatened the traditional religions. The most significant growth in the last decades of the twentieth and first decade of the twenty-first centuries has been among the Neo-charismatics and the indigenous Pentecostal churches, but few would see this as evidence of a widespread spiritual awakening. Although the most recent census data indicates that overall Christianity amounts to only 2.3 percent of the population, the Center for the Study of Global Christianity "predicts Christians will grow to almost 7 percent of India's population by 2050."[27]

Korea. Although the Korean Peninsula has been the scene of repeated spiritual awakenings since the end of the nineteenth century, and boasts some of Christianity's largest mega-churches, including the renowned Yoido Full Gospel Church in Seoul, South Korea, with a membership approaching one million, there have been few signs of a fresh revival in the closing decades of the old century and at the beginning of the new. Those affected by the early outpourings of the Holy Spirit have continued to engage in fervent evangelism and prayer and continue to see healthy results. More significant is the foreign missionary activity of the Korean churches, which has reached out both to Korean ethnics and non-Koreans, often in areas closed to Western missionaries. The world-wide impact of Korea is yet to be fully realized.

Indonesia. Although the exciting days of the famed Indonesian Revival (1965–1972), centered in Sulawesi, South Sumatra, Timor, and West Java, ended somewhat controversially, the awakening continued powerfully to affect the churches in Borneo, Papua, and Sulawesi, despite intense persecution by the Muslim majority. Laws restricting conversions from Islam to Christianity and forbidding proselytizing, especially in Muslim majority areas, limited public evangelism and the building of new churches, but not the growth of Christianity. By the 2000 census, declared Christians accounted for almost 10 percent of the population, a figure probably under-reported.[28] The rise of extremist Muslim groups at the end of the old century and the beginning of the new, while temporarily driving the Christians underground, resulted in the spread of the Christian faith in areas dominated by those fearful of the extremists. Should the political climate change, the potential for a harvest is enormous.

Despite repeated prophecies and claims of revival, there have been few authenticated spiritual awakenings affecting more than a few local churches and the immediate communities. Nevertheless, the reports that do come reassure a waiting, praying, and believing church that God still pours out his Spirit on those willing to seek him.

Endnotes

1   R. M. Riss: art. "Latter Rain Movement" in NIDPCM (2002 edn.), 832.

2   S. D. Moore: art. "Shepherding Movement" in ibid., 992.

3   G. B. McGee & B.A. Pavia: art. "Wagner, Charles Peter" in ibid., 1181.

4   D. D. Bundy: art. "Argentina" in ibid., 24.

5   J. Wimber with K. Springer: *Power Evangelism* (London, UK: Hodder & Stoughton, 1985).

6   G. W. Gohr: art. "Kansas City Prophets" in NIDPCM, 816; B. Randles: *Weighed and Found Wanting* (Cedar Rapids, IA: Bill Randles, n.d.), 97, 98.

7   Gohr, ibid.

8   Quoted in R.M. Riss: art. "Clark, Randy" in NIDPCM, 552.

9   J. White: *When the Spirit Comes with Power* (London, UK: Hodder & Stoughton, 1992 edn.), 158ff.

10 J. Kilpatrick: *The Feast of Fire: The Father's Day Outpouring* (Pensacola, FL: J. Kilpatrick, 1995).

11 Quoted in S. Rabey: art. "Brownsville Revival Rolls Onward" in *Christianity Today* magazine (February, 1998).

12 Steve Hill: Interview with "Destiny Image Digest," volume 5:1 (Shippensburg, PA: Destiny Image Publishers, Winter 1997), 14.

13 A. J. Dager: *Pensacola: Revival or Reveling?* (Redmond, WA: Media Spotlight, 1997).

14 J. Lee Grady: art. "What happened to Brownsville's Fire?" in *Charisma* magazine (Orlando, FL: Strang Communications, 2006).

15 T. Lake: art. "Todd Bentley's revival in Lakeland draws 400,000 and counting" in *St. Petersburg Times* (June 30, 2008).

16 A. Rhee: report "Revivalist claims Hundreds of Healings" (MSNBC, May 29, 2008).

17 Personal e-mail from Stephen Strader, June 8, 2008; Subject: "Jesus just raised my grandson from the dead" claimed: "Fourteen People have been raised from the dead!!!"

18 *Nightline* story: "Thousands Flock to Revival in Search of Miracles" (ABC News, June 9, 2008).

19 A. S. Gaines: art. "Thousands Flock to Alabama Revival Meetings" in *Charisma* magazine (September 2010).

20 S. Tippit: *Fire in Your Heart* (Chicago, IL: Moody, 1987), 53ff.

21 I. R. Hall: art. "Europe Eastern (Survey)" in NIDPCM, 94.

22 E. A. Wilson: art. "Latin America (Survey)" in NIDPCM, 157.

23 J. L. Allen Jr.: art. "The dramatic growth of evangelicals in Latin America" in *National Catholic Reporter* (August 18, 2006).

24 S. E. Zylstra: art. "Babies Halt the Great Commission" in *Christianity Today* magazine (July/August 2015).

25 T. Phillips: art. "China on Course to Become 'World's Most Christian Nation' Within 15 Years" in *The Telegraph* (UK) (April 19, 2014).

26 D. H. Bays & T.M. Johnson: art. "China" in NIDPCM, 64.

27 Gleanings: art. "Christians Happy that Census Shows Few Converts" in *Christianity Today* magazine (October 2011).

28 H. Beech: art. "Christianity's Surge in Indonesia" in *Time* magazine (April 26, 2010).

Part V

The Theology
of Revival

Chapter 22

A Practical Theology
of Revival

The **Purpose of Revival.** Fundamental to our theology of revival is the question: What is the purpose of revival? The purpose is twofold: *first*, the renewing of the spiritual life; and *second*, the restoring of scriptural truth. Scripture lays these two aspects down as basic to our relationship to Almighty God. To the Samaritan woman at the well Jesus said:

> A time is coming and has now come when true worshipers will worship the Father in Spirit and in truth, for they are the kind of worshipers the Father seeks. God is spirit and his worshipers must worship in Spirit and in truth. – John 4:23–24

We must always balance the experiential and the cognitive aspects of the Christian faith. What we know in our lives through the touch of God and what we know in our minds through the teaching of God are equally important. The neglect of either leads to imbalance in the development of our personal lives and has led to imbalances throughout the history of the church.

At times, revival movements have so emphasized the experiential renewing of spiritual life that they have neglected the spiritual truth.

Prior to the Reformation, this tension was a common feature of periods of renewal. The post-reformation emphasis on truth and orthodoxy often led to an under-emphasis on the experiential aspect of life, leading to a decline in spirituality. Nevertheless, from the Reformation onward, there was a steady return to both biblical faith and biblical practice. Step by step through periods of renewal God has brought the church back to the place where it is more closely approximating the apostolic pattern of the Book of Acts than ever before. The church is still not there; there still is revival yet to come. Should the Lord tarry, a succession of revivals will continue, bringing into focus other truths as yet unrealized, because we do not yet have all the truth. All the truth potentially is in the Scriptures but no one person on the face of this earth lives up to the full teaching of Scripture and can claim to have a perfect understanding of all the emphases of the Bible so that his life is in perfect balance. That is our quest and our goal but most of us will admit that we are not there yet. God still has more things to teach us, and more truth yet to awaken to our minds and to our hearts. Every time that happens, it will bring about a quickening of our spiritual life as we respond to the truth. The purpose of the revival is to bring the church back to where it began.

The Initiatives for Revival. If the purpose of revival then is to bring us back to Pentecost, back to Pentecost we must go and see that on the day of Pentecost they were all together in one place.[1] Some say that if we could just get together a human consensus then things would begin to happen. If we could just get all the people together in one place praying the same prayer, longing for the same things, moving in the same direction, then we would have our Pentecost again. We have a problem with human consensus. One thing I have discovered in over fifty years of Christian ministry is that people do not agree unless the Holy Spirit brings them into agreement. It is a human tendency not to agree. Unity is only possible by the operation of the Holy Spirit. That is why the Scripture exhorts us in Ephesians: *"Make every effort to keep the unity of the Spirit through the bond of peace."*[2] It is the Holy Spirit who brings us into the kind of united fellowship whereby despite our ignorance, we can and do pray in accordance with the will of God.[3]

If we put it to a vote we would find that everybody would vote according to their personal interests. Getting a human consensus by the ballot box is virtually impossible, and even if we do, we may not have the right consensus. Democracy in itself is no guarantee of rightness. The Holy Spirit teaches us what to pray, and how to pray; he directs us in the right way. There is a problem with human consensus that we cannot overcome by any other means than recognizing that the true initiative for revival starts with the Divine. We must have a divine revelation. That divine revelation may come through one person or to a group or to individuals scattered over a wide area. Nevertheless, it is God who reveals; it is God who discloses truth to us. The Bible is very clear in 1 Corinthians 2 that no one can know the things of God except by the Spirit of God.[4] In fact, that same Scripture contrasts what we know by the Spirit with what we know by other means and says regarding the truths of God:

> "What no eye has seen, what no ear has heard, and what no human mind has conceived"—the things God has prepared for those who love him—these are the things God has revealed to us by his Spirit. The Spirit searches all things, even the deep things of God. For who among men knows the thoughts of a man except the man's spirit within him? In the same way no one knows the thoughts of God except the Spirit of God. –1 Corinthians 2:9–11

If we all were to sit down and discuss what spiritual truth God is going to bring to the fore in the next great revival we would all have different opinions. Out of deference to one teacher we may say, "Yes, I agree with you." Then another respected teacher says, "No way!" and persuades us in a totally different direction. When the Holy Spirit reveals the truth to the hearts and minds of men, then we do not need someone to say, "Thus and so," but the Holy Spirit himself draws us, turns our hearts, and moves upon us in the direction that God wants the church to go, because that is his plan. He is bringing us back to the biblical truth, the Word of God, and as a consequence renews our spiritual life in him. We need that divine revelation, the initiative always begins with God.

But what about man? Where does man come into this? If the human consensus has problems, and we must wait for a divine revelation, what can we do? There is human preparation:

Seek the Lord while he may be found; call on him while he is near. Let the wicked forsake his way and the evil man his thoughts. Let him turn to the Lord, and he will have mercy on him, and to our God, for he will freely pardon. –Isaiah 55:6–7 NIV 1984

When God inclines the hearts of men to seek him it is because he wants to do some particular work in their midst. *"…break up your unplowed ground; for it is time to seek the LORD, until he comes and showers righteousness upon [us]."*⁵ We need to seek the Lord for that outpouring. As we seek the Lord something begins to happen. We move into line with the will of God.

Five Elements in the Incidence of Revival. What makes revival happen? Granted that God's intention is to bring us back to Pentecost and granted that we need to seek the Lord, *Step One* is always **praying *through* to God**, which is more than saying an occasional prayer on the topic. When the Lord Jesus taught the disciples about prayer he affirmed:

"So I say to you: Ask and it will be given to you; seek and you will find; knock and the door will be opened to you. For everyone who asks receives; he who seeks finds; and to him who knocks, the door will be opened." –Luke 11:9-10

This same teaching included the story of the man who came to his friends to borrow the bread and persisted in his request.

The Greek language uses the continuous form of the imperative which indicates: "You must ask and keep on asking. You must seek and keep on seeking. You must knock and keep on knocking." The person who does that is guaranteed of results. If we could have revival in five minutes' time we would all pray for five minutes for revival. If we could have revival guaranteed in five days' time we would all find time to pray for revival. If we could have revival in five years' time, there would be those who would commit themselves to praying that long for revival.

We do not know how long it will take before the revival comes. What we do know is this: God has promised spiritual outpouring if we persist, however long it takes. Jesus summarized his teaching by saying:

> "If you then, though you are evil, know how to give good gifts to your children, how much more will your Father in heaven give the Holy Spirit to those [plural] who ask him!" –Luke 11:13

We put this on an individual level in relation to a personal Pentecost. That by no means exhausts the teaching of this passage. If revival is simply an outpouring of God's Holy Spirit and since the recipients of the promise are expressed in the plural, not in the singular, we have here the key to revival. If we would see revival, then we together must pray through and touch the heart of God. When we come before the throne of God, we place ourselves where God can answer prayer.

This relationship between prayer and revival is of great significance because without a real understanding of prayer, what it is and the way it functions, we may miss the importance of praying through for revival.

The *second element* is that of **faith in God**. Faith is an integral part of the prayer, and as Jesus himself pointed out, we are to have faith in God:

> "Have faith in God," Jesus answered. "I tell you the truth, if anyone says to this mountain, 'Go, throw yourself into the sea,' and does not doubt in his heart but believes that what he says will happen, it will be done for him. Therefore, I tell you, whatever you ask for in prayer, believe that you have received it, and it will be yours. And when you stand praying, if you hold anything against anyone, forgive him, so that your Father in heaven may forgive you your sins." –Mark 11:22–25 NIV1984

It is immensely important that we have confidence in the Word of God that God will do what he has said he will do. That means that we must ascertain the will of God and act upon it. A very important element in our prayer life is undoubtedly catching a vision of what God wants to do, and moving our lives into line with that will of God, and that is what we refer to when we talk about praying through. Having done that, then we must have confidence that God will do what God has said he will do, because that is really what faith is. It is complete and total reliance upon God for what you know he has said in his Word he will do. It is important that we fulfill the conditions of the Word of God and recognize that very often the promises of God are conditional, "If you . . . then I," says God.

That takes us to the *third element*, which is **obedience**. Consider the following passage (commentary mine):

"I the LORD do not change. So you, O descendants of Jacob, are not destroyed. Ever since the time of your forefathers you have turned away from my decrees and have not kept them." *(Their failure was a failure of obedience)* "Return to me, and I will return to you," says the LORD Almighty. But you ask, "How are we to return?" *(God responds)* "Will a mere mortal rob God? Yet you rob me. But you ask, 'How are we robbing you?' In tithes and offerings. You are under a curse—your whole nation—because you are robbing me. Bring the whole tithe into the storehouse, that there may be food in my house. Test me in this," says the LORD Almighty, "and see if I will not throw open the floodgates of heaven and pour out so much blessing that you will not have room enough to store it. I will prevent the pests from devouring your crops, and the vines in your fields will not drop their fruit before it is ripe," says the LORD Almighty. "Then all the nations will call you blessed, for yours will be a delightful land," says the Lord Almighty. –Malachi 3:6–12

The issue is obedience. The test of obedience is that we turn back to God and do the things that we have not been doing. It is not the money that God is concerned about: it is the obedience. Rebellion is being unwilling to do what God has said we should do. In this instance the example that God chooses is the matter of tithes and offerings, but it could be other things in your life. What if you are tithing, but disobeying God in other areas—will God still pour you out blessings? Of course he will not. Tithing is just one part of our obedience before Almighty God. Our giving to God is an example of our commitment to God. We may withhold other areas of obedience and so miss the blessing of God. We may say: "But I tithe, why shouldn't God bless me?" The real question is: Are we faithfully obeying God in other areas?

This is not referring to salvation, but to revival, to the windows of heaven and the floodgates of blessing being opened, i.e., about restoration, not regeneration. We are talking about returning, not coming for the first time out of a life of disobedience when we turn to God in repentance and faith, receive forgiveness, and are accepted by him. Out of that faith comes a life of obedience. The Bible is absolutely clear on this point. The apostle Paul declared: *"Through [Christ] we received grace and apostleship to call all the Gentiles to the obedience that comes from faith for his name's sake."* [6] That is what we are called to—the obedience that comes from faith. Good works are no foundation for salvation. Faith in what Christ has done is the foundation. But faith that does not produce good works is dead, James appropriately says,[7] and Paul agrees, there is an obedience that comes from faith. No obedience? Then let us reexamine the foundation to see whether we have faith there.

When we are believers and live a life of rebellion and disobedience then we are called back to that proper obedience to God's requirements that the Bible lays down. We are called to live it out. We are called to return to God, to return to his decrees, to return to his requirements, and to live in the light of that. That young man on the island of Lewis in the Hebrides reading from Psalm 24 asked his fellow prayers: "Are our hands clean? Is our heart pure?" It was such a man who shall stand in the presence of the Lord and receive the blessing from God his Savior. That is a promise. But it requires clean hands and a pure heart. If we are living in disobedience, we have to put it right for revival to happen in our day and in our experience. The revived are the people who have come back in obedience. Therefore I agree, in this limited sense, with Charles Finney that revival is nothing more than a new obedience to God, i.e., if God is calling us back to obedience, we must start living it out on a daily, consistent basis to experience the full measure of God's blessing.

The *fourth element* in the incidence of revival is God's call to **humility** and **confession before God**. In the oft-quoted promise from the dedication of the Temple (commentary mine):

> "When I shut up the heavens so that there is no rain, or command locusts to devour the land or send a plague among my people, if my people, who are called by my name [*i.e., believers*], will humble themselves and pray and seek my face and turn from their wicked ways [*i.e., return to a life of obedience to God*], then will I hear from heaven and I will forgive their sin and will heal their land." [*But notice that God did not cease speaking at this point; he continued:*] "Now my eyes will be open and my ears attentive to the prayers offered in this place." –2 Chronicles 7:13–15

God is listening and watching to see whether we will do it or not. We need to bear in mind that when God commands us to do something, he does not then turn his back and say: "Well, I do not really care whether you do it or not. You just do it if you want to." He does care. He says: "Now I am going to look and see whether you are doing it. All right, who is doing it? Who is humbling himself? Who is praying? Who is turning from sin? Who is seeking the face of God? I am watching, I am listening for such prayers." He is still listening *to* those prayers as he has been listening for years *for* those prayers. Every time people begin to pray like that something begins to happen.

This matter of humility may be a hard topic for us to stomach in our day. Nevertheless, it is not hard to see that God requires it. In Isaiah 57, we usually just read verse 15, but verse 14 provides the context:

> "¹⁴It will be said: 'Build up, build up, prepare the road! Remove the obstacles out of the way of my people.' ¹⁵For this is what the high and lofty One says—he who lives forever, whose name is holy: 'I live in a high and holy place, but also with him who is contrite

and lowly in spirit, to revive the spirit of the lowly and to revive the heart of the contrite." –Isaiah 57:14–15

For the work of God to go forward we must humble ourselves. That removes the obstacles out of the way of God's people receiving a full blessing that he has for them. Tragically, our pride and self-sufficiency, our independence of mind and spirit, our self-contentedness, our self-assuredness, our self-esteem, can be an obstacle to God moving in our midst and coming into the church as a whole. We are so busy about our own things that we leave Jesus outside the door. Remember the church in Laodicea that the Lord spoke of:

"You say, 'I am rich; I have acquired wealth and do not need a thing.' But you do not realize that you are wretched, pitiful, poor, blind and naked. I counsel you to buy from me gold refined in the fire, so you can become rich; and white clothes to wear, so you can cover your shameful nakedness; and salve to put on your eyes, so you can see. Those whom I love I rebuke and discipline. So be earnest and repent. Here I am! I stand at the door and knock. If anyone hears my voice and opens the door, I will come in and eat with that person, and they with me." –Revelation 3:17–20

This is a church; not the unsaved. This is a church that is so busy congratulating itself on its wealth, its accumulation of goods, its position in the community, its robed choirs and padded pews, its multimillion dollar complex sanctuaries and facilities, that it is leaving Jesus outside the door. It does not even realize that he was never admitted into the new building, never welcomed into the beautiful sanctuary that is the wonder of the ages. He is outside waiting to come in and we are so busy listening to our choir, and congratulating ourselves that we do not hear his voice that says: "Get it all from me. I have the real gold: I have the true robes: I have the salve for your eyes. You do not even realize what your need is; you are so busy doing your own thing in the church, I am left outside."

The Lord Jesus said that kind of church comes under judgment. It may be an assembly of people but it sure is not an assembly of God. Because if it is an assembly of God, God has to be there. You cannot have an assembly of God without God. That is a fact of life. The Lord Jesus said that where two or three gather in his name, there he is in the midst, and that is where prayer will be answered.[8] We wonder why our prayers are not being answered. We do not need to wonder any longer, because if the Lord Jesus is not there, if we have left him on the outside and are not listening to his voice, then all the singing "We've got the power" does not make one scrap of difference. We do not have the power, because the power is in the presence of Jesus. It is not the proclaiming of the name of Jesus but the presence of the Jesus of the name. We must have the Lord Jesus in our midst if we would experience his power.

The Bible stresses that God dwells with the humble. He will not share his glory with somebody else. He will not share the throne with somebody else. He will not share it with a pastor; he will not share it with a deacon; he will not share it with your husband or wife; he will not share it with you; it is his throne. He invites you to dwell in his presence, but to dwell there requires humility. Bow down and the Lord will lift you up. Humble yourself and the Lord will exalt you. Puff yourself and you will be humbled. You can humble yourself or God will humiliate you. There is a difference between being humbled and being humiliated.

Humbling is something you can do for yourself by realizing who you are and what your relationship is to Almighty God, but if you will not do it then God will bring you down, and that is humiliating. And that's a little harder to take, so let's take the easy road on this one and humble ourselves rather than being brought into a place of humiliation. And confession, yes, that element of contrition, it goes beyond simple repentance, it goes beyond what we so often think in terms of. Contrition is a lifelong attitude. John Wesley liked the old-fashioned word *penitence*. Penitence is not just something that you do when you confess your sins. Penitence is an attitude of heart that marks you out throughout your whole life. We recognize who we are, we recognize what our weakness is, we recognize our dependence, we recognize our proneness to fail, we recognize what our situation is, and we walk in fellowship with God, not cocky and puffed up, but humbly, constantly seeking the face of God, constantly acknowledging that all that we have and all that we are is by the grace of God. *"I am what I am,"* says Paul, *"by the grace of God."* [9]

So often we talk about **faith** in terms of self-assuredness, a kind of ebullience and belligerence with God. That's not faith, that's presumption. Faith is reliance or dependence. The faith that says "I can do everything through Christ who gives me strength"[10] has a converse side that says "I can do nothing of myself. I am totally dependent on God." *Without me,"* says Jesus, *"you can do nothing."* [11] Separated from him we can accomplish absolutely nothing. When Jesus comes in he comes to bring us into **fellowship**, a vital relationship, a restoration to God's plan, which is exactly what God intends—and our *fifth element*: fellowship grounded in faith. God has a plan, a purpose, and his goal in all our praying, in all our believing and walking in faith, in all our obedience to God, in all our humility and confession and contrition, is to bring us back to the place where God wants us to be, because he has a plan and a purpose for our lives.

Revelation 3:20 again describes it in terms of fellowship: *"Here I am! I stand at the door and knock. If anyone hears my voice, and opens the door, I will come in and eat with him, and he with me."* And what riches there are in the fellowship of God! My, that is just incredible that he would dwell in our midst. Remember those promises from the Old Testament—I will be in their midst, they will be my people, I will be their God—those promises taken up in the book of Revelation that repeatedly assure God's people of his presence with them. That is an important element; that fellowship is only possible in the presence of God and the presence of God is only possible when we have fulfilled these elements that are part of the incidence of revival. When God's people get back to where they ought to be, we have revival.

Four Preconditions for Revival. Hopefully we will be able to see how we can prepare the way for a revival to take place in our community. *First* among the preconditions for revival is that we must **recognize the need of revival**. The solution to our problems is not more money, more prestige, better buildings, more able ministers with better training; those may be symptoms of our malaise, but the solution is in revival. When God pours out his Spirit you don't need to plead with people to give. They give. You don't need to plead with people to volunteer to serve. You can't keep them from doing it. They want to. You don't have to plead with people to come to church. Their hearts are turned toward the house of God. They want to be in church seeking the face of God. You don't even have to plead with the preachers to devote themselves to their task. Whether they like it or not, the task is going to devote itself to them and they are going to find that they can't escape from their task if they have anything like a heart for God.

If we recognize the fact that whatever the situation is, if the church is divided it will be united. If it is lazy it will be awakened. If it is failing it will be strengthened. If it is involved in sin and immorality and wracked by problem areas God will sanctify his church. It all happens in revival. Revival solves the problems of the church, but that's not why we need revival. We need revival in order to be the people God wants us to be. We need revival in order to accomplish what God has set out for his church. God has a plan and revival brings us into conformity with God's plan. That is why we need a spiritual awakening. When we recognize the need, that inevitably brings about **the humility before God**, our *second* precondition: when we recognize our need we recognize our dependence. We are totally dependent upon Almighty God, we acknowledge that we can do nothing of ourselves. We stop our foolish seeking for new techniques and methods. We stop our rushing about looking for the latest seminar or convention or teaching session on this, that, or the other. We are just tinkering with the symptoms in so many of those areas. What we need is to get down before God in humility and acknowledge that when Jesus said "I will build my church" he meant what he said. He is doing it. He *is* building his church.

Third, we need to **confess our sins and seek forgiveness**. This comes back home to us personally. What am I doing about my own personal sins? Let's face it, none of us is perfect. We all fail at times. Sin is endemic in the human condition, and even at our best we recognize that there are times when we do not do what we ought to do and we do the things that we ought not to do. Most times it is by accident that we do so. Sometimes we have to admit that it is intentional and afterward when we come to ourselves, what shall we do? Hide our sins? He who covers his sin will not prosper, Scripture says. Confess our sin? He who confesses and forsakes them will have mercy. Confess our sins and face up to God. Make restitution. Repent, says Paul, and do the works fit for repentance—works that express our repentance.

It is a difficult topic to think in terms of restitution, but there is no true repentance without restitution. Simply to say "I'm sorry" does not solve the problem. If you steal a man's livelihood, to say you're sorry leaves him still poor and you still rich. That is not enough. You must give him back what you took. Some things you may never be able to restore fully, such as his reputation. If your sin is one of gossiping or backbiting, you should do everything you can do to undo the harm that your actions have caused. That is restitution. When I encounter people who are not willing to make restitution, I seriously question the validity of their repentance. It is imperative because it is part of the biblical teaching regarding repentance. Repentance includes not just the recognition of sin and remorse for sin but also making restitution, as far as is humanly possible.

Now there will be some things for which restitution is not possible because the person is no longer available for you to make restitution—they have died or they have moved away and there is no way that you can undo what you have done in the past. Words spoken can never be withdrawn. We sometimes wish we could eat our own words but we cannot. We may have to live with the consequences of our actions. If those of us in Christian leadership positions publicly sin we may have to live with the mark against our reputation that that sin has caused, and people may never trust us again. People may be suspicious of our motives and our faithfulness in the future. We cannot demand people's confidence, but we can earn it. We can rebuild what our sin has destroyed as we faithfully serve the Lord and demonstrate the reality of our repentance.

But there is another element in true repentance and that is restoration. In the Assemblies of God we talk about rehabilitation. We need to ensure by the good offices that God has placed at our disposal that we will go on with God in a life of cleanness and holiness before him. Sometimes that involves submitting ourselves to the wise leadership and help of others who are in a position to offer us that help. Now, you need to be very careful in the matter of restoration. Tragically we hear stories about young women with moral problems going to counselors for help and those counselors taking advantage of those problems and going even further and taking them into even more drastic and problematic situations. That should not be, but sadly it does happen. Those who are involved in the work of rehabilitating the sinners need to be very careful to rely on the Holy Spirit's protection and leading. Office in itself is no guarantee of perfection nor suitability.

Fourth, **prayer** is right in there. Pray fervently for spiritual awakening. Fervent praying is effective. Elijah was noted for his fervent praying and he prayed through and saw God responding in a powerful way.

Fifth on our list of preconditions is **obedience.** The key that Evan Roberts ascertained was to determine to obey the Holy Spirit explicitly in everything; not just occasional, spasmodic, or partial obedience but explicit obedience. Roberts said this is the key to revival—to determine that from this day forward I will do exactly what the Holy Spirit tells me to do. I will put into practice the Word of God down to the very last detail.

Now, these preconditions are not sequential. They are concomitant. They happen at the same time as each other. We may in our application of them to our own lives recognize the need for revival before we recognize anything else, but once we have recognized the need for revival then we need to ensure that we are doing all of these things, that we are living a life of humility before God, that we are confessing our sins, repenting and making restitution, seeking his forgiveness, keeping short accounts with God, praying fervently in our desire for revival, and obeying the Holy Spirit explicitly. Every time we read a word of the Lord we must endeavor to live it out and to be the kind of people that God wants us to be in relation to the Scriptures, his word to us.

Endnotes

1 Acts 2:1.
2 Eph. 4:3.
3 Rom. 8:26–27.
4 1 Corinthians 2:11.
5 Hosea 10:12.
6 Romans 1:5.
7 James 2:17.
8 Matthew 18:19–20.
9 1 Corinthians 15:10.
10 Philippians 4:13.
11 John 15:5.

Chapter 23

The Application of Revival Theology

Five Results of Revival. What will be the results of such an awakening? There are five results that we should look for.

The *first result* is **a renewed sense of God's presence**. God says he will be with us. He will live with us and walk with us and fellowship with us. This renewed sense of God's presence is what revival is. Certainly, when God's Spirit has been poured out then the Holy Spirit makes us aware of the presence of God. When we look at Almighty God and see the kind of person that he is, that sense of God's presence is humbling. When Isaiah stepped into the temple and saw the Lord high and lifted up with his train filling the temple the impact on Isaiah was absolutely incredible. This pompous and well-bred young courtier was humbled before Almighty God by an awesome sense that God is here. Some would say there are four, paradoxes about the presence of God that we need to keep in focus.

First of all, God is both *transcendent yet immanent*. Too often we live as though God were only transcendent, way out there, the high and holy one, removed from contact with mankind, but God is not only way out there exalted, creator over the creature, but he is also right here with us. And we stand in the presence of the Holy God. Let me ask you, bluntly and honestly, are you conscious of the presence of God in your daily life?

I don't mean theoretically; yes, God is with us. He said: "I'll be with you always to the end of the age." I mean actually. If I were to ask you: "Are you conscious that God is right in this room right now, I mean really conscious, so that you could put out your hand and touch Him?" I think you will realize what I mean when I say that for most of our lives we live as though God were transcendent and not immanent, as though God were out there somewhere. The immanence of God may seem to be a theological theory rather than a present reality. But God is immanent, and the only thing that prevents us from being consumed by that awe-full presence is the mercy of God in which he hides his presence from us at times. But if he were to draw back that curtain and say "I am here in your midst" I wonder if we would act any differently. I wonder if we would feel any differently. I think we would.

God is *awe-full yet approachable*. Awe-full means that his presence produces a sense of awe within us. For you who are theologians and Latin scholars we're talking about the *mysterium tremendum et fascinans*. That sense of the presence of God that both repels us—"depart from me, I am a sinful man"—and yet comes to God in humility and says: "Lord, don't leave us. How can we live without you?" And we're torn between the two. When I have stood in the presence of God, that paradoxical situation is the only way that I can describe the experience that I and others have gone through. We feel our unworthiness and yet feel accepted by God.

It is beyond our understanding but the sense of God's presence, because he is, thirdly, *holy yet reconciled*. "Lord, you are of purer eyes than to behold iniquity, you cannot look upon sin, and yet you say, I'm your Father," What a God! What an incredible person God is, that we who are so unholy, can stand in the presence of God. That we who are so unholy should be accepted by a God who is so holy. We can't take it in a light and easy fashion as though, well, of course God will forgive, that's his job, that goes with the role of being God. Friends, if you think it goes with the role of being God then you don't understand what forgiveness cost, and you don't understand what sin cost. We can't treat it lightly.

And fourth, God is *orderly yet intervening*. He is a God of precise and perfect order; the whole universe runs at his word with an order that is incredible, and yet suddenly God seems to suspend everything to intervene on behalf of a worm like us. Not one sparrow falls to the ground but what God knows about it, and yet he has got whole universes to take care of. The mystery of answered prayer never ceases to amaze me. I don't expect God is going to jump to answer my prayers but he surprises me by doing that at times, and all I can say is: "This is incredible." Why would God answer prayers for me? Why would he pay attention to people like us? Yet he does, and repeatedly we get the evidence that we stand in his presence, and that God intervenes on our behalf. It brings a great sense of unworthiness with it. This consciousness of God's presence, of course, impacts our daily life in a remarkable way, because we begin to live with a greater stringency and care than we ever have done before. We learn to walk softly with God.

That brings us to the *second result*, **a return to biblical standards of holiness.** "Back to the Bible" is not just a motto, but if you live in the presence of God you come back to those old-fashioned biblical standards. We are too modern; and in our modernity we compromise; and in our compromises we lose sight of God's standard, which is the Bible itself.

Third, there is also **a restoration of spiritual power** that takes place. Remember what happened as a result of the outpouring at Pentecost? Acts 2:43 tells us that signs and wonders were performed by the apostles. They had experienced that in the days of Jesus' flesh, when he had sent them out in the ministry, but despite the power of the resurrection we have no instance of the restoration of the miracle working power until after the outpouring at Pentecost. Then the power rests once again upon the church. It is by no means coincidental that at times of revival there has been an outbreak of spiritual power. That spiritual power is not just in the working of miracles but also in the great power with which those apostles gave witness to the grace of God and the presence of the Lord in their midst. It results in conversion. It results in radical conviction of sin and transformation of individuals' lives. It results in answered prayer, not as a hope so but as an is so, amen. It becomes not just a pious expression but a personal experience, so be it, and it is. The amen is not just uttered from earth but echoed from heaven. When God says "So be it" then you can guarantee, so be it. It is so, because God said so. We need that heavenly "Amen."

Fourth, we see **a resurgence of evangelistic activity**. Effective evangelism is not crusades, programs, and methodologies; effective evangelism is an operation of the Holy Spirit, and with an outpouring of the Holy Spirit effective evangelism happens. We see evangelistic activity rising up and thrusting us forward. Friends, we need for a decade of harvest an outpouring of God's Spirit first and foremost. We don't need more crusades; we may get more crusades. We don't need more witnessing programs; they may well happen. What we need is an outpouring of God's Spirit and then evangelism becomes part and parcel of every person's life. Why? We then think in terms of the conversion of the lost; we think in terms of sharing the good news with those that are outside; we think in terms of reaching the unreached.

Fifth, we also see as a result of a revival, **a realignment of society** to God's norms. We don't just need a kinder and gentler society, we need an outpouring of God's Spirit. That will change our society. We may set a pattern for a great society, but that can never be unless God pours out his Spirit upon us and changes the hearts of men and women. That is the only time that such things will take place. Passing laws and giving presidential edicts, as helpful as they may be, will not make any difference until the Spirit be poured out upon us. Then things will begin to happen.

These are the results of revival. And as you look over the revivals that we have examined, you will see that these five evidences of a real revival emerge repeatedly and those instances where they do not emerge with clarity are instances where either the revival itself did not achieve all that God intended for it or we just do not have enough information to know everything that happened. But those well-documented revivals show these elements emerging in a phenomenal way. The revivals that we know in most recent years have evidenced every one of these results. That is what we are anticipating.

Three Ways the Holy Spirit Prepares us for Revival. The role of the Holy Spirit in revival is important if we are to experience revival in our own lives, in our congregations' lives, and in the community at large. Although this is not the place to give a full theology of the operations of the Holy Spirit in human lives, when we look at the theology of the Holy Spirit in general we see some principles that affect our understanding of his role in revival.

The preparation work for revival properly belongs to the Holy Spirit, because it is the Holy Spirit who deals with the important aspect of **conviction,** *the Holy Spirit's primary preparatory role.* That convicting power applies not just to sin, which naturally we do need in our lives as part of the preparation for our own personal walk with God, it also prepares us for an outpouring of God's Spirit. The Lord declared that when he comes, he will convict not only of sin, but also of righteousness and of judgment:

> But very truly I tell you, it is for your good that I am going away. Unless I go away, the Advocate will not come to you; but if I go, I will send him to you. When he comes, he will prove the world to be in the wrong about sin and righteousness and judgment: about sin, because people do not believe in me; about righteousness, because I am going to the Father, where you can see me no longer; and about judgment, because the prince of this world now stands condemned. –John 16:7 –11

When we say the Holy Spirit convicts of **righteousness**, we recognize that the Holy Spirit makes us aware of what we ought to be in Christ. It is as we see the *need* for revival that revival can come in our own personal lives. When we apply this aspect of the convicting work of the Holy Spirit to our lives, not only dealing with the negative aspects of sin but also with the positive aspects of preparing us for what God has ahead of us, making us aware of what his plan is, righteousness is embodied in Christ and is expressed in the life of Christ. When the Holy Spirit convicts us of righteousness, he brings to our consciousness the plan and purpose that God has and creates within us thereby a hunger and a thirst for righteousness:

Blessed are those who hunger and thirst for righteousness, for they will be filled. –Matthew 5:6

Therefore on that basis alone there is a reviving that takes place as a result of that convicting work of the Holy Spirit.

Then there is this matter of **judgment**. We think in terms of judgment as being at the end of time, but the Holy Spirit convicts us of guilt in regards to judgment. Notice very carefully the wording in John 16:7–11 does not say judgment to come *in the future*. In fact, when Jesus expounds upon the last phrase he explained: "...*because the prince of this world now stands condemned.*" When was the prince of this world judged? The crucifixion, the cross, the passion of Jesus demonstrated the judgment of God upon this world and especially upon the prince of this world, Satan. That brings the conviction of judgment forward from the end of time to right here and now. In what sense is there a judgment at this present time? There is the judgment of the cross, when we are crucified with Christ, crucified to the world and the world to us, as Galatians 6:14 appropriately points out:

May I never boast except in the cross of our Lord Jesus Christ, through which the world has been crucified to me, and I to the world. —Galatians 6:14

There is also the judgment of **commitment** in Hebrews 5 and into chapter 6, which talks about the mature in verse 14:

¹³Anyone who lives on milk, being still an infant, is not acquainted with the teaching about righteousness. ¹⁴But solid food is for the mature, who by constant use have trained themselves to distinguish good from evil.

¹Therefore let us move beyond the elementary teachings about Christ and be taken forward to maturity... –Hebrews 5:13 –6:1a

The word "distinguish" there is from the same root as the word for judgment, discrimination, or choices.

In the Welsh revival, Evan Roberts pointed out that we must put away any doubtful activities from our lives if we would experience the quickening power of the outpoured Holy Spirit. We become dull in our senses regarding the things of God. We are not always sensitive to those hindrances to our walk with the Lord and to our spiritual life. It is only when the Holy Spirit shines his searchlight on some particular aspect of our lives that we realize that those things have to go. They are out of place. They occupy a larger place in our lives than they ought. They distract us from the things of God. They shine with the spirit of the world—the glitter and the glamour that is attractive to our senses and to our physical appetites and to our life on earth—but in so doing turn our attention away from the abiding things of God. Rest assured, said the apostle John, the things which are in the world are passing away:

> Do not love the world or anything in the world. If anyone loves the world, love for the Father is not in them. For everything in the world—the lust of the flesh, the lust of the eyes, and the pride of life—comes not from the Father but from the world. The world and its desires pass away, but whoever does the will of God lives forever. –1 John 2:15-17

The one who would be the friend of the world, James 4:4 asserts, becomes the enemy of God. If there is one thing that will staunch the flow of the Spirit in our lives it is worldliness. That does not mean we live "other worldly" in a strange, antiquated way. We are not living for nineteenth-century standards of holiness, we are living for eternity.

Some people have translated the nineteenth century into an eternal rule and if women do not wear dresses down to the ground and if men do not wear just blacks, browns, dark blues, and greys, then they are worldly. That may be a matter of personal choice. If you choose to live that kind of "Puritan" lifestyle, let that be the expression of your commitment to God, not the basis of it. Discrimination does not mean that we abhor all modern inventions and want to go back in time as a witness to a bygone era of simplicity and "holiness," but rather that even in the midst of this present evil world we live as those who are not controlled by it. We are not under its authority, not subjecting ourselves to its desires, its patterns, its attitudes, and its value systems. The Holy Spirit enables us to discern those areas of our lives that need attention. That is part of the preparation of the Holy Spirit, having his awakening power operative within our lives.

Not only is the Holy Spirit preparing us by imparting to us those convictions that will enable him to flow through us and to be what he wants to be in our lives, but also there is the preparation of the Holy Spirit in what I call our **conditioning**, the *second element* of preparation. The Holy Spirit pinpoints the emphases in our lives that will enable us to be used in revival. It is not coincidental that when God begins to stir a nation, community, or even the world at large in preparation for revival, the minds of preachers begin to turn along the same lines and they begin to preach on similar biblical themes, because those are the themes that the Holy Spirit is going to emphasize in the revival to come. That means that we, who are in positions of leadership, have to be sensitive to what the Holy Spirit is saying through us to the churches and not impose upon the Holy Spirit a particular bent that we may have. We may feel that we want to minister in a particular area or along particular lines, but we need to pray through that our preaching will be in keeping with what the Holy Spirit is saying to the church.

Now that does not mean to jump on the latest bandwagon rolling down Main Street. Some people have become so eager for revival that when anybody shouts loudly, they'll join in the shouting, and they'll start shouting whatever is being said—it does not matter what. The noise is what attracts them. Friends, pray through first to see if this is the direction that God is leading and respond to his leading. Learn to listen to the Holy Spirit, because if you do not listen, you will not learn what the Spirit wants you to know, and other voices will lead you astray. We, in positions of leadership, have a great responsibility to follow that leading of the Holy Spirit. It is essential that we should do that because we can miss the coming outpouring if we ourselves are not conditioned to what the Holy Spirit wants to do.

The *third element* of preparation is in the area of **commitment**. Not just being aware of what the Holy Spirit wants to do, but committing ourselves to revival, to being revived. It is a matter of utter consecration before God. Friends, God will use the consecrated man. We need men today, and women today, who are willing to be revived and revivers. Remember how God raises up a prophetic voice to the position of leadership in order to prepare the way for a great outpouring of God's Spirit. Be willing to be that kind of person. That does not simply open the door for a ministry, because before you can speak you have to hear; before you can share you have to receive; before you can impart you have to incorporate, and that means you've got to put into your own life what the Holy Spirit is saying to you. Too much preaching is hypocritical, not intentionally so, but it is a matter of simply telling others and not doing ourselves.

We cannot expect God to use us in revival if our whole focus of ministry is upon things that we ourselves are not devoted, or totally committed to. We need that wholehearted commitment on the part of those who will be in positions of leadership. We keep short accounts with God. We walk carefully before him. We keep clean the relationships with our fellow believers and those in ministry with us. We are in fact living out a revived life. You see, God would rather use a pure vessel than an impure vessel; he would rather use a consecrated vessel than an unconsecrated vessel; he would rather use someone who is one hundred percent his than someone who is loitering on the edge of what God wants to do. He would rather use the man of faith than the man of doubt. He would rather use you when you are what he wants you to be, than use you in spite of what you are. Those who are serving God must themselves participate in that service.

I Corinthians 9:13 applies most immediately to the matter of the support that we receive for our ministry, but there's another principle that we can draw out of those very words that apply right here in relation to revival:

"Don't you know that those who work in the temple get their food from the temple, those who serve at the altar share in what is offered on the altar?" –1 Corinthians 9:13

Remember what the writer of the letter to the Hebrews says about the high priest, that when he brings the sacrifice, he first offers for his own sins, and then for the sins of the people.[2] If we would serve the Lord we must first of all participate in what God wants to do in us and *then* what he wants to do in the community. You can share far more from a heart touched by God than you can from a heart that is empty.

Oh, God may use you and flow through you, but if all you are, as the old song says, is a channel of blessing, when the blessing stops flowing what are you? Empty. You're only full while the blessing is flowing. Would to God that we would not only be channels of blessing but also filled with the presence of God in our own lives. That is why we need a commitment and that is part of the role of Holy Spirit who prepares us for revival by bringing us to the place of utter and total commitment to him. That consecrated lifestyle, where we are devoted entirely to serving the Lord, will help prepare us for what God is preparing for us.

The Sovereignty of the Holy Spirit in Revival. When we look at the role of the Holy Spirit in relation to the outpouring itself, there are several things that emerge very strongly at this point. The role of the Holy Spirit in the outpouring is a sovereign role. He is the Lord, the Spirit, and as such, he is responsible for both the timing and the expression of the revival at that time. The Holy Spirit is *sovereign*. We form in our own minds an idea of what we want a revival to be. For some it has to be a repeat of the old frontier revivals of the early nineteenth century; for others it must be another 1857 Prayer Meeting revival; for others it will be another Wesleyan-type awakening; while for others the ideal revival was 1905 in Wales; others look on a rather unusual revival such as in the Hebrides under Duncan Campbell as the ideal revival; or as in Indonesia; or in the charismatic renewal. The Holy Spirit is sovereign; it is he who will pour out upon the nations that which he has prepared the way for. A revival is geared by God to accomplish the goals that God has for the church at that time.

We've already seen that it is part of the effect of a revival to bring us to the place where God wants the church to be; a place of fellowship with him; a place of growing in grace and in the knowledge of Christ; a place of conformity to the apostolic pattern; of bringing back the church to that place of pristine power, through which we can be in our day a bride of Christ, prepared for the coming of the bridegroom. How the Holy Spirit is going to do that, and the things that need attention, God only knows, in any given revival. We have to recognize the sovereignty of the Holy Spirit in the whole of this; he is Lord in every aspect of the awakening. He is sovereign. Be prepared to flow with God. If the preparatory work has taken place in our lives, then flowing with the Holy Spirit is not a problem, because we are already committed to his sovereignty. "Whatever it takes, Lord, whatever it takes, we're going to go that way;" therefore it's no big deal to us.

But if our consecration is lacking then we may be tempted to manipulate the revival to serve our own ends rather than to serve the glory of God. We may be tempted to use the revival to build our kingdom rather than see God build the church according to the pattern that he has planned out for us. Jesus said: "I will build my church," and that does not just mean that he will put in place the bricks, the stones, and the structure. It means that he has the blueprint. He knows what he wants the church to be like. That is hard for us to grasp at times because we are so used to a very fluid and flexible attitude relating to the structures of the church, in which we say: "Well, that may be all right for that generation and that day but in our day we need a church that's like this and this and this" and so we go to our general council and we vote in new regulations and new rules and new structures and, because we have got an idea that God can work through any human structure. That may be true in a very limited way that God can use any methodology and any structure to accomplish his will, yet when Jesus said "I will build my church" he had a pattern in mind as to what he wanted the church to be like. The Bible describes the bride of Christ as *prepared* for her husband.

Christ knows exactly what he wants the church to be like. It is going to be his bride, whom he is going to spend eternity with. Do you think he doesn't care? Of course he cares, and the church becomes what Christ is making it as the Holy Spirit is poured out upon the church. That is part of the "becoming" process. He sovereignly is fashioning and forming the church into Christ's likeness, so that when Christ looks upon the church he will see it as the bride prepared for her husband. That element of divine sovereignty is one that we must not lose sight of.

The outpouring of the Holy Spirit is what makes a revival into a revival. It is the Holy Spirit's activity within the lives of those who are touched that gives the revival the *distinctive* features. Not only does the outpouring speak in terms of sovereignty, but also it speaks in terms of the distinctiveness of the revival. The Holy Spirit knows what is needed on a particular occasion and knows the emphasis that is important to the church to restore the church to where it ought to be. The distinctiveness does not come about because of the individuals involved, but rather the individuals involved in the revival and mightily used by God in the revival are selected by the Holy Spirit and taken up by him because of the particular distinctives that the Holy Spirit has in mind. The fact that some become great leaders in an awakening, and some do not, may not be a reflection on the individual, that some are more spiritual than others, or some are more holy than others, but may be because it is that kind of person that the Holy Spirit needs to use for this particular kind of revival. What we need to do is to be available to the Holy Spirit to use as he wills.

We notice in revivals how many of those who have been the prophetic voice in preparing the way for the revival do not emerge to prominence during the revival itself. Once the outpouring of the Holy Spirit has taken place, although they still have their place and their ministry, they are not right at the forefront. Observe in the great Welsh revival, the ministry of men like Seth Joshua, the leader of the forward movement in the Methodist church, under whose ministry Evan Roberts made his great consecration of "Lord, bend me and save the world." When the revival came, Seth Joshua was just one of many who were exercising an effective ministry. It was Evan Roberts, a young man, who was still in Bible college training for ministry at Newcastle Emlyn, on whose life God put his finger and said: "You're the man that I want to use as one of the focal figures for this awakening." The great evangelist R. A. Torrey, who many believed was going to be the catalyst of that great awakening, came to Cardiff and Swansea on his great crusades just before the awakening took place, and although many were stirred and got a vision of what God could do and would do, yet the revival came subsequent to his ministry. He had gone and then came the revival. Surely with the immense following that Torrey and Alexander had in their crusades, you would have expected that he would have been the one whom God would have used in the revival. But he was more of a John the Baptist, a forerunner, a prophet, exercising a ministry of putting the issues forth. Then God raised up the men that he wanted to use in that particular revival because of their kind of ministry, their kind of personality, their kind of preparation, which had been going on secretly, not even known by them themselves. Quietly God had been molding his vessels, because he knew the shape that the revival was to take.

Fifty years previously in the Mid-Century Awakening, the person who sparked off the awakening in New York was the young Dutch Reformed church missioner, Jeremiah Lanphier. What else did Jeremiah Lanphier do apart from call a prayer meeting in Manhattan and lead that prayer meeting? Do you know of anything else that he did? Do you know whether he lived a day longer or died? Do you know whether he preached all around the world or just stayed as a Dutch missioner in downtown New York? You can search the history books and Jeremiah Lanphier appears and disappears and although we can with diligence find out some of the later facts of his life, he never achieved prominence in the service of God apart from that one thing that God took him up and used him for, and that was the calling of the prayer meeting that marked the public, general phase of that awakening. He features in the history of revival in that one brief, bright moment.

The characteristics of each awakening differ one from another, and the man who may be ideal for a particular awakening with its characteristics may not in fact be the ideal man to lead the church forward from that time onward. Otherwise, what happens is the same as happened under both Wesley and under Finney, and that is that the revival expressions become institutionalized and become in themselves part of the tradition of a church. One of the greatest adversaries of a new awakening is the institutionalized old awakening. We take the new measures and make them a tradition for our day, affirming, "That's the way that it happened in the revival, therefore that's the way it's got to happen from now onward." If God did not raise up and set down his workers this would be a major problem, and at times it has been a major problem with both the Finney type of movement and with the Wesleyan type of movement, in which we will not go any further than Wesley went, but whatever Wesley did is sacrosanct. Wesley established class meetings, which were invaluable during the revival, but later degenerated into being gossip shops and a divisive influence within the church, tragically causing many problems. It was only further awakenings that were able to purify those to enable them to go forward as they ought to go.

Wesley himself visited some of the Methodist classes, the Methodist societies, and expelled all the members, because he felt they were not fit to be Methodists. In more recent days we have seen in the charismatic renewal a rising up of the cell group type of ministry with a strong shepherding type of leadership, which at a time of revival could be used by God very effectively, but subsequently could become institutionalized into such a situation that rather than expressing and advancing the revival, it hindered the revival. This prevented the work of God from going forward, because it placed in positions of leadership people, who God may have previously used in the flow of the Spirit but who subsequently entrenched themselves at the front and usurped God's authority. The authority lies in the sovereignty of the Holy Spirit, not in the hands of the individual that God has raised up. That individual is raised up to be an instrument, not to be a controller and manipulator of the revival. It becomes a temptation for us when leadership stays there on the basis of past revival usage. It becomes a temptation for us to institutionalize the revival patterns and to make a new denomination.

The Holy Spirit, Revival, and Change. In the application then, the Holy Spirit knows what he wants to do with an awakening and the changes that he is going to make to the structure of the church and to the structure of society. The world after the next awakening will be a different place from what it is now. It will be a more righteous, moral, God-fearing place. It will have characteristics that will have been inherited from the awakening. Society will have changed, because society always changes as a result of an awakening.

The immediate application of the awakening is to the church itself. The structure of the church changes. New denominations arise. New alliances of Christians arise, a new openness to fellow believers arises. The changes in the church produce changes also in society at large, not just in the community that is visited by the awakening, nor only immediate changes but even long-term changes. Things were set in motion by the great awakening of the eighteenth century that were to change the lot of the poor and dispossessed, were to bring in an education system, which would change the judicial system, were to ultimately issue in the change of the social system. Slavery with all its attendant evils was to vanish away and every revival that came placed another nail in the coffin of slavery. Society would never be the same, because God was setting things in motion. Even the landscape of national relationships, the American Revolution, came as a direct consequence of the Great Awakening in which man realized that he had an individual responsibility for his future and for his country before Almighty God. Although all who participated in the revolution were not revived people, the revolution could not have come without the people who had experienced a radical transformation of their philosophical outlook, which arose from that awakening. Who knows what kind of changes are going to come to us when this next awakening comes upon the face of the earth?

It is tragic when there are folk movements like we have recently experienced both in the mainland of Eastern Europe and in the Far East bringing multitudes into Christianity and we fail to recognize them for what they are and capitalize on them to see evangelical awakenings come to whole communities but rather look on them with great suspicion, either as a rival to the orthodoxy of the historical church, or with a measure of doubt or even apprehension because we feel that this in some way is going to water down Christianity as we know it. Folk movements may not bring people into perfect knowledge of Christ; nevertheless, where a population becomes Christianized and has copies of the Scriptures available and the opportunity of proclamation of the Word in that community, there is always the possibility of a spiritual awakening being precipitated if we bring them back to an evangelical understanding of the Scriptures, which is one of the roles of revival.

Revival not only renews the spiritual life of the church but also sees a restoration of biblical truth, and that is what has been happening throughout the world down through the centuries.

Endnotes

1   John 16:11.
2   Hebrews 5:1–3.

Conclusion

Prospects of Revival

In conclusion then, we may assuredly recognize that if we pray and earnestly seek God, as so many have done throughout history, laying aside everything that would distract us from our main purpose, God will answer our prayers and meet us in our quest for him. This may involve our carefully examining our lives under the microscope of the Holy Spirit and repenting of those things that have hindered our relationship in the past, turning away from that which distracts us in the present, and surrendering our future to his direction. David reassured his son Solomon in 1 Chronicles 28:9: *"If you seek him, he will be found by you."*

The recent stirrings on various college and university campuses, both in America and throughout the world, have awakened a renewed interest in Revival and in many places earnest seekers are experiencing spiritual renewal. Could it be that a new season of Revival and Spiritual Awakening is on the way? Only God knows the future, but we can experience his presence and power in our lives now, as we devote ourselves to seeking him.

About Dr. Ian R. Hall

With a ministry career and mission work that span well over six decades and four continents, and academic credentials and honors earned over the course of more than thirty years, Dr. Ian R. Hall is an indisputable expert on the topic of revival in all its forms, both throughout the Bible and in church history from 100 A.D. through current times.

Add to this knowledge his own personal observation and experience, and one can only begin to understand the passion with which he approaches the critical role revival plays in the health and growth of the Christian church as well as our individual spiritual lives.

Education and Ordination:
- Numerous certificates, commendations, and academic honors from British Isles Nazarene College, Manchester (England), and Elim Bible College, Capel, Surrey (England), 1963–1966

- Licensed and ordained to serve as a minister within the Church of the Nazarene and ordained by the Elim Pentecostal Church 1961–1969; credentials transferred to the Assemblies of God, USA, 1978
- Bachelor of Divinity from the University of London (England) with emphasis in church history and New Testament literature and language 1972
- Master in Philosophy (Theology) with an emphasis in early church history and Koine Greek from the University of Leeds (England) 1985
- Ph.D. in Theology with an emphasis in modern church history and evangelical Christian doctrine from the University of Leeds (England) 1994

Missions, Church and Educational Leadership:
Dr. Hall continues to serve with his wife, Sheila, in multiple pastoral, missions, teaching, and administrative leadership capacities spanning more than six decades:
- Senior Pastor, Church of the Nazarene (British Isles) 1963–1965
- Senior Pastor, Elim Pentecostal Churches (England) 1966–1978
- Pentecostal Chaplain, H.M. Prisons 1969–1975
- Lecturer, Elim Bible College, Surrey (England) 1972–1978
- Associate Professor, North Central Bible College, Minneapolis (MN) 1978–1989
- Short-term Evangelist in Western Europe, Assemblies of God World Missions 1985–1988
  - Commissioned Missionary, Assemblies of God World Missions (AGWM) 1988 – Present, Assigned to Romania, 1990
    - » Helped establish and equip Elim Christian Medical Center, Pitesti 1991–1995
    - » President, Elim Evangelical Theological Seminary, Timisoara 1996–2004
    - » President, Elim Foundation for Theological Education, Timisoara 1998–2003

> » Compassion Outreach Ministry, a Christian humanitarian aid ministry, devoted to assisting the poor families, women, children, and elderly 1992–Present
> o Missionary-in-residence, Southeastern University, Lakeland (FL) 2002–2003
> o Professor, Eastern European Bible College, Oradea, Romania, 2004–2010
> o AGWM Special Assignment short-term missions, South Africa, India, the Republic of Georgia, the Netherlands, Romania 2010–present
> o Dean/Founder of Minnesota District School of Ministry 2011–2012

Dr. Hall has also been published in multiple articles, as contributor in a number of books, and has published his own work in Romania during his mission service there.

Previously published books:
- *CALLED TO A PRACTICAL HOLY LIFE* First Published 2023 Metanoia – A Division of the Romanian Bible Society, Oradea, Romania.
- *INTRODUCTION TO HOMILETICS* – 2006 (a Berean University Graduate course)
- *PREPARING AND PREACHING BIBLE MESSAGES*, a Global University programmed textbook. First published 1994, which has been translated into twelve languages.
- *TIMES OF RENEWAL – A History and Theology of Revival and Spiritual Awakenings*, First edition published April 2023 – Metanoia – A Division of the Romanian Bible Society, Oradea, Romania.

Contributor to the following books:
- THE CONFERENCE ON THE HOLY SPIRIT DIGEST, 1983 - *The Spirit in the Old Testament* – Gospel Publishing House

- THE HOLY SPIRIT IN CHRISTIAN EDUCATION, 1988 – *The Pentecostal Revival* – Gospel Publishing House
- NEW INTERNATIONAL DICTIONARY OF PENTECOSTAL AND CHARISMATIC MOVEMENTS. – Survey of Eastern Europe, Published by Zondervan 2002

Articles published in magazines and newspapers:
- TOMORROW – THE MODERN NEWSPAPER FOR YOUNG PEOPLE – Volume 4 (2) & Volume 5 (2) – No date! Approx 1968– 1969 An Evangelistic Newspaper of the Elim Youth Movement, UK.
- ELIM EVANGEL, UK. – 1969–1980 – Numerous Articles (Approximately 40)
- PENTECOSTAL EVANGEL, USA - 1971–2003 - REDEMPTION TIDINGS, British Assemblies of God - 1972
- PARACLETE – 1981–1982
- EVANGELISTS FELLOWSHIP NEWSLETTER 1984
- ELIM REVISTA CRESTINE, TIMISOARA, ROMANIA – December 1997
- RESURSE SPIRITUALE – ROMANIAN VERSION OF ENRICHMENT, LIFE PUBLISHERS INTERNATIONAL – Several Articles
- MOUNTAIN MOVERS – AG Missions Magazine – 1991–1992

The Ministry of Ian
and Sheila Hall

I an and Sheila Hall are both
from Yorkshire, England,
where Dr. Hall was involved
in evangelism and pastoring
churches for seventeen years.
In 1978, they immigrated
to the United States, where,
for eleven years, Dr. Hall
served as associate professor at North Central Bible
College (now North Central
University) in Minneapolis,
Minnesota and ministered as an evangelist throughout the Midwest.

The couple began their missionary journey with the Assemblies of
God World Missions (AGWM) through Rev. Jerry Parsley in 1985 while
Ian was on sabbatical from North Central Bible College. From 1985 to
1988, they served in evangelism and teaching in Belgium, Germany, Italy,
Portugal, and Greece.

A well-known researcher in Pentecostal history and spiritual awakenings, Dr. Hall has been involved in several spiritual awakenings throughout his ministry.

In 1988, the Halls were appointed full-time missionary evangelists to Europe working with the national churches in Italy, Portugal, Belgium, Germany, Greece, Bulgaria, and Yugoslavia. The original intention was that they would subsequently be based in Germany, however, in December 1989, the bloody Romanian revolution known as the Christmas Rebellion removed the brutal communist leader Nikolae Ceausescu from power, leaving a door open for more missionaries to serve. Dr. Hall briefly joined Rev. Robert Mackish in Austria, the lone missionary from the Assemblies of God in Eastern Europe, before going to Romania in February 1990, during what was still a highly volatile time. Ian was the first western missionary into Romania after the Revolution. Sheila joined him in 1992.

From 1990 forward in Romania, Dr. Hall conducted evangelistic crusades, planted new churches, and taught seminars for pastors and in Bible colleges. He was also involved in establishing a Christian Medical Center in the city of Pitesti, Romania, supplying many medical supplies and equipment, including hosting Health Care Ministry teams, and raised funds for building churches in Arges. He was involved with Rev. Ioan Bochian in Bucharest establishing Biserica Emanuel, Bucharest. The church was first housed in a tent purchased from Miami Tent Company for $7,000 with money Sheila raised.

Since 1992, Sheila has been involved in Compassion Ministry, ministering to women, children, families, and orphanages, demonstrating the love of Christ by distributing food and emergency aid. Sheila was also involved in ministry to Gypsies. In 1992 she introduced Women's Ministries in Romania.

From 1996 to 2004 Dr. Hall served as president of Elim Evangelical Theological Seminary, Timisoara, Romania. Sheila served as the general administrative secretary. Dr. Hall and Sheila were responsible for raising funds for the construction of Samaria Gypsy Church, Alesd, Romania—an Assemblies of God World Missions (AGWM) project—and for providing equipment for the Samaria Gypsy Kindergarten.

Recently, the Halls have maintained a very visible presence in Oradea and were involved in helping with the construction and furnishing of the extension of the Pentecostal Church in Les, in addition to conducting very successful VBS and Kids Extravaganza Outreaches. They were involved in the finishing of Batar Pentecostal Gypsy Church in Batar, the dedication of which took place in October 2023.

In March 2023, they were asked to assist in the establishment of the Dr. James A. Sabella Roma School of Ministry, a school specifically for the training of Gypsy leaders, the first of its kind in Northern Romania, directed by Rev. Laurentiu Pascuti. Graduation of the first class of Gypsy students took place May 26, 2024.

In 2003 the Halls became naturalized American citizens. They have one son, Jonathan and two grandchildren, William and Alexa, and currently live in Lakeland, Florida.

To arrange for speaking or book signing engagements, please contact Dr. Hall directly:

Dr. Ian R. Hall
Phone: 863-603-9725
E-mail. dr.ianhall@gmail.com

Bibliography

Arthur, W.: *The Tongue of Fire, or The True Power of Christianity* (New York, NY: Harper, 1856).

Atkinson, J.: *The Great Light* (Exeter, UK: Paternoster, 1968).

Augustine: *Confessions*.

Aune, D.E.: *Prophecy in Early Christianity* (Grand Rapids, MI: Eerdmans, 1983).

Bainton, R.H.: *Here I Stand* (Nashville, TN: Abingdon, 1978 edn.).

Baker, E.: *The Revivals of the Bible* (London: Kingsgate Press, 1906).

Bede: *Ecclesiastical History of the English Nation*.

Bennett, D.J.: *Nine O'clock in the Morning* (London & Eastbourne, UK: Coverdale House, 1971).

Bettenson, H. (ed.): *Documents of the Christian Church* (London: Oxford U., 1963 edn.).

Bready, J.W.: *England: Before and After Wesley* (London, UK: Hodder & Stoughton, 1939).

Bromiley, G.W. (ed.): *The International Standard Bible Encyclopedia* (Grand Rapids, MI: Eerdmans, 1982).

Brooks, L.B.: *This Thousand Years* (South Plainfield, NJ: Bridge, 1994).

Bruce, F.F.: *The Spreading Flame* (Exeter, UK: Paternoster, 1958).

Burns, J.: *Revivals, their Laws and Leaders* (Grand Rapids, MI: Baker, 1960).

Campbell, D.: *The Price and Power of Revival* (London, UK: Parry Jackman, 1957).

Cartwright, P., Wallis, C.L. (ed.): *The Autobiography of Peter Cartwright*, (Nashville, TN: Abingdon, 1956).

Charisma (Orlando, FL: Strang Communications, 2006 & 2010).

Christian Advocate (New York, NY).

Christianity Today.

Cohn, N.: *The Pursuit of the Millennium* (Oxford, UK: Oxford U.P., 1970).

Coleman, R.: *The Coming World Revival* (Wheaton, IL: Crossway, 1995)

Coomes, D.: *The Flame Still Spreads* (Guildford, UK: Lutterworth Press, 1974).

Crowther, J.: *The History of the Wesleyan Methodists* (London, UK: Edwards, 1814).

Curnock, N. (ed.): *The Journal of the Rev. John Wesley A.M.*, vol. 2 (London, Epworth, 1938).

Dager A.J: *Pensacola: Revival or Reveling?* (Redmond, WA: Media Spotlight, 1997).

Davies, R.E.: *I Will Pour Out My Spirit* (Tunbridge Wells, UK: Monarch, 1992).

Dayton, D.W.: *Theological Roots of Pentecostalism* (Grand Rapids, MI: Zondervan, 1987), 73-74;

Destiny Image Digest, (Shippensburg, PA: Destiny Image Publishers, Winter 1997).

Didymus: *On the Trinity*.

Dorsett, M.: *Revival at Wheaton* (Wheaton, IL: International Awakening Press, 1994).

Dowley, T. (ed.): *Eerdmans' Handbook to the History of Christianity* (Grand Rapids, MI: Eerdmans, 1977).

Edwards, J.: *The Works of Jonathan Edwards: Volume 9 – A History of Redemption.* (New Haven, CT: Yale, 1989).

Eerdmans' Handbook to the History of Christianity (Grand Rapids, MI: Eerdmans, 1977).

Epiphanius: *Panarion*.

Eusebius: *Ecclesiastical History*.

Finney C.G.: *Revivals of Religion* (London, UK.: Morgan and Scott, 1913, second edn.).

Finney, C.G.: *Charles G. Finney, An Autobiography* (London, UK: Salvation Army, 1882 edn.).

Gaebelein, F.E. (ed.): *The Expositor's Bible Commentary* (Grand Rapids, MI: Regency, 1981).

Goen, C.C. (ed.): *The Works of Jonathan Edwards*, vol. 4 (New Haven CT: Yale University Press, 1972).

Goforth, J.: *By My Spirit* (Minneapolis, MN: Bethany, 1964).

Gonzalez, J.L.: *The Story of Christianity*, vol. 2 (San Francisco, CA: Harper & Row, 1985).

Graham, W.F.: *Just As I Am* (New York, NY: HarperCollins, 1997).

Hall, I.R.: *Charismatic Phenomena in the Ante-Nicene Church* (Leeds, UK: MPhil Dissertation, 1984).

Hamilton, M.P. (ed.), *The Charismatic Movement* (Grand Rapids, MI: Eerdmans, 1975).

Hardman, K.J.: *Seasons of Refreshing* (Eugene, OR: Wipf & Stock, 1994, & 2004).

Hardman, K.J.: *The Spiritual Awakeners* (Chicago, IL: Moody, 1983).

Harkness, G.: *John Calvin: The Man and His Ethics* (Nashville TN: Abingdon, 1948).

Harper, M.: *As at the Beginning* (London, UK: Hodder & Stoughton, 1965).

Harrell, D.E., Jr.: *All Things Are Possible* (Bloomington, IN: Indiana University Press, 1975).

Hebraeus, G.B.: *Ecclesiastical Chronicles* (trans. J.B. Abbeloos & T.J. Lamy, Paris: Maisonneuve, 1877).

Irenaeus: *Against Heresies*.

Island Evangelical Fellowship Minutes, (August 1975).

Jackson, T. (ed.): *Works of John Wesley*, vol. XIII (London, UK, Wesleyan Methodist, 1865).

Justin: *Dialogue with Trypho*.

Kane, J.H.: *A Concise History of the Christian World Mission* (Grand Rapids, MI: Baker, 1982).

Kilpatrick, J.: *The Feast of Fire: The Father's Day Outpouring* (Pensacola, FL: J. Kilpatrick, 1995).

Koch, K.E.: *Wine of God: Revival in Indonesia, Formosa, Solomon Islands and South India* (Montreal, Canada: Christian Evangelism Publications, 1974).

Latourette, K.S.: *A History of Christianity* (New York, NY: Harper & Row, 1975 edn.).

Latourette, K.S.: *A History of the Expansion of Christianity* (Exeter, UK: Paternoster, 1971 edn.).

Lloyd-Jones, D.M.: *Preaching & Preachers* (Grand Rapids, MI: Zondervan, 1971).

Lovelace, R.F.: *Renewal As a Way of Life* (Downers Grove, IL: InterVarsity Press, 1985).

Marshall, I.H., et.al. (eds.): *New Bible Dictionary* (Downers Grove, IL: InterVarsity, 1996).

McLoughlin, W.G.: *Revivals, Awakenings, and Reform: An Essay on Religion and Social Change in America, 1607 – 1977* (Chicago, IL: University of Chicago, 1978).

Meats, G.: *Methodist Missionaries n. 2* (Cape Town, SA: Methodist Missionary Dept., 1958).

Miller, P: *Jonathan Edwards* (New York, NY: William Sloane, 1949).

MSNBC report (May 29, 2008).

Nagler, A.W.: *Pietism and Methodism* (Nashville: Publishing House of the Methodist Episcopal Church, South, 1918).

National Catholic Reporter.

Neill, S.: *A History of Christian Missions* (Harmondsworth, UK: Penguin, 1964).

New Webster's Dictionary of the English Language (New York, NY: Delair Publishing, 1981).

New York Herald (New York, NY).

Origen: *Against Celsus.*

Orr, J.E.: *Campus Aflame* (Glendale, CA: Regal, 1971).

Orr, J.E.: *Evangelical Awakenings in Africa* (Minneapolis, MN: Bethany, 1975).

Orr, J.E.: *Evangelical Awakenings in Eastern Asia* (Minneapolis, MN: Bethany, 1975).

Orr, J.E.: *Evangelical Awakenings in the South Seas* (Minneapolis, MN: Bethany, 1976).

Orr, J.E.: lecture on the 1857 Prayer Meeting Revival at Oxford Association for Research in Revival (Regent's College, Oxford, July 26, 1977).

Orr, J.E.: *The Eager Feet: Evangelical Awakenings 1790 – 1830* (Chicago, IL: Moody, 1975).

Orr, J.E.: *The Flaming Tongue: The Impact of 20th Century Revivals* (Chicago, IL: Moody, 1973).

Orr, J.E.: *The Light of the Nations* (Exeter, UK: Paternoster, 1965).

Parker, G.H.W.: *The Morning Star* (Exeter, Devon: Paternoster, 1965).

Patrick: *The Confession of St. Patrick.*

Pollock, J.: *Billy Graham* (London, UK: Hodder & Stoughton, 1966).

Randles, B.: *Weighed and Found Wanting* (Cedar Rapids, IA: Bill Randles, n.d.).

Ravenhill, L.: *Why Revival Tarries* (Bloomington, MN: Bethany House, 2004)

Redemption Tidings.

Riss, R.M.: *A Survey of 20th Century Revival Movements in North America* (Peabody, MA: Hendrickson, 1988).

Roberts, J.M.: *The Penguin History of the World*, 3rd edn. (London, UK: Penguin, 1995).

Ryde (IW) Ministerial Fraternal Minutes, July 17, 1975.

Salway, P.: *Roman Britain* (Oxford, UK: Oxford U.P., 1981).

Shelley, B.L.: *Church History in Plain Language*, 3rd edn. (Nashville, TN: Thomas Nelson, 2008).

Smith, T.L.: *Revivalism and Social Reform in Mid-Nineteenth Century America* (New York, NY: Harper, 1957).

St. Petersburg Times (June 30, 2008).

Stenton, F.M.: *Anglo-Saxon England* (Oxford, UK: Oxford U.P., 1971, 3rd edn.).

Strader, S., personal e-mail June 8, 2008.

Sweet, W.W.: *The Story of Religion in America* (New York, NY: Harper & Row, 1950 edn.).

Tari, D.J.I.M.: *Like a Mighty Wind* (London, UK: Coverdale House, 1973).

Taylor, M.: *Exploring Evangelism* (Kansas, MO: Beacon Hill, 1964).

Tertullian: *Apology.*

The Catholic Encyclopedia (New York, NY: Robert Appleton, 1907 edn.).

The Catholic Encyclopedia (New York, NY: Robert Appleton, 1913).

The Catholic Encyclopedia, vol. 3 (New York, NY: Robert Appleton, 1908).

The New International Dictionary of Pentecostal and Charismatic Movements (Grand Rapids, MI: Zondervan, 2002).

The New International Dictionary of the Christian Church.

The Telegraph.

Tholuck, F.A.G.: *Philip Jacob Spener* (New York, NY: F.M. Barton, 1861).

Time.

Tippit, S.: *Fire in Your Heart* (Chicago, IL: Moody, 1987).

Todd, J.H.: *St. Patrick, Apostle of Ireland* (Dublin: Hodges & Smith, 1864).

Tracy, J.: *The Great Awakening: A History of the Revival of Religion in the Time of Edwards and Whitefield* (Boston, MA, 1842).

Walker, G.S.M.: *The Growing Storm* (London, UK: Paternoster, 1961).

Walker, W. et. al.: *A History of the Christian Church*, 4th edn. (New York, NY: Scribner's, 1985).

Wesley, J.: *A Plain Account of Christian Perfection* (New York, NY: Lane & Scott, 1850).

White, C.E.: *The Beauty of Holiness* (Grand Rapids, MI: Zondervan, 1986).

White, J.: *When the Spirit Comes with Power* (London, UK: Hodder & Stoughton, 1992 edn.).

Whittaker, C.E.: *Great Revivals* (Springfield, MO: Gospel Publishing House, 1984)

Wimber, J. with Springer, K.: *Power Evangelism* (London, UK: Hodder & Stoughton, 1985).

Wood, A.S.: *The Inextinguishable Blaze: Spiritual Renewal and Advance in the Eighteenth Century* (Exeter, Devon: Paternoster, 1960).

Young, N.: *The Story of Rome* (London, UK: Dent, 1907).